AA

LONDON GUIDE

Produced by the Publishing Division of the
Automobile Association

Cover: Tower Bridge, Guardsman, Westminster, Royal Wedding

Title page: Eros

Contents page: Bandsmen

Introductory page: Hyde Park

Editors: Michael Cady, Jan Clark

Consultant: Rodney Scrase DFC

Art Editor: Dave Austin

Design Assistants: KAG Design

Editorial contributors: Paul Atterbury (Buildings and Builders); Shirley Hewson (Gazetteer); Bob Smyth (Green London); John Wittich (Story of London and Walks)

Picture researcher: Wyn Voysey

Original photography: Martin Trelawny, Tim Woodcock

Phototypeset by Avonset, Midsomer Norton, Bath. Printed in Great Britain by Purnell Book Production Limited, Member of the BPCC Group

Maps and plans produced by the Cartographic Department of the Automobile Association. Atlas based on the Ordnance Survey maps, reproduced with the permission of the Controller of Her Majesty's Stationery Office. Crown Copyright reserved. Tube Map © London Transport.

ISBN 0 86145 504 5 (hardback)
ISBN 0 86145 503 7 (softback)

Published by the Automobile Association

AA Ref 53950 (hardback)
AA Ref 53947 (softback)

LONDON GUIDE

Contents

Using this Book

THE GAZETTEER
The gazetteer is divided into headings – so churches, art galleries, shops, parks, etc, are all together and can be identified easily. Each entry has a map reference so that it can be located in the map section of the book. An explanation of how to use the referencing systems is given at the beginning of the map section. Not all of the places are named on the maps, but by using the maps and the street index all places should be found easily. No opening details of places are given, but if a place is not open to the public, or is open only by appointment, then the text says so. Opening times are usually from about 10am until about 5pm (with perhaps an hour closed at lunchtime) but they change occasionally and it is sometimes advisable to check (through Tourist Offices, etc).

THE WALKS
A suggested time for each of the 16 walks has been given, but if time is taken to visit the museums, galleries and other places of interest usually mentioned, they will obviously take a lot longer. A variety of refreshment places can be found on the routes of all the walks.

THE DRIVES
There are three drives in this book – in the south-west, the north-west and the south-east. No route directions are given, but the maps clearly indicate the routes. They can be joined or left at any point. Because of one-way systems, etc the routes can only be driven in one direction; this is shown by arrows on the maps. London is an extremely busy city, and the traffic is heavy; driving in the capital is not for the beginner or the faint-hearted. The 'rush-hours' – 8am-9am and 5pm-6pm should be avoided at all costs. We suggest that these drives are best undertaken at weekends.

THE DIRECTORY
The Directory contains brief details of AA-recommended hotels and restaurants in central London (for further details consult the AA's range of Annual Guides).

MAPS AND INDEXES
The AA's own maps of London are included in this book. They are at a scale of 7 inches to one mile for Central London, and one mile to one inch for outer London. A street index of the Central London map pages is at the end of the book.

TOURIST INFORMATION
The London Visitor and Convention Bureau is London's official tourist board: all approved members – shops, hotels, tour agencies and operators – display its sign. Whatever information you need about London – what to do, where to go, how to get there, including instant hotel bookings, theatre and tour reservations – can be obtained at the LVCB's five central locations:
Victoria Station forecourt, SW1 open daily 9am-8.30pm (8am-10pm July & August)
Selfridges Store, Oxford Street, W1 (ground floor) open store hours
Harrods Store, Knightsbridge, SW1 (4th floor) open store hours
Heathrow Airport, Heathrow Central Station open daily 9am-6pm
Tower of London, EC3 (West Gate) open daily April-October, 10am-6pm.

Telephone enquiries can be made on (01) 730 3488, Mon-Fri. 9am-5.30pm.

In addition, there are several Local Authority Tourist Information Centres around the capital.

TRANSPORT
The buses and Underground are controlled by London Regional Transport, whose headquarters is at 55 Broadway, Westminster, SW1.
This authority maintains Travel Information Centres at the following Underground stations in Central London: Victoria and Piccadilly Circus (open 8.15am-9.30pm), Charing Cross, King's Cross and Oxford Circus (open 8.15am-6pm), Euston (open 7.15am-6pm), St James's Park (open 8.15am-5pm) and Heathrow (open 7.15am-9.30pm). They answer all queries about travel in London, as well as issue tickets, book tours, and sell publications. Or you can telephone (01) 222 1234 anytime, day or night.

BRITISH RAIL
Britain's extensive rail network links all major cities in the country with London. British Rail offer a full range of travel facilities at The British Travel Centre, 12 Regent Street, SW1 (tel (01) 730 3400). Here you can buy rail tickets and make reservations, book tickets for theatres and sightseeing tours, arrange accommodation, and change foreign money. The Centre is open from 9am to 6.30pm, Monday to Saturday, and on Sundays from 10am to 4pm. In addition BR Travel Centres can be found at:
14 Kingsgate Parade, Victoria Street, SW1
87 King William Street, EC4
407 Oxford Street, W1
170b Strand, WC2
(open 9am-5pm, Mon-Fri)
and at these main London terminals:
Cannon Street, Charing Cross, Euston, King's Cross, London Bridge, Liverpool Street, Paddington, St Pancras, Victoria and Waterloo.

EMERGENCY SERVICES
If you are involved in any serious accident, or if you need the police in an emergency, you should always dial 999 (these calls are free), and ask for Fire, Police, or Ambulance.

London Transport Police (for reporting thefts and other crimes which take place on London Transport): telephone (01) 222 5600.

If you are injured and require medical attention in Central London, University College Hospital (Gower Street, WC1), the Middlesex Hospital (Mortimer Street, W1), St Thomas's Hospital (Lambeth Palace Road, SE1) and the Westminster Hospital (Horseferry Road, SW1), all have 24-hour casualty departments. Several chemists have extended opening hours: these include Boots, Piccadilly Circus, W1 (Monday-Friday 8.30am-8pm, Saturday 9am-8pm), H D Bliss, 5 Marble Arch, W1 (9am-midnight daily), Underwoods, 75 Queensway, W2 (9am-10pm daily), and the Churchill Pharmacy, 268 Oxford Street, W1 (8.30am-midnight daily). All foreign visitors to Britain can take advantage of the accident and emergency services of the National Health Service without charge.

Emergency dental treatment can be obtained, at a charge, from the Emergency Dental Service: tel (01) 677 6363.

LONDON GUIDE

Introduction

Whether your interests are in the arts or shopping, architecture or royal pageantry, history or simply sight-seeing, the capital is bound to offer enough to fill up your days – or weeks. Here are the centres of government and of law, the great financial institutions and the principal homes of royalty.

It is even possible to get away from the crowds – turn off many a busy thoroughfare and you will find yourself in a quiet square, rural-seeming park or leafy courtyard where time seems to stand still. One of London's greatest qualities is its variety – it changes from street to street, from day to day; this quality is enhanced by its citizens, as cosmopolitan a mixture as is to be found in any city in the world.

The story of London

Many of the great events which have shaped Britain's history have taken place in London, and the effects of those events have often been felt far beyond the shores of Britain. Countless thousand other incidents have changed the lives of individual Londoners. Together, all those plots, intrigues, laws, customs, domestic dramas and everyday acts have made London the extraordinary place it is today.

Before Julius Caesar's invasion in 54 BC there was no Thames-side settlement which can reasonably be described as a precursor of London. There were, undoubtedly settlements all along the river, and the Thames was an important trading route with the Continent in Bronze Age times, but London is a Roman creation. Caesar crossed the Thames at what was to become Westminster, but after his departure the area was left to midges, birds and wandering tribesmen. It was not until nearly a hundred years later, in AD 43, that the Emperor Claudius established the bridgehead which was to become capital of an empire nearly two thousand years later.

Mithras – a god worshipped in Roman London

that a wall was erected to protect the inhabitants. Now that London had become a fortified, military city and no longer simply a trading port, its status in the Roman Empire was increased. It grew to become the fifth largest city in the Empire.

For the remainder of the Roman period the city grew very little outside the city wall, except to the south of the bridge across the Thames. This bridge – London Bridge – was to be the lowest crossing of the river for centuries to come. By the 5th century Rome was in decline and under threat and all the troops and able-bodied men were recalled to defend the Empire's capital. They never returned.

Britain was a Roman colony for over 400 years. During that time the Romans introduced the considerable benefits of their civilization. Among the most important of these were their carefully surfaced roads, which linked London with other Roman settlements in a network of supply routes. It was not only goods and people which travelled along these great arteries – ideas had as much impact.

Growth and destruction

All was not peaceful under Roman rule. The East Angles had been ruled, under the supervisory protection of the Romans, by King Prasutagus, the husband of Queen Boudicca (Boadicea), and on his death in AD 60, trouble broke out. On the instructions of the Imperial Agent the Queen was flogged, and her daughters were raped. The Queen rebelled and civil war broke out. Colchester and St Albans were destroyed and London was razed to the ground. Eventually Boudicca was defeated; rather than be captured, she died by taking poison.

London was rebuilt on much the same lines as before the attack. It was not until the 2nd century

After the Empire

London survived – just. There are many recorded instances of Danes, Saxons and Vikings coming up the Thames on raiding parties. They used London as a resting place during the long winter months when it was too dangerous for them to carry out their piratical activities along the coasts of England and north Europe. Although London had become almost an open city with the withdrawal of the Roman troops, there were still sufficient defences to act as a barrier against such invaders. But the citizens came to accept the interlopers, even allowing them to set up their own colonies outside the wall – the church of St Clement Danes takes its name from what was once a Danish enclave. Trade continued with many parts of the country, as well as with the Continent. By the 8th century the Venerable Bede was able to record in his *History of the English Church and People* that 'London is a mart for many nations who resort to it by land and sea'.

It was not until the Saxons had found a settled way of life in southern England that they began to make use of the natural advantages of London, and

This view of London, painted in 1620, shows the city spreading along the bank of the Thames

Remains of the old City wall, with the Barbican complex in the background

Normans and after

In the latter half of the 11th century London suffered its last invasion by a foreign power. After the death of Edward the Confessor in 1065, Harold was elected King but William of Normandy was sure the Crown was his. He defeated Harold at the Battle of Hastings. William marched towards London, but by-passed the city. He moved up the Thames Valley to Wallingford, crossed the river, and then marched back towards London, camping at Berkhamsted while he awaited the surrender of the Keys of London. On Christmas Day, 1066, he was crowned King of England in Westminster Abbey. William granted special privileges to the citizens of London, but built the Tower to remind them of his overwhelming power.

In the 12th century two of the most powerful and influential organisations in the whole of Christendom were founded. They were the Knights Templars and the Knights Hospitallers, both of whom were founded to defend the shrines of the Holy Land from attacks by Saracens. Their influence over London and its inhabitants was considerable, and they grew in power to the extent that they challenged kings, emperors and even the Pope himself. Eventually the Templars were disbanded, on orders from the Pope, and their property was handed to the Hospitallers, who held the joint lands until the Reformation.

Today, the Templars' land is occupied by the Inner and Middle Temple of the Inns of Court (where the Templars' round church can still be seen), while the Hospitallers' land is now mostly covered by houses and offices. All that remains of their buildings is the gatehouse in St John's Lane, Clerkenwell, and the much rebuilt church across the roadway from it.

A view of the Tower, with London Bridge in the background, from a medieval manuscript

Offa, King of Mercia, took London into his kingdom. Although the Saxons were mainly farmers, later they learnt to use London as a port. Government of the city at this time was by 'Folk Moot', a general meeting of all the citizens – presided over by the Bishop of London – which met three times a year.

The Templars' round church, in the Inns of Court

Scenes from the Middle Ages

In the Middle Ages London was a thriving and expanding city. It had been restricted to the area enclosed by the wall whose perimeter had been established by the Romans, except for one or two monastic establishments outside, and the Strand, once a riverside roadway, which linked the City with Westminster – where the monarch had his palace. Between the river and the Strand were the mansions of bishops and gentry. Within the wall it was crowded, noisy and busy.

From across the river, at Southwark, the city was dominated by Old St Paul's Cathedral, with the Tower on the eastern approaches. London Bridge linked the two banks of the river. It had become almost a miniature city itself – lined with shops and houses, with gatehouses at either end and a chapel dedicated to Thomas Becket forming a central feature. Hundreds of people lived on the bridge and were able to enjoy the splendid views up and down the river. The downstream pool was full of ships from all over the known world, while upstream smaller boats helped to unload ships which could not pass under the bridge and also acted as water-borne taxis for those citizens not wishing to walk over the bridge.

Visitors approaching London from the south would pass through the bridge gate, and perhaps stop to look at the heads of those who had been executed stuck on stakes above the gatehouse. Every day the gatekeeper would go to the roof to make sure they were all still there, since men were known to 'rescue' the heads of friends who had been executed. This is the origin of the phrase 'counting heads'.

Across the river

Southwark had developed from a collection of houses by the bridge to being an important suburb of the City. But it was outside the jurisdiction of the City, and became a centre for brothels, cheap drinking houses and shady activities of all sorts. With the coming of public transport in the form of coaches, Southwark became one of the termini for journeys to Rochester, Canterbury and Dover – following the line of roads laid out by the Romans. Great pilgrimages started from Southwark – as is revealed in Chaucer's *Canterbury Tales* in which the pilgrims start from the 'Tabard' in Borough High Street. In 1549 the area became a ward of the City of London and numerous felons were moved to the nearby Liberty of the Clink, which remained outside the jurisdiction of the Lord Mayor. To the Clink later came the theatres that were to be made famous as the places at which the works of Shakespeare and others were performed.

The Globe Theatre

Guilds and Guildhall

The governing of the City of London has always been in the hands of the trade guilds, or Livery Companies, who have the right to elect their own Lord Mayor and Sheriffs. This privilege continues, the ceremonies taking place each year at the Guildhall.

Many of the trade guilds can trace their origins back hundreds of years, but it was only in later medieval times that their functions and status were finally acknowledged. No one could practice a trade or craft in the City without first becoming an accredited member of the appropriate guild, and having been accepted by it had to maintain the high standard of workmanship that the Master and the Court of the Guild required. Each trade kept a tight control over its members, and official records show that punishment inflicted on wrongdoers was often harsh. In the 14th century, a spectacle maker found guilty of making imperfect glasses was sentenced to stand in the pillory in Cheapside – the main market street of London at that time – for three days, and his entire stock of glasses was smashed in front of the citizens.

Much of the history of the City has unfolded in the largely 15th-century Guildhall. Here can be seen the coats of arms of the various guilds, both old and new, while the names of the Mayors and Lord Mayors are recorded in the chevrons of the stained glass windows.

S. PAULES CHURCH

Above: the colourful coats of arms of the guilds
Left: The Great Hall of the Guildhall
Right: Gog and Magog, mythical giants in the Great Hall

The City at risk

There were over a hundred churches in London in the Middle Ages, many of which were attached to the various guilds, whose members regularly attended Mass. The churches were largely built of stone, but the houses which crowded round them were of wood. Only the richest people could afford to build in stone, and they preferred to live away from the noise and squalor of the centre of London. The wood was at continual risk from fire; and when fires started they could easily spread, with little chance of control unless lines of volunteers quickly formed a human bucket chain from the river to the scene of the fire. But the plague was more feared than fire. It struck without warning, felling rich and poor alike. Fire could be understood, but the plague was horribly mysterious. Considering the squalor and filth of the capital it is perhaps surprising that the pestilence did not strike more often. Drinking water, for example, came from the river – and the same river was more or less an open sewer.

Changing times

By the middle of the 16th century the influence of the Renaissance was spreading across the Continent from Italy, and in 1535 the Reformation took place. These two events presaged many changes in London life and living.

There were well over 100,000 people living in London by this time. Following the dissolution of the monasteries by Henry VIII, the inhabitants of all the City's monasteries and convents joined the throng. The church no longer dominated proceedings in the City, and the people took over many of its responsibilities. After the death of Elizabeth I, James VI of Scotland was offered and accepted the throne of England and the two great kingdoms of Scotland and England became the United Kingdom.

Under James the capital expanded further, with the land to the north of the Strand being built on. Exchanges, such as the Royal Exchange on Cornhill, built by Sir Thomas Gresham in the previous century, flourished with more and more of the City traders using its facilities. While there was little or no church building during the early 17th century, large houses and palaces grew up around London. Whitehall Palace, acquired by Henry VIII from Cardinal Wolsey, was partly rebuilt. All that remains of it today is the Banqueting House, which was designed by Inigo Jones and reflects the ideas introduced by the Renaissance.

London was now one of the largest and wealthiest cities in the world. The population of England and Wales at the turn of the 17th century was over four million and by the end of the century had risen to over five and a quarter million. London, including Westminster and the immediate suburbs, had a population of over 200,000 at the opening years of the century and that figure had more than doubled by its close.

The capital's size and importance attracted more and more traders, and it became the largest port in the country, providing employment for vast numbers of people. As well as trade, it was *the* centre for learning and the arts. Alongside the wealth, beauty and knowledge went poverty, disease and dirt. Plagues still struck. At such times Court and Parliament moved away from London and took up residence in Oxford.

Revolution and fire

James was not a popular king, and there were strong undercurrents of religious and political hatred throughout the country. There was an abortive attempt by his enemies to blow up the Houses of Parliament, a deed for which Guy Fawkes was executed. Eventually, during the reign of James's son – Charles I – the conflicts erupted into open rebellion, and civil war followed. London backed the Parliamentary side, and its money helped Cromwell and the Parliamentarians to win. Charles was brought to London and executed outside the Banqueting House in January, 1649.

The Commonwealth followed – 11 years of increasingly despotic rule by Cromwell. Few people regretted his passing. In May 1660 Charles II was restored to the throne, and there followed a period of great rejoicing, not least in London, where all festivities, amusements and even bright clothes had been violently suppressed.

Five years later the greatest, and last, plague hit the capital. In the following year, 1666, the Great Fire swept through the city – destroying everything in its path, including the plague. Tens of thousands were killed by the plague; thousands more lost

their homes and livelihoods in the fire. Two men have left vivid pictures of those troubled times – Samuel Pepys and John Evelyn. In their diaries the stench of both plague and fire comes uncomfortably close.

Rebuilding

A new London rose from the ashes. It was not the Renaissance city which Sir Christopher Wren had envisaged, but at least timber buildings were banned. And there were fine new buildings – notably Wren's churches, and his masterpiece, St Paul's.

Wren was very much in the spirit of his age – a brilliant mathematician, gifted scientist and architect of genius – he was a true Renaissance man. The Royal Society was founded, and helped to bring scientific and philosophical thinking into the age of reason. Businessmen financed voyages to every corner of the world. London was building an empire.

The expansion continued throughout the 18th century. People flocked to London, and contemporary writers speak with horror and amazement of its great size and wealth, and reported, with some alarm, of the swallowing up of some of the nearer villages. Soon Deptford, Paddington, Hampstead and Highgate were absorbed into the metropolis. Merchants moved out of the City, and built homes in the countryside a few miles outside the City wall. Meanwhile the intervening fields were being built over, while in Mayfair a new town was built which became the home of members of fashionable society.

18th-century facets

There was still need for caution with regard to fire, as there was no London fire brigade until the 19th century. Each parish or estate had its own fire-

During the plague, the death toll was so great that hundreds of corpses were hastily buried in pits

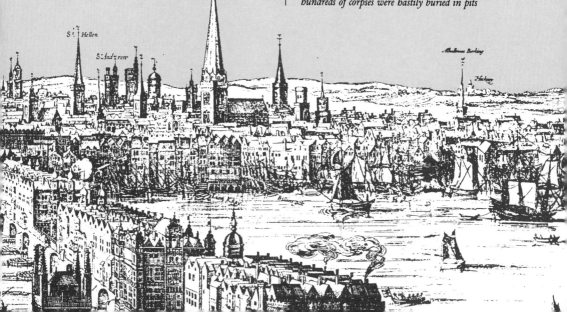

Above: London burning – the Great Fire
Left: a 19th-century fire-engine
Below: Vauxhall Gardens, gathering place for
fashionable society

engine which, on alarm, was drawn to the place of danger and the water was pumped by man power. There were also fire-brigades run by fire insurance companies. Houses had the badge of the company with which they were insured attached to their exteriors, and no other company would put out a fire in that house.

It is interesting to see how the outskirts of London expanded during the 18th century. For example, Hampstead was fast growing into a resort for the wealthy, and soon became a place of idle amusement, with cards, bowls and dice abounding. Belsize, in north London, was the forerunner of pleasure gardens such as Vauxhall and Ranelagh. One gathering of nobility and gentry at Belsize in 1772 was so large that it was estimated that between three and four hundred coaches were present. Many of the villages that were still just outside London were growing so much that places such as Paddington and Clapham had to rebuild their churches because they had become too small for their congregations.

Despite the growth, there were still many undeveloped areas. Belgravia was a swamp shown on contemporary maps as 'Five Fields', Bethnal Green was no more than a few scattered houses, while Brompton – 'Broom Town' – was still full of thickets and thorns. Holborn was still famous for its gardens, and Regent Street was an un-named path.

The 19th century

At the beginning of the 19th century London's population was just under a million; by 1901 this figure had risen to nearly 4½ million. It was a phenomenal expansion, far more dramatic than anything which had gone before. Until 1750, when Westminster Bridge was built, London Bridge had been the only bridge across the river, but in the early 1800s a spate of bridge building took place so that by 1850 nearly all London's bridges we know today had been constructed. The docks were expanded and developed, creating a vast concourse of warehouses and basins for the import and export of every conceivable kind of commodity.

When Queen Victoria came to the throne she became not only monarch of Great Britain, but also Empress of an Empire which encompassed a third of the world, and London was the teeming hub of that empire. Alongside the wealth went the inevitable poverty. Most working people lived in tiny, cramped houses or in 'rookeries' – dark, tottering areas of slums which covered hundreds of acres. Such places were ideal breeding places for disease, crime and vice. The novels of Charles Dickens paint the best pictures of life in Victorian London. He records everything in the same microscopic detail – the horror and the laughter are set side by side.

There were those who fought for the poor and needy. Outstanding among them was Lord Shaftesbury, whose tireless fight for the disadvantaged lasted for much of his life. At his funeral they lined the streets in their thousands – chimney boys, match girls, prostitutes and many others. His best memorial is in the reforms he pushed through Parliament, but more immediately visible is the statue we call Eros in Piccadilly Circus – it is actually of the Angel of Christian Charity.

Victorian London was not by any means all darkness and despair. One of the highlights was the Great Exhibition of 1851 held in Hyde Park. It was opened by the Queen, accompanied by Prince Albert, at whose suggestion the Exhibition was staged. It was visited by over six million people and the profits were devoted to the purchase of land in South Kensington and the endowment of the Victoria and Albert Museum.

The coming of the railways had an immense impact on London; it eventually enabled many people to move out of the cramped centre of the city, and the age of the commuter began.

After a raid – Paddington Station during the Blitz

War and peace

The first half of the 20th century is overshadowed by the two world wars. London suffered little material damage in World War I, but the Blitz of World War II put the capital in the front line. Of the City's 460 acres, 164 were reduced to rubble. Almost before the ashes were cold, Londoners were rebuilding their city, and the building and expansion continues just as busily today.

The days of Empire may have gone, but London remains one of the world's most important capital cities. Its population is now more cosmopolitan than ever before, and the resilience, courage and humour displayed by Londoners since the days of the Roman bridgehead are still often to be encountered. The skyline may change, but the spirit seems indestructable.

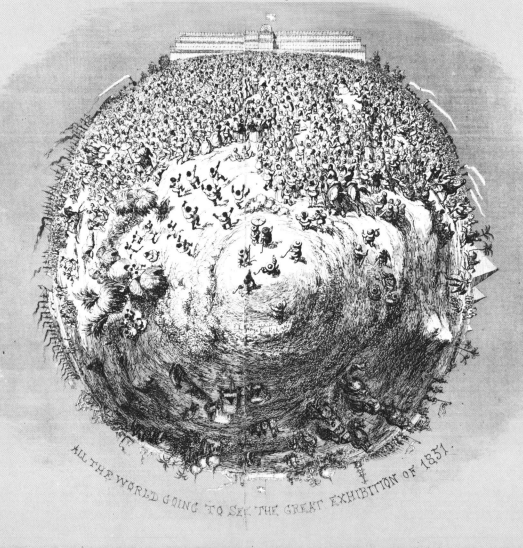

Green London

London has far more areas of natural history interest than most people would imagine. Everyone knows, of course, about the royal parks, but there are literally hundreds of other places, some of them tiny, where plants, birds, animals and insects can be sought out and enjoyed.

Wildlife in the heart of London – Tower Bridge overlooks the William Curtis Ecological Park. Insets: two common, but beautiful butterflies, meadow brown (left) and small tortoiseshell (right)

In the inner city the great parks have preserved original open space, supplemented by new landscapes as a by-product of Londoners' industrial activity. The reservoirs have created extensive lakes which are sites of national and even European significance for birdlife. The Grand Union and Lee canals are part of a 50 mile long linear park, from Rickmansworth in the north west to Waltham Abbey in the north east. The railways, which from the 1830s onwards were to occupy no less than ten per cent of the inner area, form radiating corridors of grass and scrub covered cuttings or embankments.

Since the war changes in economic patterns have

Oxeye daisies beside a railway. Such plants add colour and variety to many of London's urban landscapes

resulted in huge areas of land becoming vacant and overgrown. Ashtips of power stations, redundant railway sidings, demolished factories – many have become important if accidental nature parks. Most recently, as wildlife sites have been recognised as one of the elements that make Britain's cities more enjoyable places to live in, nature gardens have been artificially created in areas lacking natural wildspace. A wilderness on a former lorry park at King's Cross, a heathland in the former Surrey Docks and a lagoon in the Lee Valley are some of the examples described below. Urban farms are also a feature of several of London's most built-up neighbourhoods.

The geological background
London's geology is dominated by the London Clay covering the chalk basin whose rim forms the North Downs and the Chilterns. The sands and pebble beds lying between the chalk and clay outcrop as the Addington Hills and heathlands of south east London. Sandy beds also cap the heights of Hampstead in the north and Crystal Palace in the south, with alluvial gravel in the flood plain of the Thames. The Thames is the focus of the region's geography. Flowing for 40 miles from Hampton Court in the west to Dartford Creek in the east, it is fed by an intricacy of rivers and streams running down from the ridges of hills on either side of the Thames valley. In former times the uplands were covered by large forests – Middlesex in the west, Essex in the east, the Great North Wood to the south – these royal hunting forests included commons as well as woodland. Thanks to Green Belt policy, established during the 1930s to limit suburban sprawl, the encircling ring of greenery survives – though much battered by the pressure for development and new kinds of agribusiness.

Rivers and lakes, marshes and meadows

Ask anyone how many rivers there are in London and you are likely to get guesses of around half a dozen. As well as the Colne and Lee, the major Thames tributaries, people probably know of the Brent and Wandle, and maybe the Crane and Cray. Local residents will be familiar with the shorter rivers passing through their townships, the Ravensbourne through Lewisham or the Roding through Barking, for example. Few will be aware of the Hogsmill or Beverley Brook in Kingston and Richmond, or the Beam and Ingrebourne in Havering. Others are tributaries of tributaries, the Pinn feeding the Colne, and the Silk Stream and Dollis Brook converging on the Brent at Brent Reservoir. Loxford Water is an extension of the Roding and the Rom of the Beam, while to the south Pool River and the Quaggy extend the catchment area of the Ravensbourne. There are London's lost rivers too. The Fleet and Westbourne survive in the names they have given to districts, and the Tyburn in its reminder of past horrors. Yet the River Peck disappears into a culvert after only a brief above ground existence in Peckham Rye and the same fate befalls the Effra after its moment of glory in Belair Park. For long stretches even the larger streams are straitjacketed in concrete-lined banks, or used as open drains for flood water and overspill from sewage works.

Following the Thames
The Thames itself suffered almost total sterility in post-war years. Only eels were able to tolerate the oxygen-less conditions caused by the concentration of untreated sewage and the discharge of chemical pollutants. A vigorous programme of improvements since the 1960s has restored the river to a state where fish can survive again, and even the occasional seal explores as far as Kew Bridge. Starting at Teddington Lock where the rural Thames meets the tidal water from the North Sea, the visitor can spend an afternoon's birdwatching at Ham Lands. Gravel was formerly dug here, and until recently there were plans to build houses on the infilled meadows. More than 40 bird species have re-adopted the land as breeding territory. A rich variety of plants also flourish. In the middle of the river is the first of the chain of islets known as Eyots or Aits, which are observable from the shore. The thickets of alder and willow attract woodland as well as water's edge species, wrens and robins as well as coots and mallard. Muddy banks provide abundant worms and snails for fish which in turn entice grebe and heron. Lots Ait has been the subject of a public inquiry over planning proposals, and will probably not be built on. Nearby Isleworth Ait is now protected as a nature reserve.

The last sizeable grazing meadow in the upper tidal Thames is in Syon Park, one of the most important sites of scientific interest anywhere in London. A tapestry of flowers such as marsh marigold and yellow iris makes an attractive spectacle, while the population of rare snails and flies brings birds flocking. A smaller version of this type of meadow survives at Duke's Hollow next to one of the boathouses on the Boat Race course.

The former reservoirs at Lonsdale Road in the loop of the Thames at Barnes are now an eight hectare reserve where the succession of plants to 'climax vegetation' can be observed: lichens to moss layers; to grasses, herbaceous plants and shrubs; to woodland. Also known as the 'Leg o' Mutton' because of its shape, the water areas of the reserve are a feeding ground for diving ducks such as pochard, tufted duck, goldeneye and goosander. On the other side of the peninsula the quartet of Barn Elms Reservoirs are a birdwatcher's paradise (permit from Thames Water, New River Head, Rarebury Avenue, London EC1R 4TP). Teal, widgeon and shoveller are some of the ducks which are regular winter visitors, with common sandpiper, black and common tern, swallow, sand martin and yellow wagtail among other migrants.

On the south bank of the Thames at Chelsea, Battersea Park was the second of the parks to be built by the Victorians in what was then the fringe of the city. The lake here attracts a variety of water-fowl, with herons fishing from the island refuge, and a former leaf dump near the Chelsea Bridge entrance is now a nature reserve for the benefit of butterflies and nesting birds of many woodland species.

Next to the pump house which once filled the Surrey Docks, the former Lavender Dock has been re-excavated to recreate the habitats that formerly fringed the un-embanked river. From the open water of Lavender Pond the reeds give way to marsh, while on the higher ground alder is intermingled with sallow and birches. A short distance away is the newly created Rotherhithe Ecological Park, also permanently open and offering a mosaic of different habitats.

To the south of Greenland Dock (London's second oldest dock, dug as Howland Great Dock at the beginning of the 18th century), Deptford Wharf is among the half a dozen more important wasteland sites in Greater London. Like Thames Wharf at the mouth of Bow Creek on the far side of the Isle of Dogs, its mixture of demolished sheds and tipped rubble has developed as a refuge for invertebrates, small mammals and the birds which feed on them. Another former industrial site where the artificial terrain has been exploited to create a nature reserve is Thameside, on the ashtips of the old Barking power station. Orchids relish the pulverised fuel ash; flocks of birds frequent the scrub between the ditches, which are a haven for amphibians; and this large site is near to an important feeding ground for waders in Barking Bay.

On the far bank is the new town of Thamesmead. Young woodlands have sprung up since the war, and at Tripcock Park is one of London's largest reedbeds, harbouring bird species which include bearded tit and water rail. Of the moated and walled islands called tumps, built as explosives stores for Woolwich Arsenal, a handful

Below: the incomparable view from Richmond Hill.
Left: great crested grebe, often seen on lakes and reservoirs

survive as ideal nature reserves – one of them, Tump 53, has been formally recognised as such. The mudflats on the river facing the Ford works at Dagenham are a popular feeding territory for birds, while the fields in the lee of the Crossness sewage works are an (understandably) undisturbed roosting ground.

The vast expanses of marshes on either side of the Thames in this final stretch before it reaches Essex and Kent are havens for thousands of migrant birds but are threatened by commercial and housing developments. On Rainham Marsh waders include little stint, dunlin, little ringed plover, curlew sandpiper, common sandpiper, spotted redshank, redshank, greenshank, curlew, black tailed godwit, ruff and jack snipe. Several of these species can also be seen on Crayford Marsh at the mouth of the River Cray at Deptford Creek. A unique attraction here is to be found on the river side of the flood wall where a salt marsh survives, although endangered by a possible marina.

West London Rivers
Back on London's western perimeter, a stroll along the Colne takes you past half a dozen nature reserves, not all of them open to the public, which are an indication of the countryside quality of this north west corner. Stockers Lane is one of the former gravel pits in the valley bottom which teems with wildfowl during the winter, and Frays Farm Meadows where the Colne splits into different channels – one of them, the Frays River, is among the wet grasslands also attracting a massive influx of birdlife. On the side of the valley overlooking the Grand Union Canal on its way to the Thames at Brentford, Old Park Wood is a fine mature woodland and the section nearest the hospital is a nature reserve.

The upper part of the River Crane, Yeading Brook, runs through Yeading Meadows south of Northolt airfield. This is hay grassland interspersed with water-filled hollows which attracts butterflies such as small heath and skippers. On the south side of Hounslow Heath the Crane divides on either side of an island which is now the Crane Park nature reserve. Its damp woodland supports 45 varieties of larger fungi, including one found in only half a dozen other locations in Britain, and a dried out millpond shelters butterflies and grass snakes. Despite appearances, the island is wholly artificial, built to create a head of water as power for the gunpowder mills that operated here until as recently as 1926.

The Wandle
Between its source at Croydon and junction with the Thames at Wandsworth is the Wandle, once lined with mills producing paper and fabrics as well as gunpowder. By the Carshalton Ponds and pump house in the grounds of Carshalton House (now a convent) is St Philomena's Pond. Water celery, large bittercress and water sedge have been included in the replanting of the desilted lake where toads and newts cohabit with, among other species, a nationally rare snail.

To the north of the delightful Beddington Park lies the expanse dominated by the Wandle sewage works. The northernmost part of this major green

Left: the main picture is of a common blue butterfly on a fragrant orchid. The insets are of a water rail (above), skulking bird of water margins, and lupins (below) lovely plants which seed themselves in unexpected places

wedge is Mitcham Common, where in recent years local people have persuaded Merton Council to stop filling in the ponds around it and covering remnant heathland with mounds of builders' rubble.

East London Rivers
The Lee (or Lea) is fortunate to have a valley dominated by water supply reservoirs rather than sewage treatment areas. The vast expanses of the King George and William Girling Reservoirs attract correspondingly large bird roosts, but it is the group of Walthamstow Reservoirs that are most popular with birdwatchers (permits from Thames Water). As well as a famous heronry on the islands in two of the reservoirs, there is a profusion of wildfowl and gulls. The valley is a migration route for waders and over 30 species have been recorded. On the adjacent Walthamstow Marshes over 350 plant species have been identified. The Lee Valley Regional Park Authority has recognised the nature conservation interest of the area and manage it in a manner that protects its wetland character. The Authority also provides a nature trail leaflet for Bully Fen, part of an area by the Lee infilled to create the Eastway cycle track.

The vulnerability of rivers and their bankside habitats was illustrated in 1985 when an accidental spillage of chemicals into the River Roding at Woodford wiped out 95 per cent of its aquatic life along its whole length within 24 hours. The river runs through Wanstead Park, at the western end of which a stretch of the Centenary Walk links Wanstead Flats with Epping Forest through Walthamstow Forest. Eastwards, the Beam River is the spine of 'the Dagenham corridor', open land separating Romford and Hornchurch from the rest of London. Its tributary, the River Rom, forms the northern part of the chain with, to the west, the gravel diggings on Fairlop Plain which are being developed as water features in a new country park. Hornchurch Marshes, at the river mouth, are important for birds despite industrial despoliation. Almost at London's eastern boundary, the Ingrebourne River runs between Hornchurch and Upminster before reaching the Rainham Marshes. On a small tributary, Cranham Marsh is managed by the Essex Naturalists' Trust.

Two Reservoirs
In addition to the reservoirs already mentioned two of the city's most interesting lakes, Ruislip Lido and Brent Reservoir, are reservoirs of a special kind. Both are feeders for the Grand Union Canal and in the one and a half centuries since their construction each has developed a mosaic of habitats. Where the Ruislip Brook enters the Lido is one of London's only three statutory Local Nature Reserves. The sunnier part of the area is heathland – rare in the region. Brent teems with birdlife, meticulously recorded each year by London's ornithologists.

Ponds
Ponds are a disappearing element of the countryside and their city counterparts are now a valued haven for invertebrates and amphibia such as frogs, toads and the great crested newt. London has lost about 90 per cent of the ponds it had a hundred years ago, when they were an integral part of the economy. Four examples in Greenwich illustrate how even small ponds can support a myriad of plant and animal species. Lessa Pond at

Eltham is fringed by ash and willow, and the marginal vegetation includes various duckweeks, rushes and sedges. Birdbrook Road Pond at Kidbrook supports plants such as hornwort, bogbean, spearwort and monkey flower, together with no less than eight amphibian species. Nearby, Kidbrook Green is a remnant of once extensive marshland with the wet grassland supporting rushes, buttercups and hairy willowherb, and a cluster of shallow ponds is a frogs' paradise. Even the tiny pond at Dot Hill near Plumstead has its share of frogs.

Lakes in formal parks are usually of far less wildlife interest. Their concrete edges are hostile to plants and therefore unfriendly to insects and wildfowl. Even so, many uncommon species can be spotted at places like St James's Park, while the once rare great crested grebe is now a familiar sight at lakes from Hampstead Heath to Snaresbrook.

Woodlands and grasslands

While London's plants and animals have been recorded by naturalists associated with the London Natural History Society since the society's formation in 1858, the first comprehensive survey of habitats was carried out by the London Wildlife Trust on behalf of the Greater London Council in 1985. Information about over 2,000 wildlife sites in London's 33 boroughs (including the City of

London) was intended as the basis for a regional nature conservation strategy. Boroughs were to be encouraged not only to safeguard individual sites but to link them together by creating or enhancing 'green corridors', and producing 'habitat creation' reserves in neighbourhoods lacking wildlife areas. No such strategy was devised by the GLC before its abolition but a majority of boroughs are continuing to fund a Greater London Ecology Unit which is carrying on the task, assisted by the individual boroughs and voluntary conservation organisations such as the London Wildlife Trust. The first published result of the London Wildlife Habitat Survey has been the booklet *A Nature Conservation Strategy for London* which focuses on 'Woodland, Wasteland, the Tidal Thames and two London Boroughs' – Barnet and Lewisham.

Fighting for Nature

Many of London's best known natural landmarks were once the subject of bitter dispute, and confrontations continue. The best known instances of past conservation battles are Hampstead Heath and Epping Forest. The former, a delightful mixture of habitats from ponds to the oak woodland at Ken Wood, was jeopardised when the lord of the manor attempted to enclose the land in 1829 for the purpose of selling it off as building plots. It was more than 40 years later that the claim was blocked, the money found from the public purse for its purchase and the common eventually handed over to the newly created London County Council.

Queen's Wood at nearby Highgate was the scene for a similar campaign, organised by Octavia Hill, one of the founders of the National Trust. Deptford Park and Hilly Fields in Lewisham also survive as open spaces (a phrase she was the first to use), thanks to her efforts. She was also active in the laying out of dozens of churchyards as neighbourhood gardens, and even created new public open space as at Vauxhall Park. In 1911, the last year of her life, she launched the River

Left: great crested newt; it spends much of its time hiding under stones, but takes to the water in the breeding season. Below: in Epping Forest

Sydenham Hill Wood, an important nature reserve in south-east London

Wandle Open Spaces Committee. It succeeded in saving the riverside around Mitcham Bridge, and the National Trust now owns 140 acres at Happy Valley, Merton Abbey Wall, Morden Hall, Wandle Park and Watermeads, which includes a nature reserve. Epping Forest was saved by the resilience of local smallholders who suffered imprisonment for defending their commoners' rights when the ancient forest laws were challenged by those seeking enclosure and development. The Forest today is 2,430 hectares in extent, a relic of the even more extensive Forest of Waltham which stretched from the Lee to Romford. The woodland comprises mostly oak, beech and hornbeam with stretches of heathland and damp grassland in the lower areas. A Visitor Centre at High Beach offers guides to the Forest.

Woodland Reserves

The *Nature Conservation* handbook identifies 23 woodlands of 'metropolitan importance', all but nine being in the two south-eastern boroughs of Croydon and Bromley. The Croydon woods – Croham Hurst, Devilsden and Kings – are owned and managed by Croydon Council, which also looks after Selsdon Wood and its bird sanctuary on behalf of the National Trust. The 11 in Bromley include Scadbury Park near Chislehurst, recently opened as a local nature reserve, and Downe Bank, owned and run by the Kent Trust for Nature Conservation. Ancient woodland elsewhere in the south east centres round Shooters Hill where the Oxleas Woodlands are on the route of the proposed East London River Crossing link with the A2, and Lesnes Abbey Woods overlooking the Erith Marshes. On the west of London the Ruislip Woods consist of four ancient woods to the west and east of Ruislip Lido – Mad Bess Wood, Copse Wood, Park Wood and Bayhurst Wood Country Park which provides woodland trails. In Ealing, Perivale Wood is one of Britain's earliest nature reserves, managed by the Selborne Society from 1904 and purchased by them in 1926.

As the Survey points out, while ancient woodland mainly lingers on the outer fringe, 'almost all woods in London have a significant nature conservation value on a Borough or local perspective'. Two examples illustrate the continuing need to guard local wildlife areas. Gunnersbury Triangle is a young woodland which has developed in the space between three railway lines at Chiswick. British Rail, seeking to maximise the income from their land holdings, sought planning permission for factories on the site. A campaign by local residents in the early 1980s resulted in a public inquiry where British Rail lost their case. GLC funds then enabled the local borough to buy the site at non-developed valuation and hand it to the London Wildlife Trust as a nature reserve. In south London in 1985 campaigners at another inquiry succeeded in protecting some of the upper slopes of Sydenham Hill Wood, a remnant of the Great North Wood that used to extend to Croydon and survives in placenames such as Norwood and Colliers Wood. Sydenham Hill Wood is now a nature reserve, while the adjacent Dulwich Wood owned by the Dulwich College Estates Governors can be visited by keyholders.

Grasslands

Among London's most important commons and grasslands, Farthing Downs at Coulsdon at the southernmost tip of Greater London was saved as downland after another ownership battle. As elsewhere, the lord of the manor was busily selling off everything he could – marl, turf, trees – until he met with resistance from local commoners. Their approaches to the City of London persuaded the Corporation to buy out the manorial rights in 1877, and in the following year it was given *carte blanche* to buy land for recreation purposes within 25 miles of London – hence Burnham Beeches became part of its landholdings. At Farthing Downs, which together with Devilsden Wood to the south form a 100 hectare site of special scientific interest, the Corporation has produced leaflets as a popular guide to the wildlife of the area. A footpath leads out of Happy Valley to the 180 hectares of Coulsdon Common, also owned by the Corporation, and thence to Kenley Common and Riddlesdown. The down, which is covered by yew and scrub, has a patch of grassland notably rich in plant species and at its southern tip a famous geological site, the Rose and Crown Chalk Pit. However, there have been plans to build an industrial estate which would encroach into the quarry. The London boundary meanders north east through Kings and Selsdon Woods mentioned above, before diving south to take in Biggin Hill and Downe. A broad belt of open space continues northeastwards past Addington until it reaches Spring Park straddling the Croydon and Bromley boundary. Owned by the City of London, together with patches of nearby West Wickham Common, it is part of a large complex of grasslands around Hayes and Keston.

Heathland and other open areas
Heathland is scarce in London as in the rest of the country, and its specialist mix of flora and fauna is of great interest. Relict heath dominated by heather survives at Wimbledon Common and Keston Common. From here the sequence of open space extends through Bromley Common. Petts Wood, a popular National Trust woodland adjoins St Paul's Cray Common, which through lack of management is declining into secondary woodland. Adjoining Petts Wood to the west is the National Trust's most unlikely London property – the 245 acres of farm and woodland of Hawkwood, truly captive countryside. Near the last stations of the Northern Line are two areas which the Wildlife Habitat Survey has dubbed 'Countryside Conservation Areas'. The northernmost area comprises fields north of Rowley Green Common, now being jointly managed by the Hertfordshire and Middlesex Trust for Nature Conservation and London Wildlife Trust to preserve its mixture of grassland, heathland and rare sphagnum bog.

A feature of this area is Arkley Lane, one of London's few green lanes with hedgerows, ditches and the grassland of the lane itself. It runs from the London boundary past the Saffron Green Shooting Ground before climbing the Arkley ridge. The second proposed conservation area surrounds Totteridge Fields in the valley of Dollis Brook between Totteridge and High Barnet.

Parks and cemeteries, nature parks and city farms

London's parks offer almost infinite variety, from the traditional countryside scene of fields, hedges and woodlands in parts of the country parks to the formality of Hampton Court gardens. The former lie along London's northern boundary and include Bayhurst Wood at Ruislip, Stanmore in Harrow, Trent Park at Cockfosters, Hainault Forest straddling the Redbridge/Essex border and Havering at Romford. Stanmore is part of a complex of green space which survives on Harrow Weald. The heathland at Harrow Weald Common has developed as sporadic birch scrub and woodland, Stanmore Common with beech and oak. Bentley Priory, on the lower slopes, is grazing grassland with a lake in the centre which is rich in fish, water's edge plants and birdlife. Trent Park is part of the former royal hunting forest which became Enfield Chase, with woodlands to the north and a nature trail by the lakes at the heart of

Cemeteries can be superb, and virtually undisturbed, places for wildlife

the park. Hainault Forest was also a hunting forest, where replanted woodland now provides wild walks to supplement the active recreation facilities that are the other element of the country park concept. A short distance east, Havering too has been developed on the remnants of a hunting forest and offers a nature trail of the sort that usefully introduces non-experts to key aspects of natural history.

Richmond Park is the wildest of the nine royal parks, and while its deer can hardly be missed, its other mammals, including hares as well as rabbits, badgers and foxes are less conspicuous. The bird colonies include jackdaws and tree pipits, with pairs of barn, little and tawny owls together with reed warblers and water rails near the Pen Ponds in the middle of the park.

From Richmond Hill, surely among the most magnificent spots in Europe, Kew Gardens are to the north and Hampton Court Park and Bushy Park across the river to the south. The former has a 'Wilderness' and the latter a river, but both are part of the energetic landscaping that has continued from the 16th century to the present day. The canal is the Longford River, built by Charles I to bring water all the way from the Colne to supply the ponds which now attract an unexpected range of birds.

Hyde Park had a hunting history before being opened to the public by Charles I and laid out by a succession of monarchs and their consorts – most notably George I's Queen Caroline who created the Serpentine. Despite the lack of secluded areas and throngs of visitors, the count of breeding bird species is surprisingly high, and a sandbank has been constructed on the island in the lake to lure nesting kingfishers. Kensington Gardens, which makes up the western half of the park, was part of the area acquired by Henry VIII as a deer park, with Green Park and St James's Park providing a link to the river at Westminster.

Regent's Park, acquired by Henry VIII at the dissolution of the monasteries, became farmland after the Restoration before being converted by

Right: the main picture shows fallow deer in Richmond Park. The insets are of (left) a black swan and (right) a flamingo. Such exotic birds can be seen in several London parks

Nash, on behalf of his client the Prince Regent, into a speculative housing development with park attached. A model city park, it has lots going on inside it, including the Zoo which opened in 1828 and the Regent's Canal, extending the Paddington arm of the Grand Union Canal across London to the Thames at Limehouse. Primrose Hill to the north of the canal provides a splendid viewpoint but, alas, few primroses.

Wimbledon Common, together with the adjacent Putney Heath, constitute the largest area of publicly accessible wild space in London, Richmond Park apart. When acquired in 1871 the land was barren and mostly treeless, but new planting and invasion of scrub has increased its variety of cover. A host of butterflies to be seen includes small tortoiseshell, meadow brown, brimstone, orange tip, large and small whites, holly and common blue, small copper, green hairstreak, small skipper, small heath, speckled wood, painted lady, red admiral and peacock. The woodlands are reputed to contain every type of native British tree, and the fungus species are particularly numerous. Small valley bogs shelter plants such as sphagnum mosses. Reptiles are represented by the increasingly rare grass snake and the common lizard which, despite its name, isn't at all common.

Smaller Parks

Mature parklands surrounding aristocratic mansions on the routes westwards out of London, such as the Bath and Portsmouth roads, include Osterley Park, a National Trust property which is a place of considerable botanic and ornithological interest. It has a niche in history as the first spot where the great crested grebe was recorded as breeding in London after its near obliteration in the Victorian era. Syon House offers a botanic garden with an aviary and aquarium inside its Great Conservatory, and the London Butterfly House where you can see exotic butterflies even in the winter months. It also has its meadows. Gunnersbury Park is large but monotonous. Chiswick House is smaller but more picturesque and with more cover. Holland Park is the most profuse of the former private gardens. Its woodland is the nearest to central London, its undergrowth shelter for nesting birds – supplemented by more exotic specimens such as flamingoes, cranes and peacocks.

Victoria Park is north-east London's equivalent of Battersea, made in the early Victorian period on what was then the fringe of the built-up area. The Regent's Canal to the west and Hertford Union Canal along the southern perimeter add to the water areas provided by the decorative lakes and their mixture of resident and visiting duck and geese. Brockwell Park near Brixton is a park where, as its name suggests, badgers once prowled. The nearby Dulwich and Peckham Rye Parks were opened to the public in the last decade of the 19th century. The former was created by the LCC on farmland donated by the Dulwich College Estates Governors, the latter on what was Homestall Farm. Both are fine examples of landscaping, each having an arboretum, with Dulwich's well-known rhododendrons providing nesting cover. Peckham's water features, part of an elaborate layout on a Japanese theme, make it a wildlife oasis at the centre of the 'green concrete' of the encircling Rye. A short distance away is Nunhead Cemetery, the twin of Highgate Cemetery, built and managed by the same company. Overgrown since the war and

taken over by the local council in 1975, the more wooded northern half is now designated a nature reserve. Hackney's Abney Park Cemetery enjoys a similar role, while Tower Hamlets Cemetery is also likely to be managed for this purpose.

Islington and Tower Hamlets are the boroughs with least open space (apart from Kensington which has Hyde Park and Kensington Gardens on its doorstep). To make up for this deficiency organisations such as the British Trust for Conservation Volunteers have joined with local wildlife groups and schools to create nature gardens such as St Jude's at Bethnal Green. Since its creation in the early 1980s the tree, grassland and pond habitats have developed a respectable permanence. In Islington, in the shadow of the Arsenal football ground, the council has turned former railway sidings into the Gillespie Road Park. Much of the vegetation, such as brambles, was retained in the design, and the self-seeded lupins provide a mass of colour in summer. Within a stone's throw of King's Cross and on the banks of the Regent's Canal is London's most spectacular example of habitat creation. On a former coal wharf in Camley Street the GLC constructed a two acre park, planting over 5,000 trees and scooping out a large pond which has thriving populations of frogs and newts. The park is managed by the London Wildlife Trust on behalf of Camden Council, and a study centre provides leaflets describing the site. Two other city parks are at Mile End, along the Regent's Canal, and Burgess Park at Walworth.

City Farms

Children's zoos have always been a jolly ingredient of city parks, and the urban farm is an enjoyable new kind of menagerie providing a rural experience in towns. One of the earliest of London's dozen or so farms was set up by Inter-Action at their Kentish Town headquarters where among its other attractions you can now fondle a ferret. Spitalfields allows you to shear sheep, while at Vauxhall goats browse under the railway line into Waterloo. Freightliners at Highbury keeps a bull as well as the more usual cow and Surrey Docks offers produce such as honey, goose eggs and goat's milk. All have made the best of fairly desolate surroundings but Stepping Stones has the advantage of four acres at the centre of the old Stepney village. With the parish church and Stepney Green next door, they rightly boast of it as one of the pleasantest spots anywhere in the East End. No one could say the same of Mudchute in the Isle of Dogs, but it is nevertheless part of the renaissance of the former docklands. As its name indicates, the 30 acres of Mudchute were the result of dredgings from the Millwall Docks and until the advent of the farm the plan was to level the site for housing. Now it has a stable of horses plus a market garden producing vegetables for sale. From on top of the grassland mound the view north is towards the hi-tech factories of the Dockland Corporation's techno park. The farm is below to the east. Just south and filled by runoff from the spoil tip is a ditch where children collect snails and tiddlers in jam jars. Beyond is the incomparable vista of the Greenwich waterfront with Wren's Observatory on the hill above. The mixture is what makes city life such a satisfying – if often fraught – experience, and London's burgeoning wildlife is one of the most potent sources of pleasure for the city dweller.

Buildings and Builders

Any chronological study of London's architecture has to start with the Roman period, for this was the first layer of development which determined the future of the city. No complete Roman buildings survive, but the Roman influence can be seen in street patterns and in the selection of London for the site of a riverside fortress, communications centre and port.

The next layer was formed in the Middle Ages, with the establishment of Westminster as the administrative, Court and religious centre for the kingdom during the late 11th century. Wood was the standard building material and so medieval London was largely a timber-framed city. Stone was used for churches, castles and palaces – prepared with great skill by the teams of master masons who determined the nature and style of the buildings they created. There were no architects as such; the masons drew their inspiration, their skills and even their materials from France. Stone quarried near Caen was used for many of England's cathedrals, for example. The influence of France began to wane in the second part of the 15th century as a result of continual wars and religious differences between the two countries. Italy and the impact of the Renaissance began to influence English architecture. Brick became a favoured material, along with more varied types of stone, some of which now came from English sources. Skilled Italian craftsmen came to work in England, bringing the clarity, classicism and ornament of the Renaissance into buildings such as Hampton Court.

The Tudor period witnessed a great increase in the size and importance of London. The much reduced power of the church was reflected in the building of numerous royal palaces and stately town mansions, underlying the increasing move towards private land ownership. At the same time the Royal hunting grounds were established at Hyde Park, St James's Park and Green Park, giving London the green and open centre it still enjoys today. With much of the church lands confiscated and granted to private landlords, the pattern of London's future development was determined. Indeed, descendants of some of the families who began the private development of Tudor and Stuart London are still building and developing the city today.

The First Architects

This period saw the emergence of the architect. As a measure of the influence of Italy, the designer of a building became for the first time more important than the craftsmen who created it, and architects began to attain the status they still enjoy today as arbiters of public taste. Inigo Jones was in some ways,

Inigo Jones, the architect of the Queen's House at Greenwich (below)

the greatest English architect of the seventeenth century. He was born in London, the son of a Smithfield clothworker. Little is known about his early life, but he appears to have made his first visit to Italy in his late twenties as a painter. After his return he established himself in Court circles as a stage designer. To specialise in the art of theatre design would seem an unsuitable training for an architect, yet Jones made the transition quickly, no doubt helped by a second, and longer visit to Italy from 1613. While in Italy he studied Roman architecture and developed a great admiration for the classicism of Palladio. On his return to England Jones was appointed Surveyor of the King's Works, and began to plan the most revolutionary building London had ever seen. The Queen's House, Greenwich, started in 1616, was the first truly classical building in England. Jones's masterpiece in central London was the Banqueting House in Whitehall, built 1619-22, an entirely English interpretation of the Palladian style. He also introduced the most characteristic London building form, the square of houses ranged evenly around a central park. Covent Garden, part of which still survives in the form laid out by Jones from 1631, established a pattern to be followed by London builders for the next two centuries.

Wren, Vanbrugh and Hawksmoor

Three architects took over the mantle of Palladian Classicism from Inigo Jones, and they worked together so closely that they can be considered as one group. The most important of these was Sir Christopher Wren who, like Jones, had no formal training in architecture.

The Great Fire of 1666, which swept away most of medieval London, was to change Wren's life, for in 1667 he was appointed one of the Surveyors under the Rebuilding Act. Two years later he became Surveyor General of the King's Works and was knighted in 1673. A man of remarkable vision and dynamism, Wren studied architecture in France and Holland and then set about replanning London. Unfortunately the complex network of land ownership and vested interests as powerful in the 17th century as they are today, caused the plan to be rejected and so he had to content himself with rebuilding 51 city churches in 16 years.

These churches reveal his inventiveness and his daring approach to style. He invented the classical style church, and then changed it constantly to satisfy his imagination. Wren's masterpiece is without doubt St Paul's Cathedral, a building whose formal classicism, majestic dome and baroque detailing make it unique in England. Probably England's greatest church architect, Wren

Churches and other buildings by Sir Christopher Wren (left), remain an essential part of London's character. His masterpiece is St Paul's (below), a building combining technical innovation with great beauty. He also contributed to Greenwich Hospital (above), as did Vanbrugh and Hawksmoor

*St Martin-in-the-Fields: the vaulted ceiling (above)
and classical exterior (left)
Below: Horse Guards, by William Kent*

also produced remarkable secular buildings, among them the austerely simple barracks at Chelsea Hospital and the baroque splendour of the Greenwich Hospital. Wren was still working at the age of 80, lived to be 91, saw his great cathedral completed and the classical style firmly established in England.

Sir John Vanbrugh also came to architecture late in life and almost by chance. His father, a Flemish refugee, had become a successful merchant and married well, and so Vanbrugh was able to move easily in Court circles. Among other things this led him to be a spy in France, to write a series of *risqué* and highly successful comedies, and ultimately to architecture when in 1699, the Earl of Carlisle suggested he attempt a design for Castle Howard. The successful completion of this baroque extravaganza by a young and completely untrained architect resulted in Vanbrugh's appointment as Comptroller at the Office of Works and thus Wren's principal colleague. Under Wren's influence he developed a style that was the closest England ever came to adopting the ostentatious and forceful Baroque of northern Europe. Vanbrugh's work was mostly associated with country houses outside London, especially Blenheim, which was the high point of the English Baroque style. However, his own house at Greenwich is an extraordinary Gothic fortress, and he was also associated with the building of the Royal Arsenal at Woolwich from 1717.

Nicholas Hawksmoor worked with Wren and Vanbrugh on a number of commissions. A man of great talent and vision, Hawksmoor began working with Wren at the age of 18, and with Vanbrugh ten years later. He made a major contribution to Wren's work at Greenwich and was able to translate Vanbrugh's fantastic schemes for Castle Howard and Blenheim into architectural reality. In 1711 he was appointed Surveyor under the Act for Building Fifty New Churches, and designed six of them himself. They are all highly individual buildings; the best are perhaps St Anne's, Limehouse, St Mary Woolnoth, St George, Bloomsbury and Christchurch, Spitalfields. Hawksmoor also designed the west towers of Westminster Abbey.

A return to classical ideals

In the early 18th century the excesses of Baroque were definitely an acquired taste, and so it was inevitable that a reaction should set in. The next generation of architects turned their eyes firmly back towards the classical ideal. The leader of this movement was Richard Boyle, the 3rd Earl of Burlington. He designed relatively few buildings himself, the most important being his own villa at Chiswick, but his influence on both architectural and social circles was immense. It is a measure of his influence that no London buildings of significance were designed outside the classical tradition until the 1830s.

Lord Burlington was particularly associated with three architects, Colen Campbell, James Gibbs and William Kent. Campbell, who built little in London, was probably responsible for leading Lord Burlington towards Palladianism, while Gibbs was actively involved with the classic revival. His masterpiece, St Martin-in-the-Fields was in its own way just as influential as Chiswick Villa. By combining a classical portico with a steeple, it established a style for London churches that continued to be copied for well over a century. Kent's most important building in London is the Horse Guards, in Whitehall, completed after his death by John Vardy.

Georgian London

During the 18th century England became a world power, with London the heart of its mercantile empire. The wealthy country-based families acquired town houses, often sparing little expense in their design and fitting, while the spreading middle classes also required simpler versions of these grand Mayfair mansions. London spread outwards towards Bloomsbury, Marylebone, Greenwich, Hampstead, Islington, Dulwich, Kensington and Camden Town. Along the new roads and around the new squares, there appeared the typical Georgian terraced house of three or four storeys, narrow-fronted but deep, with even fenestration, a simply ornamented doorway, decorative iron railings, quickly but elegantly built of London stock bricks, manufactured in large quantities in the brickfields of Bedfordshire and elsewhere. Thousands of these simple, elegant houses survive.

Adam and Nash

Robert Adam was the greatest designer of the 18th

Top: an interior at Syon House, by Robert Adam. Above: Osterley House, also by Adam. Both buildings show his mastery of exterior and interior design

century; he was the first man to practise a total view of design, and to take responsibility for every feature of a building from the architectural exterior to the carpets and door furniture. He began to work in London in 1758, in partnership with one of his brothers, and quickly developed his own style which featured delicate mouldings, shallow stucco, decorative paintwork, and an exploitation of all the geometric forms associated with classicism. During the 1760s Adam produced three great London mansions, Syon House, Osterley Park and Kenwood, and then in the 1770s he turned his attention to inner London, designing town houses in Portman Square and St James's Square and launching his great Thames-side development at the Adelphi. This vast housing scheme was far ahead of its time and plunged Adam into insolvency. He recovered, but did not work again in London.

The imposing entrance to one of the world's treasure houses, the British Museum

The influence of Adam was immense. He popularised a vast range of decorative styles, and made design and decorative detail available to even the most humble speculative builder. Design books, commercially made plaster mouldings, mass-produced decorative architectural ornaments and cast iron fittings such as fireplaces greatly simplified the building process and made modern design a feature of quite ordinary urban housing.

John Nash was an architect of great diversity and an inspired town planner. His greatest achievement, the layout of Regent's Park and Regent Street, started in 1811, when he was sixty; it was a brilliant blend of freedom and formality which anticipated the garden city of the next century. Regent Street has been greatly changed, but the Park is still much as Nash left it. He went on to plan Trafalgar Square, Suffolk Street and Carlton House Terrace, and began the building of Buckingham Palace, but in 1830 fell from grace amid accusations of profiteering. Corrupt he may have been, but his legacy is some of the best town planning London has ever enjoyed, spacious, elegant and still working well 150 years after his death. Nash's other contribution to London was to popularise the stucco technique of building decoration which he had used as early as 1780. From the early 19th century, stucco-faced brickwork became the most common building style in London, particularly for terraced housing, partly because it could be both decorative and easily painted, and partly because it could conceal the increasingly indifferent standards of speculative building.

Greek Revival

As a reaction to the design and decoration of Adam and his followers an interest in Greek architecture had developed in the 18th century, but it was not until the early 19th century that any major Greek-inspired buildings appeared in London. Sir Robert Smirke was the leading exponent of this style. His greatest building is the British Museum (started in 1823), whose vast and dignified façade started a fashion for public architecture that was to last well into the present century.

An Explosion in Size

The 19th century altered the face of London in every way. The city changed from one that could be walked across in a morning to an uncontrollable urban monster sprawling miles out into the countryside in every direction. Architecturally London changed from an elegantly uniform city of

St Pancras, by Sir George Gilbert Scott. It is the finest railway architecture in London

terraces and squares, churches and parks into a seething turmoil in which a diversity of new buildings grew up side by side with devastating slums and squalor. Roads were improved, and many major thoroughfares were driven through the older parts of the city, the docks were greatly enlarged, bridges were flung across the Thames and embankments were built to enclose the river, canals and then railways cut their way into the centre, while public transport networks of buses, underground railways and trams spread. At the same time the development of sewage and water networks and the emergence of gas and electricity as sources of domestic and industrial power also changed the city.

Another factor which influenced change was new building technology. The extensive use of structural cast iron from the 1830s for other than industrial buildings gave architects new freedoms of scale and style. Industrial mass production techniques affected both structure and ornament, and both architects and builders were increasingly able to specify or order all the components they needed from catalogues. Terracotta and other man-made materials began to replace stone for commercial, public and domestic buildings, particularly from the 1860s. The ready availability of sheet glass enabled windows to be increased in size, and allowed for the production of huge, entirely glazed structures. Books covering every aspect of architectural history, design and decoration were readily available, and their use was encouraged by the new government-sponsored schools of art. In fact, some architects were now able to exert more influence through books and published designs than actual buildings. The Victorian period was a great melting pot, from which emerged some of the most dynamic building London had ever seen.

Victorian Architects

In the early years of Victoria's reign, speculative building was rife, but the standards and design principles of the 18th century were maintained by some builders. Thomas Cubitt, who started life as a carpenter, rose to become London's greatest speculative builder. He formed the first of the large building companies, using a pool of permanently employed craftsmen to carry out his grandiose schemes. Bloomsbury, Barnsbury, Belgravia and Pimlico were largely created by Cubitt and his brother Lewis from the 1820s.

In the hands of Cubitt and others such as Sir Charles Barry, classicism survived, but it was now only one of a handful of styles that architects could pursue. The architecture of the past was constantly studied, revived and adapted to suit current needs, but it is wrong to dismiss the Victorians as mere revivalists. Certainly they exploited the past, but often in a dynamic and entirely novel way. Probably the most popular Victorian building style was the Gothic. From the 1830s medievalism was the rage, a reflection in part of the enthusiasm engendered by the many religious movements of the period. There was an upsurge in church building, mainly prompted by the increasing population of London and its steady spread into areas where no churches existed. For many architects, Gothic was the only suitable style for modern churches, particularly among those with High Church or Catholic interests such as A. W. N. Pugin, George Edmund Street and William Butterfield.

Pugin was a brilliant and influential designer, and a fervent supporter of 13th and 14th century Gothic. Most of his work was outside London, but his crowning glory was the Houses of Parliament, designed in partnership with Sir Charles Barry. With the building of the Houses of Parliament, Gothic became the official style for the grandest of public and private buildings. The style was soon applied to museums, banks, hotels, offices and railway stations. Though universally popular it was never dull, as each architect managed to develop his own particular version.

Thus, Street, primarily a church builder, was able to adapt his interpretation of 13th century Gothic to suit the Law Courts. Butterfield was drawn to the aggressive and colourful Gothic of northern Europe, and developed a polychromatic

George Gilbert Scott   J W Bazalgette

style based on sharp colour contrasts between various brick
and stone finishes. All Saints, Margaret Street is the prime
example of this. More inclined to the styles of English and
French Gothic was Sir George Gilbert Scott, a man of
prodigious output. The son of a clergyman, Scott worked
extensively as a church builder and restorer, but still found
time to design the St Pancras Hotel and Station (by far the
most adventurous and dramatic railway building in London)
and the Albert Memorial. Another enthusiast for colourful
Gothic was Alfred Waterhouse, who had already enjoyed
considerable success in Manchester, his home town, before
moving to London in 1865. A keen admirer of
terracotta and coloured brick, Waterhouse is best
known for the Natural History Museum and the
Prudential Assurance building in Holborn.
Stylistic versatility was exhibited particularly in
the railway stations, huge and imposing structures
designed to reflect the miraculous power of
mechanical transport. The greatest was Euston,
fronted by Philip Hardwick's monumental
Greek triumphal arch (demolished by British
Rail in 1961). Lewis Cubitt's King's Cross is
classical in feeling with its two great
engineer's arches signifying arrival and
departure. St Pancras apart, the most exciting
and original station is Paddington, a Gothic
cathedral in cast iron, designed by the Great
Western Railway's engineer, Isambard
Kingdom Brunel. Indeed, many of the
greatest features of Victorian London were
designed by engineers rather than
architects. Brunel's father, Marc, built
the first Thames tunnel, opened in 1843
and still used by underground trains. Sir
Joseph Paxton, a Derbyshire gardener
turned engineer, designed the Crystal Palace
while John Rennie, the son of a Scottish
farmer, built three Thames bridges,
Waterloo, Southwark and London (all

*The Albert Memorial – Sir George Gilbert Scott's
architectural tribute to the Prince Consort and the
best aspects of the Victorian era*

Edwin Lutyens   *Norman Shaw*

The familiar landmark of Battersea Power Station dominates the south bank of the Thames

subsequently destroyed). Finally, the engineer who had the greatest impact on Victorian London was Sir Joseph Bazalgette. His visible memorial is the Thames embankments, but his most famous work, the London sewage and water supply system, remains invisible, and still hard at work over a century later.

Buildings small and large

Prior to 1800 the largest buildings in London were St Paul's and Westminster Abbey. The next century saw the creation of hundreds of larger, more decorative rivals, designed for a great variety of purposes. Changes in scale affected housing as well. During the last decades of the century attempts were made to remove London's desperate slums. Some disappeared under major new road schemes, such as Shaftesbury Avenue, Charing Cross Road and Victoria Street, while others were replaced by new blocks of low cost flats, some built by philanthropists such as George Peabody, others by the London County Council (formed in 1889).

The other answer to slums and to overcrowding was to spread London ever outwards into the country. Huge new suburbs in semi-rural settings were built, linked to the centre of the city by railway and underground networks. The best of these, such as Bedford Park and Hampstead Garden Suburb, followed the garden city principles laid down by architectural philosophers such as Philip Webb, William Morris and Ebenezer Howard. Rural and vernacular traditions also inspired the Arts and Crafts movement, a potent architectural force at the end of the century. Architects such as Richard Norman Shaw and Sir Edwin Lutyens returned to the early English forms of the Stuarts, and of Wren and the Queen Anne period, as well as to regional building styles and local materials. Shaw came from a conventional architectural background, but he soon put aside the influence of Victorian Gothic. He turned to the English vernacular, designing Bedford Park in West London. Laid out in 1880, this idiosyncratic rural village planted in the outskirts of London was the first garden suburb. At the same time Shaw used a more decorative Queen Anne style in designing a range of distinctive London houses, notably Lowther Lodge, Kensington (now the Royal Geographical Society) and Swan House, Chelsea Embankment. Later Shaw moved away from his vernacular styles and developed the extravagant Baroque style exhibited by the former HQ of the Metropolitan Police on the Victoria Embankment, now known as Norman Shaw Building and the Piccadilly Hotel.

Lutyens followed a similar path, developing from an original exponent of the domestic vernacular style into a modern master of the Baroque and 17th-century Classicism. This pattern of development, from work with Unwin at Hampstead Garden Suburb from 1909 to the Cenotaph and the Midland Bank headquarters during the early 1920s, shows Lutyens' command both of the grandiose and of small scale detail.

The late Victorian and Edwardian era produced the last great period of London's development. Despite the ravages of the 20th century, London is still in many respects an Edwardian city, with a wealth of monumental, finely constructed and elegantly detailed buildings. These can be seen at their best in Piccadilly and St James's and throughout the City.

Into the 20th century

For London, the 20th century has seen a period of decline. Certainly the city grew steadily larger, its sprawling suburbs gradually swallowing more of south-east England, but the architectural coherence of previous centuries of growth has been lost.

In the 1920s, as a result of the First World War, England had fallen behind much of Europe, both creatively and financially. Architects struggled to maintain the style and quality of the Edwardian era, and sometimes succeeded. At the same time they had to take note of the Modernist philosophies coming from Europe and the United States. Some architects managed to blend both forces together, for example, Lutyens, Sir Herbert Baker, Sir John Burnet and Sir Giles Gilbert Scott. Scott, grandson of the great Victorian gothicist Sir George, was almost a prodigy, rising to international fame when he won the competition for Liverpool Cathedral at the age of 24. Dynamic, adventurous and rarely a slave to past styles, Scott later produced a powerful modernist style seen at its best in Battersea Power Station (1929) and Waterloo Bridge (1939). Another architect to make the transition was Charles Holden. He designed a series of underground stations in a geometric style, for example Arnos Grove and Osterley, but his masterpiece is the headquarters of London Transport in Broadway, Victoria. Built from 1927, this features sculpture by Epstein, Henry Moore and Eric Gill.

Compared to other European cities, London has very few Art Deco buildings of note. Some of the best examples of this genre were the cinemas, notably the Odeon chain with their jazzy tiling and rounded forms inspired by ocean liners. Other good buildings in this style are the Hoover factory of 1932 by Willis Gilbert and Partners, the Royal Masonic Hospital designed by Sir John Burnet in 1930, the remarkably ship-like Olympia

exhibition hall by Joseph Emburton, and the black-glass-clad Daily Express building in Fleet Street. Other architects reacted against such decorative modernism, for during the 1920s and 1930s another style of contemporary architecture had taken root.

The New Architecture
Inspired in particular by Germany and the Bauhaus design school, International Modernism swept across Europe and into England. Architectural philosophers such as Le Corbusier, Mies van der Rohe, Walter Gropius and others developed a style of new urban architecture that relied on pure form, abstract geometry, modern materials and techniques and a highly mechanical finish. All ornament was shunned as decadent and unnecessary. It was a functional style, and its natural form was the vertical high rise tower block. Some avant-garde English architects began to experiment with this style during the 1920s, but the real impetus came during the early 1930s when a number of architects, fleeing Nazism, came to England; among them Gropius, Chermayeff and Lubetkin. All were highly influential and from this period on International Modernism became the only acceptable style for forward-thinking architects. In the 1930s the effect was interesting, producing buildings such as the High Point flats in Highgate and the Penguin Pool at London Zoo.

However, the real impact of this style was not felt until after the Second World War. The LCC architectural department followed Modernism in the general terms, producing the Festival Hall in 1951, and from 1952 the vast but carefully planned Alton housing estates at Roehampton, where tower blocks were placed in a landscape setting. In the 1960s planners and developers, faced with the increasing problem of traffic and the

Towards the 21st century? Richard Rogers' Lloyds Building in the City

shortage of office space, set about developing London in the name of Modernism. Repetitive tower blocks marched across the face of London, and little concern was shown for scale, skyline and quality. Vast office developments were matched by vast housing estates, with planners and architects under pressure from political sources to build quickly and cheaply.

By the late 1970s, the tower block was discredited, particularly for housing, a reaction hastened by the collapse of Ronan Point. More important was the realisation that the past was not something simply to be destroyed. Preservation, conservation and the blending of old and new became an acceptable philosophy. In many cases this has saved buildings, particularly of the 19th century, that would otherwise have been lost.

Post Modernism
As well as enjoying the pleasures of architecture past, architects also developed a new style, European and American in origin. Post-Modernism has now come to London: a blend of interpretations of styles from different periods of history combined with a love of materials and modern technology, it produces buildings that are as entertaining, diverse and as richly detailed and colourful as those of the Victorian or Edwardian periods. Used at first for small scale terrace housing, shop fronts and industrial buildings, Post-Modernism has now reached maturity in London with James Stirling's Tate Gallery extension and Richard Rogers' Lloyd's Building. These are major additions to the extraordinary collection of architecture that has helped to form London. What future generations make of it remains to be seen.

LONDON GUIDE

Gazetteer

Entries in this Gazetteer can be located
on the maps by using the reference
included below the name.
An explanation of how to use the references
is given on page 72.

Above: the Natural History Museum

Left: Royal Weddings are opportunities to witness London's magnificent ceremonials

CEREMONIES

Everyone knows about Changing the Guard at Buckingham Palace, but London has literally dozens of other ceremonies. Some are dazzling state occasions, while others are attended only by a few participants and curious onlookers. A selection of the most colourful and most interesting is given here.

Daily Ceremonies

Ceremony of the Keys
Tower of London

The Ceremony of the Keys has taken place every night for the last 700 years. The Tower is still officially owned by the Queen as a palace and fortress and is therefore closely guarded and securely locked at night. The ceremony is performed by the Chief Yeoman Warder of the Tower and an escort of Guards. It takes the form of a series of challenges and replies, and ends with the keys of the Tower being deposited for the night.

Applications for a pass to attend this ceremony, which lasts for about 20 minutes from start to finish, should be made in writing to the Resident Governor.
Nightly just before 10pm

The Changing of the Guard
Buckingham Palace

Starting at 11am at St James's Palace, the detachment of Old Guard forms up in Friary Court. After an inspection, the Drummers beat the call 'The Point of War' while the colour is brought on. The Old Guard marches up The Mall to Buckingham Palace, led by their Corps of Drums, while the Buckingham Palace detachment of the Old Guard falls-in and is inspected in the Palace forecourt by the subaltern. They await the arrival of the rest of the Old Guard, who then form up on the right of the Buckingham Palace Guard. The actual 'Changing' begins on the stroke of 11.30. The New Guard, headed by their regimental band, marches into the Palace via the North Centre Gate, to a central position facing the Old Guard. Accompanied by the band the New Guard marches in slow time towards the Old Guard. Having paid each other military compliments, the Captains of the Guards march towards each other to carry out the symbolic ceremony of handing over the Palace keys.

After saluting the Senior Captain on parade, the officers of both Guards go to the Guardroom to hand over their responsibilites. For about half an hour the band plays on. When each new sentry is posted, complete orders are read to him by the corporal, and when the new sentries take over at St James's, the sentries who have been relieved march into Buckingham Palace to complete the Old Guard. At 12.05 the Guards are brought to attention. The Old Guard departs from the central gate to return to their barracks after exchanging compliments with the New Guard. Now the detachment of the New Guard marches off to start their guard duties.
Daily in summer; alternate days in winter

Mounting the Guard
Horse Guards, Whitehall

A detachment of the Household Cavalry guards the old entrance to the demolished Whitehall Palace – an area partly occupied by Horse Guards, a handsome 18th-century building whose east front faces onto Whitehall. Mounting the Guard is a colourful spectacle with the mounted Cavalrymen immaculate and impassive on their elegant horses.
11am weekdays; 10am Sundays

Royal Events

Royal Epiphany Gifts Service
Chapel Royal,
St James's Palace

For this ceremony the Sovereign (or a representative), is accompanied by the Yeomen of the Guard. The contents of three purses, which symbolise the gifts of the three Wise Men, are distributed to the poor of the parish.
6 January

State Opening of Parliament
Houses of Parliament

After a general election, and before each new session of Parliament the Sovereign attends the State Opening of Parliament, a ceremony dating

Guards prepare for the nightly closing of the Tower in the ancient Ceremony of the Keys

On Horse Guards Parade, the world-famous ceremony of Mounting the Guard is carried out by the Household Cavalry

from the mid-16th century. The Royal procession moves from Buckingham Palace to the Palace of Westminster, where the ceremony takes place in the House of Lords. Before the arrival of the procession, the Yeomen of the Guard search the cellars of the Houses of Parliament – a precaution that dates from the Gunpowder Plot of 1605.
Mid-November

Trooping the Colour
Horseguards Parade

The Sovereign's official birthday is celebrated by Trooping the Colour. The Colours (flags) of one of the five Foot Guards' Regiments are trooped before the Sovereign. Years ago this was necessary so that the regiments could recognise their own colours in battle. At the end of the ceremony, the Sovereign rides to Buckingham Palace ahead of her Guards.
Second Saturday in June

Ceremonies Large and Small

Admission of Sheriffs
Guildhall

The election of two sheriffs and other officials of the City takes place with much pageantry. The Lord Mayor and other city officials attend a church service before proceeding to the Guildhall where members of the livery companies are assembled for the presenting of the chains of office to the sheriffs.
28 September or preceding Friday

Cakes and Ale Sermon
St Paul's Cathedral

Members of the Stationers Company walk in procession from Stationers' Hall to St Paul's Cathedral, where their chaplain preaches the Cakes and Ale Sermon in deference to the wishes of John Norton, a member of the Worshipful Company of Stationers who died during the reign of James I. Cakes and ale are distributed before or after the service.
Ash Wednesday

Doggett's Coat and Badge Race
River Thames – London Bridge to Chelsea

The oldest annually contested event in the British sporting calendar, this race celebrates the accession of George I to the English throne. In 1715 Thomas Doggett, comedian and manager of London's oldest theatre, the *Drury Lane*, bequeathed a badge of silver and money to pay for a livery coat for the winner of a race for single sculls.
End of July

Election of the Lord Mayor
Guildhall

There is a service at St Lawrence Jewry after which the current Lord Mayor goes in procession to the Guildhall, and, with the Aldermen, makes the final selection from the candidates nominated by the livery companies. When the selection is made, the Lord Mayor and the Lord Mayor elect ride in the state coach to the Mansion House.
29 September

Installation of the Lord Mayor
Mansion House and Guildhall

The current Lord Mayor and the Lord Mayor elect both attend a luncheon at the Mansion House attended by liverymen of each of their companies. Afterwards they go in procession to the Guildhall where they officially change places and transfer the insignia of office, and the City starts another year.
8 November

John Stow's Quill Pen Ceremony
St Andrew Undershaft

This ceremony commemorates the writer of *Survey of London* (1598). The Lord Mayor and other dignitaries attend, and during the service the Lord Mayor places a fresh quill in the hand of Stow's statue, which depicts him at work on his *Survey*.
On or near 5 April

The Lord Mayor's Show
The City

This is the most famous City pageant. The Lord Mayor, elected annually, is head of the Corporation of London, the City's administrative body, and is host to visiting Heads of State and celebrities. This important office makes him or her the first citizen of the City, taking precedence over everyone except the Sovereign. The procession dates from the 14th century and the Lord Mayor rides in the state coach in order to be 'shown' to the citizens.
Second Saturday in November

Oak Apple Day
Chelsea Royal Hospital

Charles II founded the Hospital for non-commissioned army officers, and their colourful uniforms are a familiar part of Chelsea life. On Oak Apple Day the pensioners parade for inspection and all wear a sprig of oak. They give three cheers for their founder, Charles II, whose statue is decorated with oak boughs.
29 May

The Lord Mayor's State Coach, built in 1757 and still in use

Old Bailey in session
Central Criminal Court

The opening session of the Central Criminal Court is attended by the Lord Mayor of London, who leads a procession from the Mansion House, attended by the sheriffs, the swordbearer, the common crier and the City Marshal.
6 January

Quit Rents Ceremony
Royal Courts of Justice

This, the oldest ceremony in London, involves the City Solicitor making token payments for two properties. The rents are two faggots of wood, a billhook and a hatchet for land in Shropshire, and six horseshoes and 61 nails, for a forge which once stood in the Strand.
October

CHURCHES AND CATHEDRALS

The life of medieval cities revolved around the Church. Before the Fire of London in 1666 there were an astonishing 126 churches in the City's 'Square Mile'. Some of those had been destroyed before 1666, but the Fire razed or damaged 87, including Old St Paul's. Sir Christopher Wren rebuilt 51 of them – a unique architectural achievement. Disaster struck again in the Blitz of World War II, when 19 churches were gutted or destroyed, including surviving medieval churches, ten of Wren's churches and some of the Victorian era. Many of the outstanding churches are in the City, but there are fine churches of great architectural and historic interest in many other parts of London. A selection of some of the best is given on the following pages.

All Hallows-by-the-Tower
Byward Street, EC3
Map Ref: 79K
Part of the wall of a church which stood on this site in the 7th century can be seen in the crypt here, as can fragments of Roman paving and the remains of two Saxon crosses. The body of the church was gutted in the Blitz, but much of interest remains.

All Hallows
London Wall, EC4
Map Ref: 79L
The Roman and medieval walls of London form part of the boundary of the churchyard here. The beautiful 18th-century interior of the church was badly damaged in the Blitz and restored in the 1960s.

All Saints
Margaret Street, W1
Map Ref: 76J/K
This unusual, brick-built church was erected in 1849. It was designed by William Butterfield, whose strikingly original use of bricks is continued in the church's interior.

All Souls'
Langham Place, W1
Map Ref: 76J
This church was built in 1822 as part of John Nash's great design produced for the Prince Regent, later George IV. Nash laid out a ceremonial route from Carlton House Terrace, through Regent Street to Regent's Park.

Brompton Oratory
Brompton Road, SW7
Map Ref: 80F
Built at the end of the 19th century, this huge Roman Catholic church is in the Italian Renaissance style. The nave is 51ft wide, and the interior decoration – much of which was executed by Italian artists and craftsmen – overwhelmingly lavish.

Holy Trinity
Sloane Street, SW1
Map Ref: 81L
This church's designer, J D Sedding, was the principal architect of the Arts and Crafts Movement inspired by William Morris and many of the ideas of that movement have been used in this church. The magnificent stained glass windows were designed by Edward Burne-Jones and made by William Morris.

St Andrew-by-the-Wardrobe
Queen Victoria Street, EC4
Map Ref: 78P
Its curious name derives from its proximity to the King's Great Wardrobe or Storehouse established in the time of Edward III. The church was designed by Wren and finished in 1695, but burnt out in 1940. It was restored in the late 1950s, and many of the furnishings in place now were brought from other churches to replace those destroyed in the Blitz.

St Andrew Undershaft
St Mary Axe
Leadenhall Street, EC3
Map Ref: 79M
This church is first mentioned in the 12th century. Its name is derived from a tall shaft or maypole which until 1517 was set up each Mayday outside the church. The church was rebuilt between 1520 and 1532 and is typical of its period.

Two views of Brompton Oratory. Left: The entrance façade and (below) the interior, showing the baroque splendour of the vast nave

St Clement Danes Church, and statue of Gladstone

St Anne and St Agnes
Gresham Street, EC2
Map Ref: 78K
This attractive little church was first mentioned in 1200. Wren rebuilt it between 1676 and 1687 after the Great Fire and it is now used for Lutheran services.

St Anne Limehouse
Commercial Road, E14
Map Ref: 79H/M
Nicholas Hawksmoor, pupil and colleague of Sir Christopher Wren, built this spectacular church in 1712.

St Bartholomew-the-Great
West Smithfield, EC1
Map Ref: 78K
Part of a grand Norman priory church, this is one of the oldest churches in London. It was founded for Augustinian Canons in 1123 by Rahere, a courtier of Henry I who became its first prior.

St Bartholomew-the-Less
West Smithfield, EC1
Map Ref: 78K
This is the chapel of St Bartholomew's Hospital. All that remains of the pre-Fire building are the original 15th-century tower and the vestry, which were incorporated into the present building by George Dance the Younger in the 18th century.

St Benet
Paul's Wharf, Upper Thames Street, EC4
Map Ref: 78P
Used by Welsh Episcopalians since 1879, this handsome little church was completed by Wren in 1683. It has a fine brickwork exterior and a charming steeple. The galleried interior has a simple beauty.

St Bride
Fleet Street, EC4
Map Ref: 78J
The name Bride is a corruption of Bridget, a 6th-century Irish saint. The old church (12th-century) was a fine medieval building with a lofty pinnacled tower on the south side. Wren rebuilt it with a symmetrical exterior with the highest, and one of the most beautiful, of his many steeples, called the 'wedding cake' steeple because of its shape.

St Clement Danes
Strand, WC2
Map Ref: 77R
A church has stood here since the 9th century. It was rebuilt by Wren in 1680 and again after virtual destruction in the Blitz. In the 115-ft tower are the bells immortalised by the nursery rhyme 'Oranges and Lemons'. It is the RAF church.

St Edmund The King and Martyr
Lombard Street, EC3
Map Ref: 79Q
Dedicated to St Edmund, a king of East Anglia who was killed by the Danes in 879, this church has a distinctive Wren spire.

St Ethelburga
Bishopsgate, EC4
Map Ref: 79L
Best preserved of the pre-Fire churches, this tiny building is entered through a 14th-century doorway.

St Etheldreda, or Ely Chapel
Ely Place, EC1
Map Ref: 78J
Originally built in the 13th century, this beautiful little chapel deteriorated over the centuries, and was almost completely destroyed in the Blitz. The façade and some of the Roman foundations remain and are incorporated in the present structure. The chapel has two stories and a massive vaulted undercroft dating from 1252. It is the oldest pre-Reformation Roman Catholic church in London.

St George, Hanover Square
St George's Street, W1
Map Ref: 76N
This is an impressive classical-style building with a galleried interior lit by 16th-century Flemish windows. The church has been fashionable for weddings since the 18th century and among those married here were Disraeli and Roosevelt.

Thomas Archer's tower for St John's, Smith Square, surrounded by four graceful pillars

St Giles-in-the-Field
St Giles High Street, WC2
Map Ref: 77L
In 1731, Henry Flitcroft, who was William III's gardener, beat Hawksmoor and Gibbs to win a competition to build the present church. It has a fine 161-ft Baroque steeple and superb interior fittings.

St Helen Bishopsgate
Great St Helens's, EC3
Map Ref: 79L
This church may have a Saxon foundation. In 1212 a Benedictine nunnery was established in St Helen's which was used jointly by the nuns and parishioners, between whom was a screen; this dual usage is shown by the church's unusual structure – two naves separated by a single arcade, the lofty western arches dating from about 1475.

St James's
Piccadilly, W1
Map Ref: 76P
This Wren church has a magnificent galleried interior beneath a barrel-vaulted ceiling. There is marvellous woodcarving, the work of Grinling Gibbons.

St James-the-Less
Thorndike Street, off Vauxhall Bridge Road, SW1
Map Ref: 82K
G E Street was one of the most accomplished Victorian architects. He built this splendid church in 1860. Its plain exterior hides a majestic vaulted interior which is lit by windows made by the famous firm of Clayton and Bell.

St John
Smith Square, SW1
Map Ref: 83L
When Queen Anne gave Thomas Archer instructions on how to build this church, she is reputed to have kicked over a stool, pointed at it and said, 'Build me one like that!'

St Katherine Cree
Leadenhall Street, EC3
Map Ref: 79M
This classical church, dating from 1628, escaped both the Great Fire and the Blitz. It has a curious mixture of styles, the classical pillars and arches contrasting strangely with the shouldered gothic windows and vaulted plaster ceiling.

St Lawrence Jewry
Gresham Street, EC2
Map Ref: 79L
Wren rebuilt this church in 1687 on the site of a medieval church, and it was one of his largest and most expensive to construct. The name Jewry comes from Jews living in the area before their expulsion from England in 1290. It is the Guild church of the Corporation of London and pews are set aside for the Lord Mayor, Sheriffs and other City dignitaries.

St Magnus the Martyr
Lower Thames Street, EC3
Map Ref: 79Q
The church here stands at the head of the old London Bridge, the footway to which passed under the tower. The steeple is one of Wren's most complex and striking designs.

St Margaret Pattens
Rood Lane, Eastcheap, EC3
Map Ref: 79Q
St Margaret Pattens may be so called because the clogs (called pattens) worn to keep shoes out of the mud were sold nearby, but it may also refer to a benefactor named Patynz or Patins. The beautiful, simple spire by Wren is 199ft high – his third highest.

Inside and outside the dome of St Paul's

St Margaret Westminster
Parliament Square, SW1
Map Ref: 83G
Dating from the 16th century, this church has been the official church of the House of Commons since 1614. It is especially noted for its wealth of monuments.

St Martin-within-Ludgate
Ludgate Hill, EC4
Map Ref: 78K
Originally, this church adjoined Ludgate and the west wall is part of the medieval city wall. Inside there is magnificent carved woodwork by Grinling Gibbons.

St Martin-in-the-Fields
Trafalgar Square, WC2
Map Ref: 77Q
The medieval church on this site was surrounded by fields, as the name suggests. It was extensively rebuilt by Gibbs in the early 18th century and is the parish church of Buckingham Palace. Gibbs' combination of classical portico and tower was a novelty in its day and has been widely copied since.

St Mary Abchurch
Abchurch Lane, EC4
Map Ref: 79Q
First mentioned in the 12th century, then rebuilt by Wren, this church was badly damaged in 1940 when the famous painted dome was nearly destroyed. This painting, by William Snow, painter-stainer and carver, is unique in a City church. It has been beautifully restored.

St Mary-at-Hill
off Eastcheap, EC3
Map Ref: 79Q
Only partly destroyed in the Great Fire and repaired by Wren, this church is unassuming on the outside, yet the interior is one of the finest in the City.

St Mary-le-Bow
Cheapside, EC2
Map Ref: 78K
The crypt here, dated about 1090, was the basement of what was apparently one of the earliest stone churches in London. It was badly damaged in the Blitz, but Wren's steeple survived, and its beautiful spire is crowned by a 9ft weathervane. The famous Bow Bells were originally rung as a curfew and those who are born within the sound of these bells are said to be true Cockneys.

St Mary-le-Strand
Strand, WC2
Map Ref: 77R
James Gibbs designed this lovely little Baroque church, which stands on an island in the Strand. It was completed in 1717, and retains some of its original interior furnishings.

St Mary Woolnoth
Lombard Street, EC3
Map Ref: 79Q
First mentioned at the end of the 12th century, this church was partially damaged in the Great Fire of London and subsequently restored by Wren. It was completely rebuilt by Nicholas Hawksmoor between 1716 and 1727, and shows his unique style at its best.

St Olave
Hart Street, EC3
Map Ref: 79R
This medieval church was saved during the Great Fire by Samuel Pepys and Admiral Sir William Penn, who had the surrounding buildings torn down. Pepys and his wife are buried here. The church is entered from Seething Lane via a gateway decorated by skulls, which Dickens described as belonging to the church of St Ghastly Grim in *The Uncommercial Traveller*.

A medieval roof boss in Southwark Cathedral

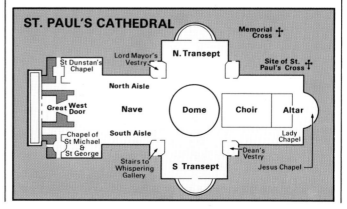

The tomb (1408) of John Gower in Southwark Cathedral

St Paul's Cathedral
St Paul's Churchyard,
Ludgate Hill, EC4
Map Ref: 78K
A church has stood on this famous site since the 7th century. The Normans replaced the wooden church in the 11th century, and it became a focal point of religious life in London. The church eventually fell into disrepair through neglect and was used as a market place and thoroughfare for pedestrians. By the 17th century it was in such bad repair that Inigo Jones was commissioned to restore it, but work was interrupted by the Civil War. Sir Christopher Wren was subsequently commissioned to continue the work, but on 2 September 1666 the Great Fire broke out and most of the building was gutted.

In 1672 Wren began work on the designs for a new cathedral. Completed in 1710, it stands today as Wren's masterpiece and one of the finest churches in the world. The crowning beauty of the building is the dome, which rises 365ft above ground level and is 112ft in diameter. Around it is the famous Whispering Gallery, where a hushed message can be clearly heard on the other side.

The cathedral contains numerous chapels, and hundreds of monuments. The oldest of these is to John Donne, which was saved from Old St Paul's. Almost filling the North Aisle is the huge monument to the Duke of Wellington, who is actually buried in the crypt. Also in the crypt is the tomb of Lord Nelson. Perhaps the most poignant monument is that to

Wren, which, in translation, reads: 'Reader, if you seek his monument, look around you.'

St Peter-upon-Cornhill
Bishopsgate Corner, EC3
Map Ref: 79L
Occupying the highest land in the City, this is believed to be the oldest church site in London – perhaps dating back to the 2nd century. Wren rebuilt it after the Great Fire, and among its many fine interior fittings is an outstanding chancel screen designed by Wren and his 16-year-old daughter.

St Stephen Walbrook
Walbrook, EC4
Map Ref: 79Q
One of Wren's greatest works, this church has what is believed to be the first dome built into any English church. It was wrecked in World War II, but has been restored and is now the headquarters of the Samaritans.

Southwark Cathedral
Borough High Street, SE1
Map Ref: 85C
Although a church has stood on this site since the 7th century, it only attained cathedral status in 1905. Despite considerable rebuilding, especially during the 19th century, parts of the cathedral date back to the 16th century, and there are some features from the 13th century and before. The interior is rich in monuments. One of the earliest is a wooden effigy of a knight dating from about 1275. John Harvard, the founder of Harvard University in the USA, was born in Southwark and is commemorated by a chapel here.

Union Chapel
Compton Terrace, Upper Street, N1
Map Ref: 88G5
This strikingly-designed Congregational chapel was designed by James Cubitt and completed in 1876. Its octagonal interior seats 1,800 and it has been called the 'cathedral of Congregationalism'. It contains a piece of the rock on which the Pilgrim Fathers landed in America.

Wesley's Chapel
City Road, EC1
Map Ref: 79G
John Wesley himself laid the foundation stone of this chapel on 21 April 1777, when he was 74 years old. It was opened for public worship a year later and is the mother church of world Methodism.

ST. PAUL'S CATHEDRAL

Memorial Cross ✝

Lord Mayor's Vestry
N. Transept

St Dunstan's Chapel

Site of St. Paul's Cross ✝

North Aisle

Great West Door

Nave

Dome

Choir

Altar

Chapel of St Michael & St George

South Aisle

Lady Chapel

Stairs to Whispering Gallery

Dean's Vestry

Jesus Chapel

S Transept

Westminster Abbey
Old Palace Yard, SW1
Map Ref: 83G

Edward the Confessor enlarged this Benedictine medieval monastery to make a church fit for the coronation of English kings. He died eight days after its consecration, on the feast of St Peter, 28 December 1065. His successor, Harold, was crowned here the following week and every successive sovereign has been crowned here since, with the exception of Edward V and Edward VIII, who were never crowned.

The only part of Edward's original building to be seen today is the Norman Undercroft, which now houses a museum, and the Chapel of the Pyx, which was once used as the Royal Treasury. Henry III added a Lady Chapel at the east end in 1220, and then in 1245 decided to rebuild the whole abbey in honour of Edward. This building was finished in 1269 and was modelled on French cathedrals such as Rheims and Amiens. From the 13th century until the reign of George II the abbey was used as the burial place of English kings and queens.

Enlarged and beautified at the end of the 14th century, work was carried on throughout the 15th century, but the designs of Henry III were strictly adhered to. The

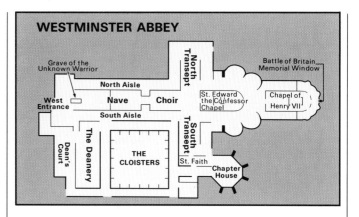

Lady Chapel was pulled down in 1503 and sixteen years later the spectacular Henry VII Chapel rose on the site.

The architecture of the Abbey is one of the finest achievements of English builders. The fabric is of Reigate stone with piers of coloured

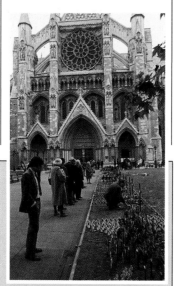

Westminster Abbey's north font

Purbeck marble. The nave is the tallest Gothic nave in the country.

There are over 1,000 monuments in the abbey and these have always been a matter of controversy. Although cluttering the beautiful lines of the building, the memorials provide a unique history of English monumental sculpture from the 13th to the 19th centuries.

In the centre of the Royal tombs is the now battered tomb of the founder of the Abbey, Edward the Confessor; the Coronation Chair built round the Stone of Scone stands opposite. Nearby are the tombs of Edward I, Edward II, and Henry III. Henry VII's tomb is in the chapel which bears his name; in side chapels nearby are Mary Tudor, Elizabeth I, Richard II and Henry V. There are sad little tombs to Royal children, including the ill-fated Princes who were murdered in the Tower.

The Abbey is noted for the concentration of burials and memorials to musicians, statesmen and actors. Writers and poets are buried in Poets' Corner – Geoffrey Chaucer was buried in the Abbey in 1400 and since that time writers and poets have been buried or commemorated around him.

Elsewhere there are memorials to Pitt, Disraeli, Gladstone, Lord Baden-Powell, General Gordon of Khartoum, Clement Attlee, Ramsay MacDonald, Ernest Bevin, and Winston Churchill.

Westminster Cathedral
Ashley Place, Victoria Street, SW1
Map Ref: 82K

It took until 300 years after the Reformation before government by diocesan bishops was restored to Roman Catholics in Britain. In 1884 Cardinal Manning bought the site, and between 1895 and 1903 this imposing symbol of Catholic importance was built in a striking Italian-Byzantine style. It has a 284-ft campanile and the widest nave in England, and the interior is lavishly decorated with yellow, red and white marble. Eric Gill's Stations of the Cross, made between 1913 and 1918, adorn the main piers and are the outstanding works in the cathedral.

The Abbey 'Family'

Every year some 3½ million people visit Westminster Abbey, but it is very much a church dedicated to regular worship as well as to playing a part in great events in the life of the nation.

Keeping the abbey clean and beautiful, preparing for daily services and continuing the original Benedictine tradition of hospitality are tasks involving a small army of dedicated workers – people who can be described as members of the abbey 'family'. Who are they and what do they do?

Enter the Abbey and first you will see the Marshals, identified by their maroon gowns. At key points within the nave and royal chapels they guide and direct the flow of visitors, passing on information about some particular memorial and sometimes having to remind visitors that they are in a living church.

Also in evidence and wearing black cassocks – long tunics – are the Vergers. Their main duty is to care for the interior of the Church and to prepare for services. The Vergers, both men and women, also lead the clergy in procession at services, carrying their verge or wand of office. But the Vergers at the abbey have another important role: they act as guides for the 'super-tour'. At fixed departure times every weekday, small parties are given a personally-conducted tour of the abbey and its precincts.

It is then that the Vergers' intimate knowledge of the building and its history can help to illustrate to the visitor just what the abbey means.

Every hour, on the hour, a priest leads those in the abbey in a brief act of prayer. He wears a scarlet cincture or belt around his black cassock. These priests – the incumbents of one of the abbey livings – spend a week at a time at the abbey and are ready to give spiritual guidance to those who seek their help.

The government of the abbey, care of its fabric and finances is administered by the Dean and Chapter of Westminster. The Dean and the four Canons who form this body are assisted by a number of clergy – minor canons and lay officers. Together they are known as the Collegiate Body. All its members wear scarlet cassocks, a sign that Westminster Abbey is a 'royal peculiar' and as such exempt from the jurisdiction of the Archbishop of Canterbury and the Bishop of London, responsible only to the sovereign.

CITY INSTITUTIONS

Despite changing economic circumstances, 'the City' remains one of the world's most important financial and trading centres. Vast modern buildings dominate much of the City today, but there are still many reminders of a long and fascinating history.

Commerce and Finance

For centuries the City has been the centre of Britain's financial and commercial activities. **The Bank of England** was founded in 1694 when City merchants decided that an independent national bank was needed. In 1743 the new building was opened in Threadneedle Street; this was expanded by Sir John Soane at the turn of the 18th century and modernised in 1925 and 1939. The Bank was nationalised in 1946 and now prints and issues notes and administers the National Debt.

The Stock Exchange is the modern venue for financial dealings. Founded in 1773, it is now on the corner of Throgmorton Street and Old Broad Street. It is possible to observe the proceedings from the Visitors' Gallery.

The Stock Exchange replaced **The Royal Exchange** which was opened in 1568 and used as a meeting place for City merchants. Today it is the home of the London International Futures Exchange. The proclamations of new sovereigns and declarations of war are traditionally made here.

Lloyd's of London, the most famous underwriting business in the world, was started by Edward Lloyd in 1773 in a coffee house in Lombard Street. Today its huge, ultra-modern building occupies an extensive site in Lime Street and underwrites billions of pounds of insurance world-wide. The famous Lutine Bell, salvaged from a frigate in 1799, is traditionally rung once for the loss of an overdue vessel and twice for its safe arrival.

Sir William Tite designed the present Royal Exchange in 1841; it is the third Exchange to stand on this site

The coat of arms of the Grocers' Company

The Corporation of London

Since 1215 the City of London has had the right to elect its own mayor annually. The government of the City is administered by the Corporation acting through the Court of Common Council, which is an elected body presided over by the Lord Mayor. The City is broken down into 25 wards and the ratepayers from each ward elect one alderman and a number of councilmen to the Court of Common Council; 131 councilmen make up the court together with 25 aldermen. These aldermen form the Court of Aldermen which administers justice within the City. The liverymen elect two sheriffs for the City annually, and only aldermen who have served as sheriff are eligible as candidates for the office of Lord Mayor.

The Guildhall
Map Ref: 79L
The Court of Common Council meets at the Guildhall. In 1411 the livery companies raised money for its construction. Wren restored it after the Great Fire and George Dance the Younger added the new façade in 1788. Damaged in the Blitz, it was given a new roof in 1953. The Great Hall is now used for the Lord Mayor's Banquet and other civic functions; it retains its original walls and the banners of the 12 Great Livery Companies hang from the ceiling. Beneath the Hall is a magnificent 15th-century crypt. Admission free.

Livery Companies

The Livery Companies started as friendly societies or guilds for a particular trade in the City and most date from the 14th century. With the growth in importance of these companies their leading members took to wearing a uniform or livery. The original 12 Great Companies are: Mercers, Grocers, Drapers, Fishmongers, Goldsmiths, Skinners, Merchant Taylors, Haberdashers, Salters, Ironmongers, Vintners and Clothworkers. Today there are in excess of 90 and the Companies still exercise a strong influence on their trade or craft.

Only two Livery Halls escaped damage in the Blitz – the Apothecaries and the Vintners, while others have been restored or rebuilt. Special visits can often be organised to these Halls through the City Information Centre in St Paul's Church Yard.

The Mansion House
Map Ref: 79Q
This Palladian-style mansion is the home of the Lord Mayor during his year of office. Built in 1739, its principal rooms are the Egyptian Hall and the Saloon. The Corporation plate and insignia, Sword of State and Mace are kept in the building.

Visits can be arranged by prior application.

The Old Bailey (Central Criminal Court)
Map Ref: 79K
This was built in 1902 on the site of the infamous Newgate Prison. Major criminal trials have been held here ever since and the public may view the proceedings in No 1 Court.

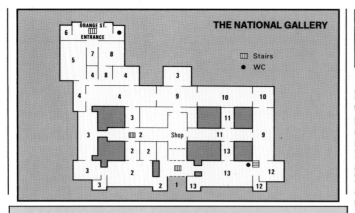

GALLERIES

Housed in London's three national picture galleries are some of the finest works of art in the world. As well as these great collections, there are also many smaller galleries with works of equal merit.

The National Gallery
Trafalgar Square, WC2
Map Ref: 77Q

The gallery houses one of the finest collections of the world's masterpieces, with all periods of European painting represented. There is a selection of English paintings, but the national collection of British art is at the Tate. The National was founded in 1824 after King George IV and the connoisseur Sir George Beaumont had persuaded the government to buy 38 splendid pictures – among them works by Raphael, Rembrandt and Van Dyck – which had belonged to the Russian-born merchant and philanthropist, John Julius Angerstein, who had died the year before. The government bought the collection for £57,000 and added to it 16 pictures (including two Rembrandts, four Claudes and works by Rubens, Wilkie and Richard Wilson, donated by Sir George Beaumont). They were housed in Angerstein's house in Pall Mall until a more suitable gallery could be built. The site chosen for the gallery was in Trafalgar Square on the site of a Royal mews and the gallery was constructed between 1832 and 1838 by William Wilkins. Since then it has had a number of extensions to cope with its growing collection.

The first director was Sir Charles Eastlake, who added considerably to the original pictures by buying pictures of the Italian Renaissance and earlier pictures of the greatest interest. By 1870 both Rubens and Rembrandt were well represented and soon afterwards works by other Flemish and Dutch masters were added as well as those by painters of the Spanish School and representative British painting. Numerous important purchases have been made during this century, and the gallery now owns over 2,000 pictures from the time of Giotto to that of Van Gogh. Admission free.
Nearest Underground: Charing Cross, Leicester Square and Embankment

The National Portrait Gallery
St Martin's Place, WC2
Map Ref: 77Q
See feature on this page.
Admission free.
Nearest Undergrounds: Charing Cross, Leicester Square and Embankment

The Tate Gallery
Millbank, SW1
Map Ref: 83L
Sir Henry Tate, the sugar magnate, paid for the construction of a gallery to house the growing

The National Portrait Gallery

The idea of a National Portrait Gallery was first proposed in Parliament in 1845. The gallery was established in 1856, and the first portrait to enter the collection was the Chandos portrait of William Shakespeare. It is only since 1896, and then after a number of moves, that the Gallery has been established in St Martin's Place, around the corner from the National Gallery.

Visitors to the gallery are asked to take the lift to the top floor, where the collection begins. On these upper floors it is possible to display the portraits in rooms which are decorated in a style reflecting the historical period, but progressively, as one moves down to the ground floor and the 20th-century gallery, pressure on space is such that the only option has been to introduce revolving turntables as a means of accommodating likenesses of all those who are thought worthy of inclusion.

The portrait of Richard II as a boy is historically the earliest on show. It is a copy of the original, which is to be seen in Westminster Abbey. There follows an extensive cover-age of the Tudor period with a Holbein cartoon of Henry VIII, the stretched out portrait of Edward VI seen only in proper perspective when viewed from a peephole at the side, and the group of paintings of Queen Elizabeth I.

The collection continues with rooms devoted to the early Stuarts, to the Civil War and the period of the Restoration and then to person-alities in the arts and literature of the 18th century. There is a delight-ful range of portraits of members of the Kit-Cat Club – people such as Walpole, Congreve and Vanbrugh.

On the first floor are the Victor-ians and then the Edwardians, and here is the first photograph, of Isam-bard Kingdom Brunel. On the lower mezzanine are paintings of the Royal Family – group portraits of George VI and his family contrasting with an earlier state portrait of George V, his wife and two eldest children.

Of a much more recent vintage are the portraits of Queen Elizabeth II by Pietro Annigoni, of the Prince of Wales and Diana, Princess of Wales, both by Bryan Organ. Fin-ally, there is a very large collection of 20th-century figures right up to Ian Botham, the cricket all-rounder. Photographs predominate over paintings and sculpture in these later

The portrait of HRH The Princess of Wales before her marriage, painted by Bryan Organ

displays. Some of the works in the gallery are undoubtedly master-pieces – but subjects are included for their importance as people in history rather than artistic quality. It all adds up to a fascinating array of great British faces.

collection of British art begun by
Sir Francis Chantrey earlier in the
19th century. The gallery was
completed in 1897. Tate also
offered the nation 67 paintings and
three sculptures which were mostly
the work of his fellow Victorians.
In 1910 Sir Joseph Duveen paid for
a wing to house the paintings of
J M W Turner which the painter
had left to the nation and were
previously housed in the National
Gallery. In 1926, Duveen's son,
later Lord Duveen of Millbank,
paid for a further extension for the
modern foreign collection. He then
paid for a third enlargement for the
long sculpture gallery, which was
built in 1937. A further
enlargement has recently been
completed.

The gallery contains two national
collections: British painting and
20th-century painting and sculpture.
The British paintings include works
by Hogarth, Blake and the Pre-
Raphaelites. The collection of
works by Turner is now housed in
the specially-built Clore Gallery.
The foreign collection includes
representative work from the
Impressionists to the present day
and includes paintings by Cézanne,
Matisse, Picasso, Braque, Chagall,
Klee, Mondrian, Pollock and Stella.
Sculpture is represented by Henry
Moore, Barbara Hepworth and
Alberto Giacometti, among others.
The modern collection traces the
development of art from
Impressionism to post-war European

*Mr and Mrs Andrews, painted by
Thomas Gainsborough, one of the
finest British masterpieces in the
National Gallery*

and American art.
Admission free.
Nearest Undergrounds: Westminster
and Pimlico

Other Art Galleries and Smaller Collections

Courtauld Institute Galleries
Woburn Square, WC1
Map Ref: 76F
Part of Samuel Courtauld's personal
art collection was given to London
University at the time of the
Institute's foundation, and the rest
bequeathed on his death in 1947.
These bequests were the foundation
of this superb collection of
paintings. The gallery is housed in a
redbrick building constructed in
1958 to the designs of Charles
Holden. It is most famous for its
Impressionist and Post-Impressionist
pictures, but there are also works by
Goya and Rubens and a collection

of Old Master drawings. The art
critic Roger Fry presented a
collection of 20th-century British
and French paintings to the
University and these are displayed
here. Among them are works by
the Bloomsbury Group, of which
he was a member.
Admission charge.
Nearest Undergrounds: Euston
Square and Russell Square

Dulwich College Picture Gallery
College Road, SE21
Map Ref: 92J13
The oldest public picture gallery in
England and one of the most
beautiful galleries in London, it is
housed in a building designed by
the distinguished architect Sir John
Soane in 1811. There is a notable
collection of Dutch paintings,
including three by Rembrandt. In
addition, paintings by Lely,
Hogarth, Gainsborough and
Reynolds, Canaletto, Poussin,
Raphael and Rubens make this a
very representative collection of
European art.
Admission charge.
Nearest Station: West Dulwich

1. 16 C. - 18 C.	14. Aspects of European
2. Exotic & Sublime	Art 1910-1930
3. Blake	15. Impressionism,
4a. Closed -	Post-Impressionism
Refurbishment	16. Abstraction c. 1910-40
4b. British 19 C	17. Surrealism
5. British Watercolours	18. Recent Acquisitions
6,7,8. British 19 C	19. European Masters
9. Pre-Raphaelites	c. 1940-60
10. Late Victorian	20. German Art c. 1900-40
11. 20 C sculpture, art	and Abstract
since 1970	Expressionism
12. Cubism, Futurism,	21. Dubuffet, etc
Vorticism	22. Rothko
13. British Painting	23. Giacometti etc
1880-1920	24. Print Room Gallery

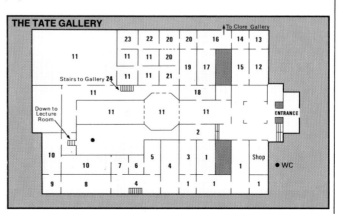

THE TATE GALLERY

Hayward Gallery
The South Bank Complex, SE1
Map Ref: 83D
The purpose-built gallery was opened in 1968. It is run by the Arts Council and puts on temporary exhibitions of interest and quality.
Admission charge.
Nearest Underground: Waterloo

Institute of Contemporary Arts
Nash House, 12 Carlton House Terrace, SW1
Map Ref: 82B
Situated in elegant Carlton House Terrace, this gallery holds interesting exhibitions of an *avant-garde* nature.
Admission charge.
Nearest Undergrounds: Piccadilly Circus and Charing Cross

The Iveagh Bequest
Kenwood House, Hampstead Lane, NW3
Map Ref: 88C9
In 1764 the great architect Robert Adam converted this house for the Earl of Mansfield into a magnificent Classical-style mansion set in beautiful grounds. Lord Iveagh purchased the mansion in 1925 and gave it to the nation in 1927 together with his collection of paintings which include works by Frans Hals, Vermeer, Reynolds, Gainsborough and Rembrandt.
Admission free.
Nearest Undergrounds: Hampstead, Archway, Golders Green (then bus)

Leighton House Art Gallery
Holland Park Road, W14
Map Ref: 88V1
The great Victorian artist, Lord Leighton, designed this house as his home. It has an exotic interior with an Arab Hall decorated with ancient tiles from Rhodes, Damascus and Cairo. Many of his paintings are displayed, together with works by Burne-Jones and other late 19th-century artists and craftsmen.
Admission free.
Nearest Underground: High Street, Kensington

The Queen's Gallery
Buckingham Palace Road, SW1
Map Ref: 82E
Originally this building was a conservatory designed by John Nash in 1831. It has a constantly changing exhibition of works of art from the Royal Collection.
Admission charge.
Nearest Undergrounds: St James's Park and Victoria

A painting from 'Dreams of a Summer Night', one of the temporary exhibitions for which the Hayward Gallery is famous

Royal Academy of Arts
Burlington House, Piccadilly, W1
Map Ref: 76P
The Academy puts on some of the finest travelling exhibitions to be shown in London. It was founded by George III in 1768 and was moved to Burlington House from the National Gallery in 1869. The Summer Exhibition, which promotes the work of living artists, is held annually from May to August and is a highlight of the summer season. The Academy owns a splendid collection of masterpieces by such artists as Michelangelo and Constable.
Admission charge.
Nearest Undergrounds: Green Park and Piccadilly

Serpentine Gallery
Kensington Gardens, W2
Map Ref: 80B
This attractive gallery is in the centre of Hyde Park. Monthly exhibitions of contemporary art organised by the Arts Council are held here.
Admission charge.
Nearest Undergrounds: Lancaster Gate and South Kensington

The Thomas Coram Foundation For Children
40 Brunswick Square, WC1
Map Ref: 77G
Captain Thomas Coram founded this hospital for destitute children in 1739. Various works of art were presented to the Foundation for display in the Court Room to attract the public and raise funds. Of particular interest is the portrait of Coram by Hogarth, which was the first gift. The present building was completed in 1937 and houses a vast number of exhibits which have been presented to the Foundation.
Admission on application.
Nearest Underground: Russell Square

The Wallace Collection
Hertford House, Manchester Square, W1
Map Ref: 75M
Originally founded by the 1st Marquis of Hertford, this magnificent collection was greatly enlarged by the 4th Marquis who spent a lifetime amassing works of art from France. His natural son, Richard Wallace, brought the collection to England in the second half of the 19th century. His widow presented the collection to the nation and it was opened to the public in 1900. Housed in an elegant 18th-century town house, the collection is world famous for its 18th-century paintings and furniture by French artists and crafsmen. There are also paintings by Frans Hals (including *The Laughing Cavalier*), Rubens, Holbein and Titian, and an immense variety of arms and armour, porcelain, clocks, miniatures, and other decorative arts.
Admission free.
Nearest Undergrounds: Bond Street and Marble Arch

Whitechapel Art Gallery
Whitechapel High Street, E1
Map Ref: 88K3
This gallery was founded to contribute to the cultural life of the East End. It has received much acclaim for the excellence of its temporary exhibitions. The building has an ornate *art nouveau* façade.
Admission free.
Nearest Underground: Whitechapel

William Morris Gallery
Forest Road, Walthamstow, E17
Map Ref: 89N11
This gallery is devoted to the work of the great Victorian artist-craftsman, poet and free thinker William Morris. There are many exhibits from the Morris Company, and the Frank Brangwyn collection of pictures. Brangwyn worked with Morris and presented the gallery with many of his own works.
Admission free.
Nearest Station: Blackhorse Road

MUSEUMS

It would be possible to spend a lifetime exploring London's museums, and still not see all that they had to offer. As well as containing objects of every conceivable description, the museum buildings themselves are often of great interest.

Artillery Museum
The Rotunda,
Woolwich Common, SE18
Map Ref: 93T18
The museum contains a collection of guns, muskets, rifles and artillery. Admission free.
Nearest Stations: Woolwich Dockyard and Woolwich Arsenal

Bear Gardens Museum
Bear Gardens, SE1
Map Ref: 78P
On the site of an ancient bear-baiting pit, this museum is housed in a 19th-century warehouse and has a permanent exhibition relating to Elizabethan theatre. It also illustrates the history of Bankside as an entertainment area. Admission charge.
Nearest Underground: London Bridge

HMS *Belfast*
Symons Wharf,
Vine Lane, SE1
Map Ref: 85D
The *Belfast* is the largest cruiser ever built for the Royal Navy. Her weight is 11,000 tons and she was built in 1938. She was opened to the public in 1971 after being saved from a breaker's yard. Admission charge.
Nearest Underground: London Bridge

The massive bulk of HMS Belfast *dwarfs the Thames tugs*

A reminder of bear-baiting days

Bethnal Green Museum of Childhood
Cambridge Heath Road, E2
Map Ref: 89L4
The museum is located in a light and spacious prefabricated Victorian hall and its exhibits include toys, dolls' houses and model soldiers. Admission free.
Nearest Underground: Bethnal Green

The British Museum
Great Russell St, WC1
Map Ref: 77L
Behind the somewhat forbidding façade of the British Museum is one of the greatest collections of treasures anywhere. It was founded in 1753 from the bequest of a

Treasures of the British Museum

physician, Sir Hans Sloane, and its expansion over the following century was little short of astonishing. During this time some of the greatest pieces were acquired, including the Elgin Marbles and the Rosetta Stone, the Hamilton collection of Greek vases and most of the Assyrian sculptures.

The museum now has major collections of Greek and Roman Antiquities, Prehistoric and Romano-British Antiquities, Egyptian Antiquities, Western Asiatic Antiquities, Oriental Antiquities, Medieval and Later Antiquities, Coins and Medals and Prints and Drawings.

The present building was designed by Smirke in the early 19th century. It also houses the British Library, a copyright library with immense and constantly expanding stocks (it receives, by law, a copy of every work published in the UK). Admission free.
Nearest Underground: Russell Square and Tottenham Court Road

Cricket Memorial Gallery
Lord's Ground, NW8
Map Ref: 74B
A must for cricket enthusiasts or those wanting to know more about England's most enigmatic game, this gallery has a collection of pictures and other memorabilia. Of special interest is the first urn to contain the 'Ashes' (the ashes of the burnt stumps of the 1882-83 cricket test match series between England and Australia) for which the two countries still compete. Admission charge.
Nearest Underground: Lords

The *Cutty Sark*
Greenwich Pier SE10
Map Ref: 93P17
This last and most famous of the tea clippers was built at Dumbarton in 1869 for the London shipowner Captain John Willis. She was still carrying cargoes when she was bought and restored in 1922. Since 1954 she has rested in a specially made dry dock at Greenwich. The name comes from the 'cutty sark' or chemise worn by the witch in Robert Burn's *Tam O'Shanter*. Admission charge.
Nearest Station: Greenwich

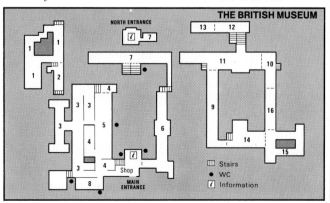

THE BRITISH MUSEUM

Basement
1. Greek & Roman
2. Western Asiatic

Ground Floor
3. Greek & Roman
4. Western Asiatic
5. Egyptian
6. British Library
7. Oriental
8. Special Exhibits

Upper Floor
9. Greek & Roman
10. Western Asiatic
11. Egyptian
12. Prints & Drawings
13. Oriental
14. Romano-British
15. Medieval & Later
16. Special Exhibits

NORTH ENTRANCE

Shop

MAIN ENTRANCE

▥ Stairs
● WC
ℹ Information

Above: old trolley buses on display at the London Transport Museum. Left: the distinctive tower of the Horniman Museum

The Geological Museum
Exhibition Road, SW7
Map Ref: 80K
This is the national museum of earth sciences. It illustrates the general principles of geological science and shows the regional geology of Britain and the mineralogy of the world. This dry description belies the lovely and intriguing things to be seen here.

Established in 1837 after a Geological Survey of Great Britain, the museum moved in 1935 to its present building. The main hall contains exhibitions entitled The Story of the Earth, Britain Before Man and British Fossils. There are also magnificent displays of gemstones and of metaliferous ores.
Admission free.
Nearest Underground: South Kensington

Horniman Museum
London Road, SE23
Map Ref: 93K13
The building is an interesting Art Nouveau structure built in 1901 and the museum itself is named after its founder, Frederick J Horniman, a tea importer who collected exotic objects in the course of his travels. There are ethnographical and natural history exhibits and musical instruments from all over the world.
Admission free.
Nearest Station: Forest Hill

Imperial War Museum
Lambeth Road, SE1
Map Ref: 84J
This museum was founded shortly after World War I to commemorate the dead with a display of relics from the war. Since then its scope has been expanded to cover all wars since 1914 that have involved Britain and the Commonwealth. The building stands on the site of the old Bethlehem Hospital for the Insane – the original Bedlam. Apart from objects of war such as tanks, weapons and uniforms, there is an outstanding collection of British 20th-century art mostly commissioned by the War Artists Advisory Committee.
Admission free.
Nearest Undergrounds: Lambeth North and Elephant and Castle

The London Dungeon
28–34 Tooley Street, SE1
Map Ref: 85C
Located in old vaults under railway lines, this museum recreates horrific scenes of historical torture and murder.
Admission charge.
Nearest Underground: London Bridge

The London Transport Museum
Covent Garden, WC2
Map Ref: 77Q
Situated in the newly-renovated Victorian complex that was once Covent Garden Market (now moved to Nine Elms), this museum tells the story of London's transport. Buses, trams and railway locomotives are on show and there is an interesting collection of posters. The great age of London

Transport's art, the 1920s and 1930s, is very well represented.
Admission charge.
Nearest Undergrounds: Covent Garden and Leicester Square

Madame Tussaud's
Marylebone Road, NW1
Map Ref: 75H
Brought over to England from Paris by Madame Tussaud in 1802 this most popular museum found a permanent home in London in 1835. The waxwork exhibits include historical figures, politicians, entertainers, sportsmen and Royalty. The Chamber of Horrors with its reconstruction of crimes never fails to frighten and chill.
Admission charge.
Nearest Underground: Baker Street

Dame Edna Everage, one of the personalities immortalised in wax at Madame Tussaud's

Museum of Instruments
Royal College of Music, Prince Consort Road, SW7
Map Ref: 80F
Situated in the wonderful Victorian building of the Royal College of Music are rare and beautiful musical instruments dating back through several centuries.
Admission free.
Nearest Underground: South Kensington

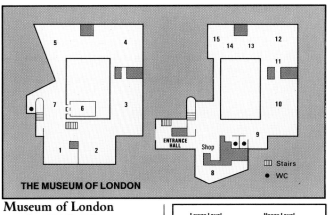

THE MUSEUM OF LONDON

Museum of London
London Wall, EC2
Map Ref: 78K
Dedicated solely to the history of
London, this museum is housed in a
purpose-built modern complex and
is an integral part of the Barbican
development. The origins of the
museum are archaeological. The
Corporation of London established
the Guildhall Museum as an
addition to its library. Exhibits
poured in and after World War II
the museum outgrew the Guildhall
and had two temporary homes
before moving to its present home
in 1976.

The archaeological exhibits were
augmented by exhibits from
Kensington Palace. This diverse
material gives a dramatic panorama
of London's long history from
prehistoric days to the present time.
Modern techniques together with
sound and visual displays are used;
the dramatic reconstruction of the
Great Fire is particularly
memorable. There are period
rooms, shops and vehicles to
illustrate life in London through the
ages.
Admission free.
Nearest Undergrounds: Barbican
(closed on Sunday) St Paul's
Moorgate and Mansion House

The Musical Museum
368 High Street, Brentford
Map Ref: 91P17
A fascinating collection of
automatic pianos and other old
instruments is gathered here in an
old church near Kew Bridge.
Admission charge.
Nearest Underground: Kew Bridge

Museum of Mankind
6 Burlington Gardens, W1
Map Ref: 76P
The museum is a department of the
British Museum and has a
magnificent collection of the art and
material culture of tribal, village and
other pre-industrial societies from
most areas of the world outside
Western Europe. Large,
spectacularly arranged exhibitions
form a vital part of the museum's
annual cycle.
Admission free.
Nearest Undergrounds: Piccadilly
Circus and Green Park

Lower Level	Upper Level
1. Late Stuart London	8. Special Exhibits
2. Georgian London	9. Thames Prehistory
3. Early 19 C. London	10. Roman London
4. Imperial Capital	11. The Dark Age
5. 20 C. London	12. Medieval London
6. Treasury	13. Tudor London
7. Lord Mayor's	14. Early Stuart London
Coach	15. Great Fire 1666

National Army Museum
Royal Hospital Road, SW3
Map Ref: 81Q
The exhibits in this museum show
the history of British, Indian and
Colonial forces from 1485 onwards.
Admission free.
Nearest Underground: Sloane Square

National Maritime Museum
Romney Road,
Greenwich, SE10
Map Ref: 93P17
This museum is situated in a
building which was once a royal
palace, surviving parts of which date
back to the 15th century. Designed
by Sir Christopher Wren, with later
alterations by Vanbrugh and
Hawksmoor, it contains interesting
galleries of naval history and special
sections devoted to Admiral Lord
Nelson and Captain Cook.
Admission charge.
Nearest Station: Greenwich

National Postal Museum
King Edward Street, EC1
Map Ref: 78K
This museum contains one of the
most comprehensive collections of
postage stamps in the world.
Admission free.
Nearest Underground: St Paul's

The Natural History Museum
Cromwell Road, SW7
Map Ref: 80K
This was originally built up from a
collection by Sir Hans Sloane
housed at the British Museum. Sir
Joseph Banks bequeathed a large
botanical collection in 1829 and
when the British Museum
expanded, a separate natural history
museum was required. The present
museum was opened in 1881. The
building, covering four acres, is in a
19th-century Romanesque style
faced with terracotta slabs bearing
animals, birds and fishes moulded in
relief.

The west wing houses galleries
devoted to birds, corals and
sponges, insects and butterflies,
starfish and fish. There is also the

*The Natural History Museum is a
superb example of Victorian
architecture in the Romanesque style*

Hall of Human Biology and the
Whale Hall, which has models or
skeletons of many types of whale
suspended from its ceiling. There is
an extensive fossil collection and an
ecology gallery. On the first floor is
the Mammal Gallery and Mineral
Gallery. A favourite with everyone
is the display of reconstructed
skeletons of prehistoric animals such
as the brontosaurus and
tyrannosaurus.
Admission free.
Nearest Underground: South
Kensington

1. Birds.	13. Fossil Sea Reptiles
2. Insects	14. Ecology
3. Marine Invertebrates	15. Fossil Mammals
4. Whales	16. African Mammals
5. Human Biology	17. Origin of Species
6. Dinosaurs	18. Mammals
7. Spiders	19. Man's place in
8. Fishes and Reptiles	Evolution
9. Special Exhibits	20. Minerals, Rocks
10. Fossil Invertebrates	and Gemstones
11. Wildlife in Danger	21. Meteorites
12. Fossil Fishes	22. British Natural History

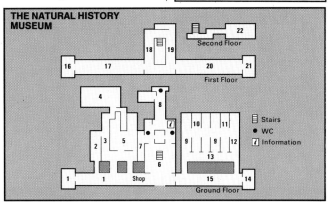

THE NATURAL HISTORY MUSEUM

The RAF Museum, Hendon

It was in 1910 that the London Aerodrome factory was opened at a site out in London's countryside. This early airfield served as a base for the defence of London against the bombing raids of German airships in World War I. But it was the Air Displays of the 1920s

One of the aircraft at Hendon

and the 1930s which made Hendon famous. In a colourful garden-party atmosphere, pilots of the RAF gave highly professional aerobatic displays and helped establish the value of this new branch of the military forces. Today much of that grass airfield has been built over, but the half a million visitors who make the trip to Hendon every year can see something of life in the RAF from its creation in 1918, right up to the present day.

There are three museums – the RAF Museum, the Battle of Britain Museum and the Bomber Command Museum. The first of these concentrates on the story of the RAF.

The collection of historic aircraft is housed in a giant shed – originally two World War I hangars – and the display ranges from the Sopwith FI Camel of World War I to the prototype of the Harrier of today.

In the Battle of Britain Museum, pride of place is given to the Spitfire and the Hurricane. A large hangar houses German bombers and their escorting fighters on one side, while facing them are the aircraft of Fighter Command. On the first floor of the museum the Operations Room of No. 11 Group has been re-created as it was at the height of the Battle of Britain – 11.30 hrs on 15 September 1940. In the Ground Floor gallery are a number of scenes from civilian life.

The Bomber Command Museum traces the development of the Command from the early biplanes – the De Havilland 9a of World War I, the Lancaster, Mosquito and Halifax of World War II, to the Valiant and the Vulcan of the post-war era. There is a reconstruction of the office of Sir Barnes Wallis, the brilliant inventor who created the Wellington bomber and the bouncing bomb used in the Dam Buster Raid, and a display commemorating the Head of the Command, 'Bomber Harris'.

A huge projector shows the galaxies at the Planetarium

The Planetarium
Marylebone Road, NW1
Map Ref: 75H
The heavens are depicted on a huge copper dome here and there is an interesting commentary accompanying the spectacle. Admission charge.
Nearest Underground: Baker Street

Pollock's Toy Museum
1 Scala Street, W1
Map Ref: 76F
Two interconnected houses here contain a wonderful museum of childhood including dolls, teddy bears, board games and toy theatres. Admission charge.
Nearest Underground: Goodge Street

Public Record Office Museum
Chancery Lane, WC2
Map Ref: 78J
This is the national repository of records with many documents dating back to the Norman Conquest, including the Domesday Book. The museum incorporates glass and monuments from the Rolls Chapel and other treasures. Admission charge.
Nearest Underground: Chancery Lane

Royal Air Force Museum
Aerodrome Road, Hendon, NW9
Map Ref: 87S12
See feature on this page. Admission free.
Nearest Underground: Colindale

The Science Museum
Exhibition Road, SW7
Map Ref: 80F
The collections in this endlessly fascinating museum cover the application of science to technology and the development of engineering and industry from their beginnings to the present day. The ground floor galleries are given over to the development of motive power. On the first, second, and third floors are galleries dealing with astronomy, chemistry, nuclear physics, navigation, photography, printing, electricity and communications. Among other exhibits is the Apollo 10 Space Capsule. Popular with children is 'Launch Pad', which provides an introduction to scientific ideas through the medium of exciting 'hands-on' exhibits. Admission free.
Nearest Underground: South Kensington

1. Development of Motive Power	20. Printing and Papermaking
2. Hot Air, Gas and Oil Engines	21. Nuclear Power and Physics
3. Exploration	22. Computing
4. Transport	23. Navigation
5. Fire Fighting	24. Sailing and Marine Engineering
6. Hand & Machine Tools	25. Docks and Diving
7. Iron & Steel	26. Optics
8. Glass	27. Heat & Temperature
9. Telecommunications	28. King George III Collection
10. Textile Machinery	29. Photography & Cinematography
11. Plastics	30. Electricity and Magnetism
12. Agriculture	31. Geophysics and Oceanography
13. Gas	32. Clothes for the Job
14. Meteorology	33. Aeronautics
15. Time Measurement	
16. Mapmaking	
17. Astronomy	
18. Weighing, Measuring and Lighting	
19. Chemistry	

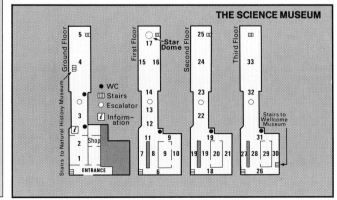

THE SCIENCE MUSEUM

Sir John Soane's Museum

There can be few places which give such fascinating insights into the life of a highly cultured gentleman and architect, who lived just over 150 years ago, than a visit to 13 Lincoln's Inn Fields, the home of Sir John Soane RA.

Items on display range from the sarcophagus of Pharaoh Seti I, the father of Rameses the Great, to the mock-gothic tomb to Fanny, the pet dog of the great tragedienne, Sarah Siddons; from the paintings of Canaletto and Watteau to the satirical compositions of William Hogarth – the *Rake's Progress* and the *Election*; from the 16th-century Italian Renaissance miniature of Giulo Clovio to the extensive collection of architectural drawings of the Adams Brothers and of Soane himself – 20,000 in all.

What makes this museum especially exciting is the way in which Soane organised the house to be full of surprises. There are rooms at different levels, mirrors which open new dimensions, a hole in the floor to disclose the stone coffin of the Pharaoh, small rooms and narrow passages. This is an exploration in space, an extraordinary jumble where ingenuity overcomes lack of space, where every effort is made to disorient us, and it all works just as Soane intended.

Sir John Soane's Museum
13 Lincoln's Inn Fields, WC2
Map Ref: 77M
See feature on this page.
Admission free.
Nearest Underground: Holborn

Thamesworld
53–55 Greenwich Church Street, Greenwich SE10
Map Ref: 93P17
Many kinds of audio-visual techniques are employed here in order to re-create the River Thames in history, as it is today, and as it might be in the future.
Admission charge.
Nearest Station: Greenwich

Victoria and Albert Museum
Cromwell Road, SW7
Map Ref: 80K
Known affectionately as the V & A, this vast museum is one of the cultural and educational institutions started after the Great Exhibition of 1851. Objects and works of art from this Exhibition formed the nucleus of the Victoria and Albert, Science, Geological and Natural History Museums grouped at the end of Exhibition Road. The brainchild of Prince Albert and Sir Henry Cole, the V & A is today by far the most complex of London's museums, but it is one of the most enjoyable, providing something for everyone.

There is a fine collection of Western and Oriental sculpture and applied art objects, Japanese lacquerwork, Persian miniatures, furniture, sculpture, bronzes and tapestries (including Raphael's tapestry cartoons). The Henry Cole Wing is divided into levels to house the museum's collection of 18th- and 19th-century British paintings. The V & A also has an extensive collection of watercolours.
Admission free, but voluntary donations encouraged.
Nearest Underground: South Kensington

The V & A's graceful tower

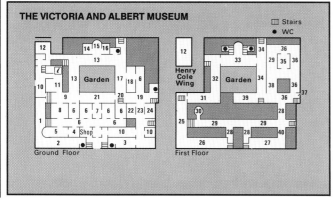

THE VICTORIA AND ALBERT MUSEUM

🛤 Stairs
● WC

Ground Floor

Henry Cole Wing

First Floor

1. Continental 17 C.	21. Gothic Art
2. Continental 18 C.	22. Victorian Cast Court
3. Continental 19 C.	23. Fakes & Forgeries
4. Woodwork Collection	24. Italian Cast Court
5. Raphael Cartoons	25. English Renaissance
6. Eastern & Asian Art	26. British 1650-1750
7. Medieval Treasury	27. Carvings & Bronzes
8. Dress Collection	28. Stained Glass
9. High Renaissance	29. Armour & Ironwork
10. Sculpture	30. Musical Instruments
11. Boilerhouse Project	31. British Art
12. Prints & Photographs	32. Theatre Museum
13. Renaissance Italy	33. Silver
14. Morris Room	34. Enamel & Metalwork
15. Gamble Room	35. 20 C. Collection
16. Poynter Room	36. Tapestries etc
17. Renaissance N.Europe	37. Fans
18. Medieval Tapestries	38. Jewellery
19. Carpets	39. Library
20. Spanish Art	40. Glass Vessels

Above: Buckingham Palace and the Queen Victoria Memorial from St James's Park. Right: entrance to the Royal Mews

PALACES

From earliest times the Royal Family was constantly moving and building and rebuilding their homes. London, as the capital city, has many Royal homes past and present. The earliest is the Tower of London and the current Royal home is Buckingham Palace.

Buckingham Palace
Buckingham Palace Road, SW1
Map Ref: 82E
The principal residence of the sovereign overlooks the west end of St James's Park and is backed by a private garden of 40 acres. The dignified classical façade, 360ft long, was reconstructed in 1913 by Sir Aston Webb. It is enclosed by a large forecourt patrolled by sentries of the Brigade of Guards in full dress uniform. When the Queen is in residence, the Royal Standard is flown at the mast-head. The colourful ceremony of Changing the Guard is performed daily in the forecourt.

The palace takes its name from Buckingham House, built in 1703 for John Sheffield, Duke of Buckingham, and purchased in 1762 for George III. The house was settled on Queen Charlotte in 1775, and it passed to her son George IV, who commissioned John Nash, the court architect to remodel it in 1824. Though the name was changed to Buckingham Palace, the new mansion (completed in 1830) was little used until the accession of Queen Victoria in 1837, after which it became the permanent London residence of the Court. The interior of the palace, never open to the public, contains many splendid apartments, some decorated under the direction of Queen Mary. The State Apartments include the Throne Room, the State Ballroom and the Picture Gallery which contains a selection of valuable paintings from the royal collection.

The Royal Mews in Buckingham Palace Road is open to the public twice a week. On view are carriage horses, royal cars and carriages including the Gold State Coach used at the Coronation, and the Glass State Coach used for Royal weddings.
Admission charge to Royal Mews.
Nearest Undergrounds: Hyde Park Corner and St James's Park

Clarence House
St James's, SW1
Map Ref: 82B
The building is one of the less successful by John Nash, who designed it for William IV, then Duke of Clarence. The much altered interior was restored in 1949 for Princess Elizabeth, who occupied the house until her accession in 1952. It is now the home of Queen Elizabeth, the Queen Mother.
Not open to the public.
Nearest Undergrounds: Charing Cross and Green Park

Hampton Court Palace
Hampton Court, Surrey
Map Ref: 91L8
This huge palace was built by Cardinal Wolsey outside central London on the River Thames. Construction began in 1514. The Palace is of red brick and is nearly 700ft long and 400ft wide – it contains over 1,000 rooms. As Wolsey's favour with Henry VIII declined, he gave the Palace to the king in an attempt to retain his friendship. Henry took the Palace but imprisoned Wolsey for high treason the following year. The King enlarged and beautified the Palace and successive monarchs used it regularly. William and Mary, who did not like Whitehall Palace,

One of the King's Beasts flanking the entrance to Hampton Court Palace

employed Sir Christopher Wren to rebuild the eastern part of the building. George II was the last monarch to use Hampton Court. It is a marvellous museum of great works of art and paintings by such masters as Mantegna and Verrio. The grounds are spectacular and a joy to visit throughout the year (see also page 53). Part of the Palace is used as Grace and Favour apartments for servants of the Crown.
Admission charge.
Nearest Station: Hampton Court

Kensington Palace
Kensington Palace Gardens, W8
Map Ref: 80A
Kensington Palace stands on the extreme west side of Kensington Gardens. It was partly rebuilt for William III by Sir Christopher Wren and added to by William Kent. It was the principal private residence of the sovereign from 1689 until 1760 and the birthplace of Queen Victoria. The Prince and Princess of Wales and Princess Margaret have apartments in wings of the palace. The State Apartments with their fine pictures and furniture are on view to the public. Admission charge.
Nearest Undergrounds: High Street Kensington and Lancaster Gate

Lambeth Palace
Lambeth Palace Road, SE1
Map Ref: 83M
Not a Royal Palace but an ecclesiastic one, this has been the London residence of the Archbishops of Canterbury for 750 years. The buildings were begun by Archbishop Hubert Walter (1193–1205), and Stephen Langton (1207–28) was the first archbishop to live here. The palace has been extensively altered and added to by many of his successors, but it still retains its medieval atmosphere. The entrance is a fine Tudor gateway of red brick usually called Morton's Tower after the cardinal who built it in 1490.
Not open to the public.
Nearest Underground: Waterloo

The Orangery in the Gardens of Kensington Palace. Built in 1704, its brickwork is of the highest quality

Lancaster House
Stable Yard, St James's, SW1
Map Ref: 82B
Lancaster House was begun in 1825 by Benjamin Wyatt for the 'grand old Duke of York', who died in 1827 before he could either pay for it or occupy it. Originally named York House, it was purchased by one of the Duke's creditors, the Marquess of Stafford (afterwards Duke of Sutherland) and completed by Sir Robert Smirke in 1840. Sir Charles Barry was responsible for much of the lavish decoration. The house is now used by the government for conferences, banquets and other entertaining. Admission charge. Open when not being used for official functions.
Nearest Undergrounds: Green Park and Charing Cross

Marlborough House
Pall Mall, SW1
Map Ref: 82B
The entrance to Marlborough House is on the south side of Pall Mall. It was built by Sir Christopher Wren in 1710 and was the home of Queen Mary from 1936 until her death in 1953, but has not been used as a residence since. It now houses the Commonwealth Secretariat. The chapel is notable for its royal pews and Carolean panelling. Visitors are admitted to the chapel when services are held there.
Open by appointment.
Nearest Undergrounds: Charing Cross and Green Park

St James's Palace
St James's, SW1
Map Ref: 82B
The Palace is a rambling and picturesque brick mansion of Tudor origin built round several courtyards. It was formerly the official London residence of the sovereign and the scene of all important Court functions. Foreign ambassadors are still accredited to the Court of St James. The palace takes its name from a leper hospital dedicated to St James the Less and mentioned early in the 12th century. This was dissolved in 1532 and in its place Henry VIII built a royal palace. Henry VIII transferred his affections to his new Whitehall Palace and St James's Palace only became the official residence of the sovereign when Whitehall was burned down in 1698.
Not open to the public.
Nearest Undergrounds: Charing Cross and Green Park

Friars Court, part of St James's Palace

The Palace of Westminster (Houses of Parliament)

Map Ref: 83G

The Houses of Parliament, or more correctly **The Palace of Westminster**, is the seat of the supreme legislature in Great Britain and Northern Ireland. Designed by Sir Charles Barry, who was assisted by A W Pugin, the buildings were begun in 1840 and the first parliament was opened here by Queen Victoria in 1852. It is elaborate late-Gothic in style and the stone used was magnesian limestone from Anston in Yorkshire. The building cost over £3 million and covers an area of about 8 acres. Besides the House of Commons, in the northern part and the House of Lords, in the southern part, it contains innumerable offices, committee rooms, libraries and dining-rooms. It also acts as the residences of the Speaker of the House of Commons, the Serjeant at Arms and other officers. It incorporates Westminster Hall and the crypt of St Stephen's Chapel, practically the only parts of the former royal palace to survive the fire which destroyed the previous building. At the north end of the building stands the splendid Clock Tower which rises to 320ft. The hours are struck on the great bell of 'Big Ben', cast in Whitechapel and named after Sir Benjamin Hall, the first Commissioner of Works at the time it was hung.

Westminster Hall is a noble and beautiful hall originally built by William II. It was rebuilt by Richard II who employed the architect Henry Yevele. The splendid hammerbeam roof of twelve bays is the finest of its kind in the world and was built of oak.

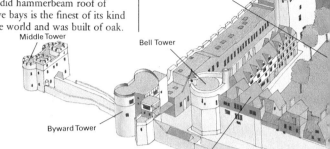

The chief court of English law sat in the hall from the late 13th century until 1825.

In front of Westminster Hall is a fine bronze statue of Oliver Cromwell and to the south is the equestrian statue of Richard I.

Opposite the huge Victoria Tower of the Houses of Parliament is the entrance to the moated **Jewel Tower** the last surviving domestic part of the Royal Palace of Westminster. It was probably built in 1366 and was used as the treasury for the private jewels, plate and other valuables of Edward III. Admission free.

Nearest Underground: Westminster

The Tower of London

Tower Hill, EC3

Map Ref: 79R

Originally built by William the Conqueror to impress the citizens of London, the Tower was begun in 1070 but in those days would have looked very different. For example, its outer walls would have been of wood. Only the central Tower or White Tower dates from the original building by Gundulph. The White Tower is one of the earliest and largest buildings of its kind in Western Europe, being 90ft high and having 15ft thick walls. The beautiful Norman chapel of St John is an outstanding example of Romanesque architecture. Sporadic building and improvements to the Tower went on throughout the centuries. In Henry III's reign from 1216 to 1272, there was a great spate of building and the first mention of the royal palace south of the White Tower was made. In Edward II's reign the defences were strengthened.

The Tower has been a palace, a prison and a place of execution. Prisoners were taken from the Tower via Traitors Gate to their place of execution. Famous prisoners include Thomas More, Princess Elizabeth, Walter Raleigh,

Left: the Houses of Parliament, or Palace of Westminster. Below: the Tower

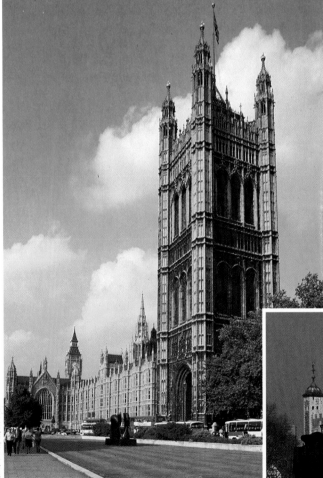

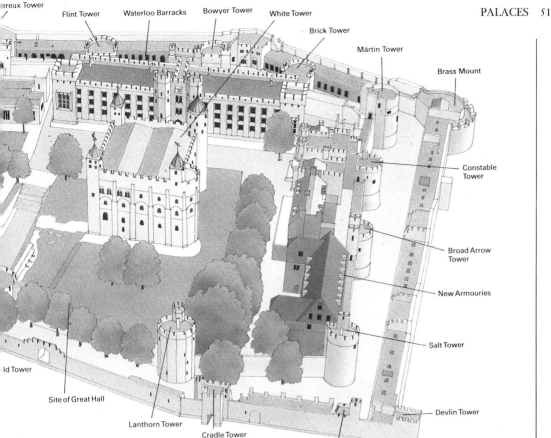

Flint Tower · Waterloo Barracks · Bowyer Tower · White Tower · ereux Tower · Brick Tower · Martin Tower · Brass Mount · Constable Tower · Broad Arrow Tower · New Armouries · Salt Tower · Devlin Tower · Well Tower · Cradle Tower · Lanthorn Tower · Site of Great Hall · Id Tower

Anne Boleyn, Catherine Howard, and more recently Rudolph Hess, the deputy leader of the Nazi Party In the past, the Tower has housed the royal armouries, the Mint and the Royal Observatory, the Royal Menagerie, and the Public Records. It still guards the Crown Jewels and is a barracks and a museum. Today the Tower's fine museum of armoury is world famous; it traces the history of western armour from medieval times to the Stuart period and includes a fascinating collection of Oriental armour. The Crown Jewels are on view in the Jewel House. The Wellington Barracks within the Tower are used by regiments performing public duties. The Yeomen Warders are privileged retired non-commissioned officers who are in charge of the daily running of the Tower; the origin of their nickname 'beefeaters' is obscure, but may come from medieval times when they tasted the food given to the sovereign to ensure it wasn't poisoned. Admission charge.
Nearest Underground: Tower Hill

A Flemish gun, one of the superb pieces of ordnance in the Tower

Yeoman Warders in day-to-day dress

The Yeomen Warders of the Tower of London

Yeomen Warders are popularly known as Beefeaters, probably because of their role in Tudor times as Yeomen Waiters at the Royal Table. The day-to-day wear of the Yeomen Warders is a blue uniform with dark red facings and embroidery. This was first introduced in 1858. The uniform which features on the postcards and posters is the state dress uniform of scarlet and gold – with white ruff, red, white and blue ribbons at the base of the hat and similarly coloured rosettes on garters and shoes. On full dress occasions, the weapon carried by the Yeomen Warders is the partisan, an 8ft long pike with gold tassel decoration. It is a weapon which was in common use in 1485, the year a victorious Henry VII began the new Tudor dynasty. The Chief Warder's badge of office is a silver mace on which is a replica of the White Tower. On State occasions, his Second-in-Command, the Yeoman Gaoler, carries a ceremonial axe. This axe has been carried in procession for over 400 years, in earlier times when escorting prisoners from the Tower to trials at Westminster.

Apart from the control of admissions and the guiding of visitors, Yeomen Warders have a number of ceremonial duties. These include a daily parade, and at 10 o'clock at night a ceremony in which the Chief Warder, wearing a long scarlet watchcoat, takes responsibility for the Ceremony of the Keys. With an escort of guardsmen, he carries out the ritual ceremony of locking the Tower for the night.

Among the less frequent ceremonies is the Beating of the Bounds. This takes place every three years on Ascension Day. Following a service in the Church of the Tower – St Peter ad Vincula – the Governor, Chaplain, Yeomen Warders, residents and choir process to each of the 31 boundary stones marking the limits of the Tower Liberty. At each of these the choirboys hit the marker with wands.

The Yeomen Warders, all ex-servicemen, link tradition with the modern responsibility of welcoming visitors. Their skill and expertise adds immensely to the enjoyment of a visit to the Tower.

PARKS AND GARDENS

London is one of the greenest cities in the world. Not only does it have ten royal parks, some of which are so large they feel just like 'proper' countryside, but it also has hundreds of public parks and a host of smaller gardens. A selection of some of the best is given on the following pages. For information on those parts of 'green' London with a natural history interest, see the article beginning on page 13.

Battersea Park
Albert Bridge Road, SW11
Map Ref: 92C/D17
This is a 200-acre park between Albert and Chelsea Bridges, originally laid out in 1852. Much of the Victorian landscaping remains, including a 13½-acre lake. Other features include a garden for the disabled, an 'old English' garden, heather, herb and alpine gardens and a show glasshouse. There are also many recreational facilities.
Admission free.
Nearest Station: Battersea Park

Bushy Park
Teddington, Middlesex
Map Ref: 91L9
Fallow deer and red deer are among the principal attractions of this walled park, which has large areas of rough grass, bracken and huge old trees. More formal in nature are the Woodland Gardens, which lie along the Longford River. Covering nearly 100 acres, these gardens have rhododendrons, azaleas, camellias, ericas and water plants.
Admission free.
Nearest Station: Teddington

The Chelsea Physic Garden
Chelsea, SW3
Map Ref: 81Q
This has been an important centre for the study of horticulture since its foundation in 1673. While preserving its history and identity, the garden aims to stimulate interest in horticulture and botany.
Admission charge.
Nearest Underground: Sloane Square

Chiswick House Grounds
Chiswick, W4
Map Ref: 91R17
A 17th-century Italian-style garden, with a serpentine lake, yew hedges and a famous collection of camellias.
Admission free.
Nearest Station: Chiswick

Dulwich Park
Dulwich, SE21
Map Ref: 92J13
Excellent collections of rhododendrons and azaleas – at their best in mid-May – are the special features of this park, which also has a lake, an aviary, a tree trail and a garden for the disabled. Many sporting facilities are included in the park's 72 acres.
Admission free.
Nearest Stations: North Dulwich and West Dulwich

Golders Hill
Hampstead, NW3
Map Ref: 88B9
Flamingoes, pea fowl and an animal enclosure with goats and fallow deer can all be seen here. The park includes the Hill, a tranquil garden alongside Inverforth House and West Heath, with many fine plants and a pergola walk.
Admission free.
Nearest Underground: Hampstead

Below: the Buddhist Peace Pagoda in Battersea Park
Bottom: in the grounds of Chiswick House

Summer colour in the Sunken Garden at Hampton Court

Greenwich Park
Greenwich, SE10
Map Ref: 9317P
Superb views over the Thames are among the best things about this lovely park. Scattered among the trees and open grass are flower gardens and a small wilderness area – complete with deer. The park is the setting for the Old Royal Observatory and the Greenwich Meridian.
Admission free.
Nearest Station: Greenwich

Ham House
Richmond, Surrey
Map Ref: 91N13
Surrounding this grand 17th-century house are extensive gardens, authentically restored to their original appearance in 1979, with a parterre where box-edged beds are filled with lavender, and an orangery.
Admission free.
Nearest Station: Richmond

Hampton Court Palace Park and Gardens
Hampton Court,
East Molesey, Surrey
Map Ref: 91L8
Henry VIII's famous gardens and parkland, with a Tudor knot garden, the maze, and a huge, ancient vine. Charles II created the Long Water in French canal style, and there is a very old Pond Garden. The Rose Garden and the Wilderness Garden are delightful.
Admission free.
Nearest Station: Hampton Court

Tulips at Holland Park. The Dutch theme is misleading; the Holland in the title is actually a district of Lincolnshire

Holland Park
Holland Park, W11
Map Ref: 881V
This 55-acre park has a Dutch garden dating from 1812, with tulip displays in spring, an iris garden and a yucca lawn. There is also an orangery, and a natural woodland garden with interesting bird life.
Admission free.
Nearest Underground: Holland Park or Kensington High Street

Horniman Gardens
Forest Hill, SE23
Map Ref: 93K13
Set on the side of a hill, this 26-acre park has views over central London. There are sunken rose and water gardens and animal and bird enclosures.
Admission free.
Nearest Station: Forest Hill

Hyde Park and Kensington Gardens
Bayswater Road, W8
Map Ref: 80A/B
Famous for the Serpentine, an artificial lake with boats and swimmers as well as water birds, Hyde Park is the largest of the central London parks. It also contains Speakers' Corner – close to Marble Arch – and Rotten Row, once a promenade for the rich and fashionable. Despite the park's popularity, it has an impressive tally of resident and breeding birds. Kensington Gardens merge into Hyde Park, and are most famous for the statue of Peter Pan and for the Orangery. There is a beautiful sunken garden in front of Kensington Palace.
Nearest Underground: Lancaster Gate and Hyde Park Corner

London Zoo is one of the best institutions of its kind in the world, with a remarkable variety of inhabitants

many bird species including herons. Running round the northern perimeter of the park is the Grand Union Canal.

In the north-eastern corner of the park is London Zoo, with one of the finest collections of living creatures in the world.
Admission free to park; charge for zoo.
Nearest Underground: Regent's Park

Richmond Park
Richmond, Surrey
Map Ref: 91Q13
Charles I enclosed the park as part of a royal estate and successive monarchs developed it for hunting. Today the deer wander free in the beautiful woods and spinneys. The park is used for riding, walking and golf, but it also contains the marvellous Isabella Plantation, which is full of heathers, magnolias, camellias, rhododendrons and azaleas. Richmond is the wildest of the royal parks, its hundreds of acres of open grassland and trees home to a host of bird and animal species.
Admission free.
Nearest Station: Richmond

Kenwood, The Iveagh Bequest
Hampstead Lane, NW3
Map Ref: 88C9
In the gardens of Kenwood House, which cover 200 acres, are a lime avenue, rhododendrons and herbaceous borders, lakes, and splendid woodlands. The gardens form an integral part of the 790 acres of Hampstead Heath.
Admission free.
Nearest Underground: Hampstead (then bus)

Regent's Park
Regent's Park, NW1
Map Ref: 75C/D
This park was laid out as part of Nash's scheme for a garden city, and it retains much of its Regency character. The focus of the overall design was the Inner Circle, which encloses the lovely Queen Mary's Garden with its attractive little lake, cascades and rockery plants. The subterranean Tyburn River fills the large lake on the south-western side. The islands in the lake are home to

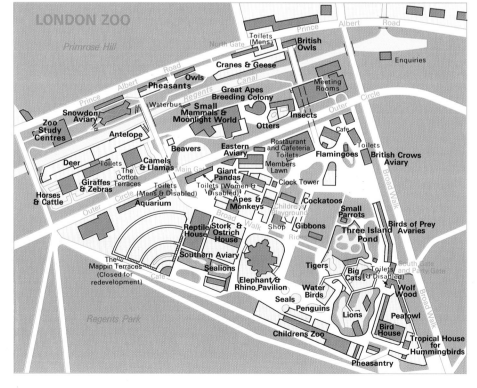

Royal Botanic Gardens
Kew, Richmond, Surrey
Map Ref: 91P16
Established on 300 acres beside the
Thames, these world-famous
gardens combine unrivalled research
facilities with great beauty. Plants of
every kind and description can be
seen here, some in glasshouses
where the temperatures are very
carefully controlled. Best known of
the houses is Decimus Burton's
marvellous steel and glass Palm
House, built in 1844 and still
serving its original function. As well
as formal areas, there are lakes and
woodland walks.
Admission charge.
Nearest Station: Kew

*Top: Digging the rose beds in front of the Palm House at Kew Gardens.
Above: the bandstand in St James's Park*

St James's Park
The Mall, SW1
Map Ref: 82B/F
Lawns and colourful plants in beds
and borders are spread under the
trees here. The Queen Mother's
Rose Walk and the large ornamental
lake with its exotic and native
waterfowl are the highlights of this,
perhaps the most immediately
attractive of the central London
parks. Many of the birds are tame
and will feed from the hand.
Admission free.
Nearest Underground: St James's Park

Syon Park Garden
Brentford, Middlesex
Map Ref: 91N16
These extensive gardens, with their
lake and garden centre, belong to
Syon House. Syon's horticultural
reputation goes back to the 16th
century when the use of trees as
purely decorative contributions to
its layout was looked upon with
amazement. The water gardens and
six-acre rose garden are among the
highlights here.
Admission charge.
Nearest Station: Syon Lane

Tradescant Trust Museum of Garden History
Lambeth Palace Road, SE1
Map Ref: 92F18
This newly-created period garden is
in the churchyard of St Mary-at-
Lambeth, which contains the graves
of the elder and younger John
Tradescant, gardeners to Charles I.
The garden contains plants
introduced to England in the 17th
century.
Admission free.
Nearest Underground: Lambeth
North

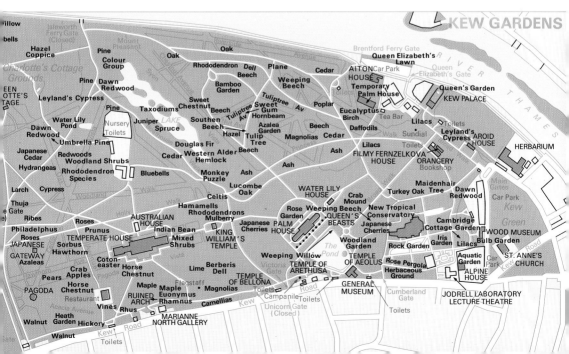

SHOPPING IN LONDON

Many come to the capital just for the shopping, and the best shops are famous the world over. Described here are the principal shopping streets.

Bond Street
W1
Map Ref: 76N
Known as the 'High Street of Mayfair', it is divided in two – Old and New Bond Street. New Bond Street has fashion boutiques – **Kurt Geiger, Yves St Laurent**, and **Fenwicks**. **Sotheby's**, London's famous auction house, is an interesting experience even if you just want to view the fine art collections. Further on is **Asprey's**, specialists in fine, rare articles and antiques. Beyond Burlington Gardens the street becomes Old Bond Street, home of art dealers and shops selling oriental rugs.

Charing Cross Road
WC1
Map Ref: 76K
The street for scholars and musicians with very good new and secondhand bookshops to browse in including **Foyles**, with over 4 million books, and **Waterstones** an excellent new bookstore. There are many musical instrument and record shops.

King's Road
SW3
Map Ref: 80P
This is the most fashion-conscious street in London. The King's Road, which stretches for over a mile, is packed with clothes and shoe shops. A good department store is **Peter Jones** at **Sloane Square**. At the far end of the King's Road the emphasis changes to antique shops.

Knightsbridge
SW1
Map Ref: 81G
This is the most luxurious of London's shopping streets, best known for the largest department store in Europe – **Harrods**, where you can buy anything. **Harvey Nichols** is a good department store expecially for clothing, and the rest of the street is lined with fashion

shops such as **Charles Jourdan, Rayne** and, for woollens, the **Scotch House**. **Beauchamp Place**, off Knightsbridge, is known for its unusual fashion boutiques and designer shops such as **Janet Reger** and **Bruce Oldfield**.

Oxford Street
W1
Map Ref: 75B/M
This is the home of the major London department stores and offers an enormous selection of fashion shops. **Selfridges**, is good for home interiors, designer collections and large food hall. Next door is the largest branch of **Marks and Spencer**, which specialises in high-quality clothes as well as food and household effects. **Debenhams**, another department store, has inexpensive luggage and furnishings. Just next door is **D. H. Evans** which has an excellent selection of separates, the Designer Room and the Astral sports department. **John Lewis**, 'never knowingly undersold', promises that if you buy something here and find it cheaper elsewhere, John Lewis will refund the difference. **British Home Stores** has a first-class lighting department and clothing section. For music enthusiasts the **HMV** store is the best-stocked record shop in the area.

South Molton Street (just off Oxford Street) has high-fashion boutiques and *al fresco* cafés.

The landmark every shopping enthusiast heads for

Piccadilly
W1
Map Ref: 82A
Lillywhites, located right on the Circus, is one of London's best sports shops. **Simpsons** are suppliers to the Royal Household of top-quality tailored clothes. **Hatchards** is a large bookshop and next door **Swaine, Adeney Brigg & Sons** sell quality leather goods, umbrellas and riding equipment. The largest store here is **Fortnum and Mason**, renowned for its food hall. **The Burlington Arcade**, next to the Royal Academy, is an elegant covered shopping street, excellent for antiques and jewellery.

Antique dolls are among the collectables in the exclusive shops of Burlington Arcade

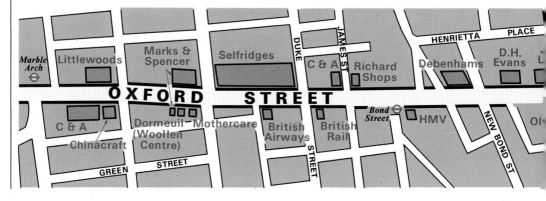

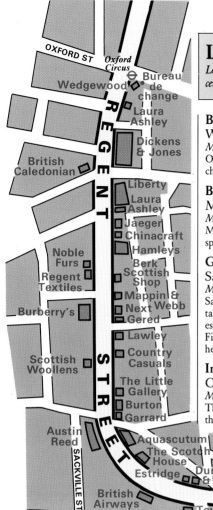

LONDON'S SPECIALIST SHOPS

London has a great variety of specialist shops. Below is a short selection of central London shops with a difference.

Bendick's
Wigmore Street, W1
Map Ref: 75M
Over 30 different types of chocolates are made here.

Button Queen
Marylebone Lane, W1
Map Ref: 75M
Modern and antique buttons are the speciality of this shop.

Gieves and Hawkes
Savile Row, W1
Map Ref: 76P
Savile Row, home of gentlemen's tailors, is the setting for this historic establishment which began in 1771. Fine hand-made suits can be bought here.

Inderwick's
Carnaby Street, W1
Map Ref: 76P
This shop, established in 1797, is the country's oldest pipemakers.

John Lobb
St James's Street, SW1
Map Ref: 82B
Specialists in hand-made shoes. The original Wellington boot is on show here.

James Lock
St James's Street, SW1
Map Ref: 82B
The oldest shop in London opened in 1764 as a hatters. The bowler hat was invented here.

London Silver Vaults
Chancery Lane, WC2
Map Ref: 77M
A maze of silver dealers for trade and public.

Paxton and Whitfield
Jermyn Street, W1
Map Ref: 76P
An international cheese store opened in 1797.

Purdey
South Audley Street, W1
Map Ref: 75R
The most famous handmade guns for sportsmen.

G. Smith and Sons
Charing Cross Road, WC2
Map Ref: 77Q
Tobacconists specialising in snuff.

James Smith
New Oxford Street, W1
Map Ref: 77L
A shop specialising in umbrellas, custom-made sword sticks and ceremonial maces.

Turnbull and Asser
Jermyn Street, W1
Map Ref: 76P/82B
Shirtmakers to the Prince of Wales.

Twinings
The Strand, WC2
Map Ref: 77R
An immense selection of teas and coffees in the smallest building along the street.

Regent Street
W1
Map Ref: 76J
A street of quality shops including **Dickins and Jones**, a large department store renowned for its fabrics, and, next door, the famous **Liberty's**, with its old-world ambience, selling fine textiles, rugs and clothing. A little further down is **Jaeger**, selling classic clothes, and then a delight for children – **Hamleys**, a gigantic toyshop. Across the road is **Burberry's**, the raincoat store. Other stores include **Laura Ashley, Aquascutum, Austin Reed** and **Garrards**, 'The Queen's Jeweller', which is responsible for cleaning the Crown Jewels. **Regent Street** is most attractively lit at Christmas.

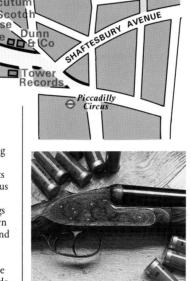

Superb craftsmanship and attention to detail are hallmarks of Purdey's guns

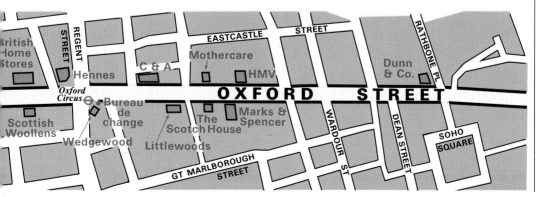

STREET MARKETS

Market life in London is exciting even if you do not buy anything. The markets cater for all tastes and budgets – selling antiques, crafts, clothing, fruit, vegetables – and almost anything else. Some of the markets are still on their original historic sites.

Berwick Street
Berwick Street, W1
Map Ref: 76K/P
This is the best fruit and vegetable market in London, set in the heart of Soho. Prices are low and quality high; there are also food stalls selling cheese, shellfish and other produce. Monday – Saturday.
Nearest Underground: Tottenham Court Road and Piccadilly Circus

Brixton Market
Electric Avenue, SW9
Map Ref: 92G15
The market has a Caribbean air as

Berwick Street Market

many West Indians live in the area. It is a lively and densely packed market of covered arcades and open-air stalls. Secondhand clothes, often designer-label rejects, and household goods are available. Monday–Saturday (Wednesday morning only).
Nearest Underground: Brixton

Camden Lock Market
Camden, NW1
Map Ref: 88D6
Along the Lock's cobbled paths are

stalls selling clothes, antiques, pottery and textiles. It has a village atmosphere with plenty of cafés and restaurants, some with live music. Saturday and Sunday.
Nearest Underground: Camden Town

Camden Passage
Islington, N1
Map Ref: 88G5
Saved from demolition in the 1960s, this market has some of the best antique shops and stalls in London. It is excellent for dealers and browsers interested in furniture, jewellery, prints and Victorian clothes. There are also specialist traders such as the only playing card and banknote dealers in Britain. Wednesday and Saturday.
Nearest Underground: Angel

Columbia Road
Shoreditch, E2
Map Ref: 79D
A mass of fresh flowers and plants of all descriptions, this market is a must not only for gardening enthusiasts but also for town dwellers who want a bargain or an excellent choice of houseplants. Sunday morning.
Nearest Underground: Old Street

Greenwich Antiques Market
Greenwich High Road, SE10
Map Ref: 93N17
A good antiques and craft market. Saturday and Sunday.
Nearest Underground/Station: New Cross or Greenwich

Street Furniture

Bound up with the history of London as a city is the development of its street furniture – items that adorn the streets either for purposes long since outdated, or which have practical use today. Wrought and cast iron, stone and steel, concrete and plastic, such items provide a fascinating gallimaufry.

In the City are parish boundary and property marks. These are of stone affixed to a wall at ground level or cast iron plates 9"-12" across and usually at first floor height. They show boundaries of the parishes even where the church has long since disappeared. Similar marks are used to indicate the boundaries of Wards, into which the City is divided.

Marks were also used on houses from the early 1700s onwards for a different purpose – to identify a property as being insured against fire. Companies such as the Sun Fire Office and the Royal Exchange Assurance issued cast iron, tin and copper marks. They were there to guide the private fire brigade of the company who would take action only for the properties which bore the appropriate symbol.

The 1762 Improvement Acts made it a requirement that house numbering and street lighting become the responsibility of Vestries. Today, some of the 18th-century houses in London's West End proudly display not only iron railings and balconies of

Lamps on Westminster Bridge

grace and charm, but also lamp holders and extinguishers, sometimes erroneously described as 'snuffers'. There link-boys could put out the flaming torches which they used to light the way for their carriage or sedan chair borne masters. Examples of such ironwork are to be seen over the doorway of No 10 Downing Street, in Duke of York Street, St

James's and behind Westminster Abbey in Barton Street and Cowley Street. The modern development of street lighting dates from 1807, when gas lamps were erected, first in Pall Mall and later in adjoining streets. There are many gas lamps still in use in Central London, although some of the early standards bearing the cypher 'George IV' and in some instances 'IIII Geo', have been converted to electricity.

The paving of the residential streets and the use of coal for house heating helped develop yet another item of street furniture – circular coal plates. These are usually 12" or 14" in diameter and gave direct access to the cellar behind and underneath the house. Such plates frequently bear the name of the maker.

For the benefit of the horse-drawn traffic of London, another development was the heavy granite drinking trough. The Metropolitan Drinking Fountain and Cattle Trough Association provided 500 such troughs in London. Those still in position today are generally used for decoration and filled with flowering plants. There is one exception in Hyde Park: that is still full of water and is much used by horses ridden in the Park.

Jubilee Market
Covent Garden, WC2
Map Ref: 77Q
This central London market opened when the original Covent Garden market moved to Nine Elms. Now established, it has a good variety of crafts at weekends as well as records, souvenirs, fruit and vegetables.
Nearest Underground: Covent Garden

Leather Lane
Holborn, EC1
Map Ref: 78E
One of the City's most famous lunchtime markets with a noisy atmosphere. It is particularly good for clothes, hardware, fruit and vegetables.
Monday – Friday.
Nearest Underground: Chancery Lane or Farringdon

New Caledonian Market
Bermondsey Square, SE1
Map Ref: 85H
Known more familiarly as Bermondsey Market, this colourful antiques market sells mainly to international dealers but offers good bargains if you can spot them. It begins in the early hours of the morning and has a good selection of silver, pottery, porcelain, coins and medals as well as furniture.
Friday morning.
Nearest Underground: London Bridge

Petticoat Lane
Middlesex Street, E1
Map Ref: 79M
During the week this street is known as Middlesex Street. On Sunday it changes into a colourful, noisy market street. Its name dates from the 17th century when the area was full of clothes dealers. New clothes, leather, hi-fi and household goods are now the specialities.
Sunday morning.
Nearest Underground: Aldgate or Aldgate East

Browsing among the antiques and bygones in Portobello Road

Portobello Road
Notting Hill, W11
Map Ref: 87V3
Named after Puerto Bello on the Gulf of Mexico, Portobello has always been renowned for its antiques. During the 1960s it was the centre of the London hippy scene. Today it boasts one of the best antique markets in London

Sunday morning bargain hunters in the East End's colourful Petticoat Lane market

with street entertainers providing music among the stalls.
Monday – Saturday (Friday: antiques, Saturday: general).
Nearest Underground: Ladbroke Grove or Notting Hill

Ridley Road
Hackney, E8
Map Ref: 88J7
The Jewish and West Indian communities run the stalls in this well-known East End market. They sell cheap fruit and vegetables and there are specialist kosher and Caribbean shops.
Tuesday–Saturday (Thursday morning only)
Nearest Station: Dalston Kingsland

Roman Road
Roman Road, E3
Map Ref: 89M5
Quality clothes are offered here and this market has quickly become fashionable.
Tuesday, Thursday and Saturday.
Nearest Underground: Mile End

Shepherd's Bush
W12
Map Ref: 87U1
The market, in a long, wide alley beside the railway, is a feast of junk, hardware, fruit and vegetables. It has echoes of an Arab street market in the exotic foods for sale.
Nearest Underground: Shepherd's Bush

TRADE MARKETS

London's wholesale markets have a unique history, but sadly many of them have now moved away from central London. You have to arrive at dawn to catch the atmosphere.

Billingsgate
North Quay, West India Docks, Isle of Dogs, E14
Map Ref: 89N2
In the 13th century a Royal Charter was granted for the sale of fish, and Billingsgate was established. The arcaded building in Lower Thames Street is now a listed building and the market has been moved to the Isle of Dogs.
Nearest Station: Greenwich

Borough
Southwark, SE1
Map Ref: 85C
This claims to be the oldest fruit and vegetable market. Edward VI granted it a Royal Charter, and a second market replaced it in the 16th century. Today the market occupies buildings beneath the railway arches of the viaduct serving London Bridge station.
Monday to Saturday.
Nearest Underground: Borough or London Bridge

Leadenhall Market
Gracechurch Street, EC3
Map Ref: 79Q
This market, founded in the 14th century, stands on the site of the Roman basilica. Its name comes from the lead-roofed 14th-century mansion of Sir Hugh Neville that once stood near this site.
Predominantly a meat and poultry market, it also offers fish, vegetables and plants for the City's workers.
Monday – Friday.
Nearest Underground: Bank and Monument

New Covent Garden
Nine Elms, SW8
Map Ref: 83Q
London's best known fruit, vegetable and flower market occupied Covent Garden until 1974, when the market was moved to Nine Elms. Today it is in a modern building which has increased efficiency, but much of the atmosphere has been lost.
Nearest Underground: Vauxhall

Smithfield
Charterhouse Street, EC1
Map Ref: 78J
The largest meat, poultry and provision market in the world, this is the only trade market in London to have remained on its original site. It derives its name from Smoothfield which was originally an area outside the City. Until the last century, cattle came into London on the hoof, but in 1867 this was stopped and the present Central Meat Market was built by Sir Horace Jones. The 'bummarees' or meat porters have their own police force and public house, which is licensed from 6.30 am.
Nearest Underground: Farringdon

Spitalfields
Commercial Street, E1
Map Ref: 79H
Established in 1682 under licence granted by Charles II to John Balch, the market was located in what was a fertile area and so all kinds of produce were sold. The City Corporation bought the market at the beginning of the 19th century. They carefully designed it as a fruit and vegetable market (specialising in bananas), with heated cellars underground for ripening.
Nearest Underground: Liverpool Street

Covent Garden – Choosing flowers in the Flower Market.
Below: Covent Garden today

Covent Garden

William Boston, an obscure monk of Peterborough, was appointed Abbot of Westminster in 1533. He was the pliant instrument of Henry VIII and three years later he signed away much of the property of the abbey to the King. Among these transfers was Covent Garden. Here the monks had grown fruit and vegetables for their needs. It had been the custom to sell any surplus to the local population, and in this was the beginning of the market.

In 1552 Covent Garden and a 7-acre field to its north – the Long Acre – was given to John Russell, First Earl of Bedford, by Henry's son, Edward VI. It was to remain in the family ownership until 1918.

Early in the reign of Charles I, the Fourth Earl of Bedford secured the approval of the King to a proposal that the area be laid out to provide 'habitacions fitt for Gentlemen and men of ability'. Inigo Jones, the King's Surveyor, put forward designs for houses, arcades and a church around an open square.

The central open space continued to be used as a venue by traders in market garden produce, and in 1670 Charles II granted the Bedford family the right to hold a market.

The surrounding houses ceased to be used by the wealthy and the titled for whom they had been designed. The central market space became a shambles of wooden shops and booths; by the 19th century a change was essential. Acts of Parliament paved the way for the construction of the Central Market Building. For almost 150 years this was to be London's main fruit and vegetable market, but by the 1950s and 60s congestion was intolerable. From midnight to mid-day the market and the nearby streets were thronged with porters, produce and trucks in an area designed for horse drawn carts and pedestrians. It was a relief when, in 1974, the market finally moved to a new 68-acre site south of the River Thames.

In a bold move, the Greater London Council, then responsible for the government of London, decided upon restoration of this whole central area, with shops and restaurants, boutiques and stalls. The area between the market and St Paul's Church has become a popular spot for performances by buskers, musicians and magicians.

It is not just the Central Market Building which is of interest. In the Old Flower Market Building is housed the London Transport Museum, and in the Jubilee Hall on weekdays is a general market.

ASSOCIATION FOOTBALL

Wembley Stadium
Empire Way, Wembley
Map Ref: 87Q7
The stadium was built in 1923 as part of the British Empire Exhibition. It seats 100,000 and is probably most famous for the annual Cup Final between the two football team finalists from the whole of England. As well as being used for the Littlewoods Challenge Cup and international football fixtures, it also hosts many other events such as women's hockey matches, the Gaelic Games, speedway and twice-weekly greyhound racing. It can be adapted for pop festivals, boxing, gymnastics, and horse shows. In 1948 the Olympic Games were held here, and in 1966 England won the World Cup Soccer Final at Wembley. Tours available.
Nearest Underground: Wembley

ATHLETICS
Meetings are held mainly at Crystal Palace National Sports Centre and Wembley (see above). The former is purpose-built with an all-weather track and covered accommodation for spectators.

Crystal Palace National Sports Centre
Crystal Palace Park, SE19
Map Ref: 92K10
Nearest Station: Sydenham

THE BOAT RACE
Putney to Mortlake
An annual event between the universities of Oxford and Cambridge, where crews of eight row the four-mile course on a Saturday shortly before Easter.

CRICKET

Lord's Ground
St John's Wood Road, NW8
Map Ref: 74B
The game was first played in Tudor times, but it was not until 1744 that rules were drawn up. Lords is the home of the Middlesex County Cricket Club and the famous Marylebone Cricket Club. The name Lord's comes from the groundsman, Thomas Lord, who laid the turf. International matches – Tests – are played here between Commonwealth countries and counties competing for the Gillette Cup and the Benson and Hedges Cup play their Finals here.
Nearest Underground: St John's Wood

The Oval
Kennington Park Road, SW11
Map Ref: 83R
The home of Surrey County Cricket Club and the venue for the final Test in a series.
Nearest Underground: Oval

SPORTING VENUES

The British national game is football, a game so old that no one is sure of its origins. There are 12 League clubs in the capital. Rugby is also very popular and there are 10 London clubs where first class games can be watched during the winter months. For those who enjoy the gentler summer game of cricket there are two major Test cricket grounds, Lord's and the Oval. Athletics are well catered for with five stadiums. Just outside Central London there are three major race courses where flat and steeplechase race meetings are organised throughout the year. There are also six greyhound racing tracks, two speedway tracks and two major tennis venues.

GREYHOUND RACING
Races are either on the flat or over hurdles; pure-bred greyhounds chase after an artificial hare on an electrified rail at speeds of up to 40mph. The most famous tracks are:

Harringay
Green Lanes, N4
Map Ref: 88H10
Nearest Station: Harringay Stadium

Walthamstow
Chingford, E4
Map Ref: 89N13
Nearest Station: Highams Park

HORSE RACING
Race meetings are as much society occasions as they are sporting events. Most famous is Royal Ascot, held at the end of June; also in June, at Epsom, are two of the most famous British races – the Derby and the Oaks.

Ascot Racecourse
Ascot, Berkshire
Off map
Nearest Station: Ascot

Epsom Racecourse
Epsom, Surrey
Off map
Nearest Station: Epsom

Kempton Park Racecourse
Sunbury-on-Thames, Greater London
Map Ref: 90G9
Nearest Station: Kempton Park, Sunbury

Sandown Park Racecourse
Esher, Surrey
Map Ref: 90K5
Nearest Station: Esher

RUGBY UNION FOOTBALL
Rugby Football is said to have started in 1823 when W W Ellis, a pupil at Rugby School, picked up a soccer ball and ran with it. Guy's Hospital claims to have the world's oldest Rugby Club, formed in 1843. There are a number of rugby grounds in London, but the most famous is Twickenham, where the Internationals, the Oxford and Cambridge match, the Inter-Services championship and the Hospitals Cup are played.

A match between London clubs – Arsenal and Tottenham Hotspur

Twickenham
Whitton Road, Twickenham
Map Ref: 90/91K14
Nearest Station: Twickenham

SPEEDWAY
The sport was introduced to Britain in the 1920s. It developed from dirt-track racing in open fields. The bikes are 500cc, run on pure methanol and have no brakes!

Hackney Stadium
Waterden Road, E15
Map Ref: 89N7
Nearest Station: Hackney Wick.

Wimbledon Stadium
Plough Lane, SW19
Map Ref: 92B11
Nearest Underground: Wimbledon Park

TENNIS
Once a year, for two weeks at the end of June, the All-England Lawn Tennis and Croquet Club at Wimbledon sees top players from all over the world compete for the Wimbledon Championships on grass. The complex includes 30 grass courts, nine hard courts and two indoor courts. The Wimbledon fortnight attracts over 300,000 spectators. The Club is also used for other major events including the Davis Cup.

The All-England Lawn Tennis and Croquet Club
Somerset Road, SW19
Map Ref: 91V12
Nearest Underground: Southfields

SQUARES

Squares are among the best places to get away from the hurly-burly of London. They are often unexpectedly quiet, and frequently interesting to explore.

Belgrave Square, SW1
Map Ref: 81H
Belgrave Square is one of the largest in London. Essentially a small park enclosed by railings, it is used by the residents who live in the beautifully designed terraced houses built by Thomas Cubitt in the 19th century.

Berkeley Square, W1
Map Ref: 76N
Most of the Georgian houses which once stood here and were lived in by famous people such as Clive of India and Alexander Pope have

The statue of George II in Roman costume by Van Nost stands in Golden Square

given way to modern development. The beautiful plane trees are almost 200 years old.

Bloomsbury Square, WC1
Map Ref: 77L
The name of this square probably derives from the medieval manor of Blemund'sbury. The Earl of Southampton bought the manor in 1545, and the square was laid out by his descendants in 1661. It was

the first open space to be called a square. Humphry Repton planted the gardens in 1800.

Clerkenwell Green, EC1
Map Ref: 78E
Centre for radical protest meetings long before the growth of 'Speakers' Corner', this square is in the historic area of Clerkenwell. The former Middlesex Court of Sessions dominates one side and the Marx Memorial Library the other. Here Fagin taught Oliver Twist to pick pockets.

Fitzroy Square, W1
Map Ref: 76E/F
Designed by the famous Adam brothers in the 18th century, some of the terraces here preserve their original work.

Golden Square, W1
Map Ref: 76P
Originally called 'Gelding', this is the centre of the woollen trade.

Gordon Square, WC1
Map Ref: 76F
The area is associated with the circle of 20th-century writers and intellectuals known as the Bloomsbury Group. Residents included Virginia Woolf, economist John Maynard Keynes and Lytton Strachey.

Grosvenor Square, W1
Map Ref: 75R
This area is known as 'Little America' as it is dominated by the large modern building of the American Embassy. The open garden in the middle was designed by the 18th-century architect William Kent. It contains a memorial to Franklin D Roosevelt.

The effigy of a Knight Templar in the Temple Church

Inns of Court

The Inns of Court originated in the reign of Edward I. In his reign the clergy no longer practised in the courts of justice and their place was taken by professional students of law. The Inns had the exclusive privilege of admitting law students to practise as advocates in the courts of England and Wales. By dining in hall a certain number of days in each term and passing their examinations they were 'called to the Bar'. After this they could plead for others in a court of law. Originally there were twelve inns of court; today there are four, Gray's Inn, Lincoln's Inn and the Inner and Middle Temple, which remain independent of each other. Each is governed by its 'benchers' under the presidency of a treasurer.

Middle and Inner Temples stretch down to the Thames from Fleet Street. The name Temple derives from the Knights Templar, a religious fellowship who protected pilgrims on the roads to the Holy Sepulchre. They held this land until they were dissolved in 1312. The property passed to the Knights Hospitallers, and was subsequently leased to lawyers. The earliest building, the Temple church, dates from the 12th century. Middle Temple Hall is a wonderful 16th-century building. The large complex contains 17th- and 18th-century buildings of great interest. Most are used by lawyers as offices and some are private apartments. In spite of damage during the Blitz, the area is still architecturally and historically fascinating.

Hanover Square, W1
Map Ref: 76J/N
Hanover Square once contained elegant Georgian houses, but many of these have now been replaced by modern offices.

Leicester Square, WC2
Map Ref: 76P
The Earl of Leicester built Leicester House on this site in the 17th century; before that it had been open fields used for fighting duels. In Victorian times the fields were laid out as a garden with a statue of Shakespeare in the centre.

Lincoln's Inn Fields, WC1
Map Ref: 77M
Lincoln's Inn Fields were laid out in the 17th century and were famous for duelling. Lord William Russell was executed here in 1683. There are many handsome buildings, including the Sir John Soane's Museum and the Royal College of Surgeons.

Parliament Square, W1
Map Ref: 83G
The square faces the Houses of Parliament and contains the statues of many British politicians and foreign statesmen. It was originally laid out by Sir Charles Barry in 1850.

Portman Square, W1
Map Ref: 75M
Set in an area once sought-after by high society, this square took 20 years to build. Beneath the attractive garden in the centre is an underground car park.

Russell Square, WC1
Map Ref: 77G
This is the largest of the Bloomsbury squares and was laid out by James Burton in the early 19th century. Few of the original buildings survive, and the area is now dominated by the buildings of London University. The central gardens were laid out by Humphry Repton.

St James Square, SW1
Map Ref: 82B
A particularly lovely garden noted for its trees with an equestrian statue of William III forming the focal point.

Smith Square, SW1
Map Ref: 83L
This square is named after Sir John Smith, who owned and developed the land. In the centre is a fine church built by Thomas Archer in the 18th century. The Conservative party has its headquarters here.

Soho Square, W1
Map Ref: 76K
The name Soho comes from a hunting call meaning 'after him'. Charles II's illegitimate son, the Duke of Monmouth, had a mansion here and when he and his followers made a bid for the Crown at the Battle of Sedgemoor, 'Soho' was their battle-cry. The French Protestant Church founded in 1550, and protestants fleeing from persecution in Europe, originally gave the area its foreign flavour.

Tavistock Square, WC1
Map Ref: 76F
Charles Dickens lived in this square for nine years and wrote several of his novels here. The fascinating

Jewish Museum faces the gardens, which have a copper beech planted by Pandit Nehru in 1953 to mark the unveiling of the statue of Mahatma Gandhi.

Trafalgar Square, WC1
Map Ref: 77Q
Famous for its pigeons and dominated by Nelson's Column, Trafalgar Square is often the setting for meetings and rallies and is generally teeming with people. The National Gallery lies along the north side of the square.

Vincent Square, SW1
Map Ref: 82K
Named after William Vincent, the Dean of Westminster from 1802-15, it was traditionally a place where young men practised skills such as archery, wrestling and tilting. Westminster School has its playing fields in the centre and the headquarters of the Royal Horticultural Society is here.

Woburn Square, WC1
Map Ref: 76F
More a long strip than a square, this area contains many modern buildings, including the Warburg Institute and the Courtauld Institute Galleries, with its superb collections of French Impressionist paintings and other fine works.

Feeding the pigeons (inset) in Trafalgar Square

STATUES AND MONUMENTS

London's statues and monuments commemorate famous men, women, events, and in some cases, legendary figures or characters from fiction.

Achilles
Hyde Park, W1
Map Ref: 81D
This statue to the most famous of all the Greek heroes was designed by Sir Richard Westmacott and made from cannon captured during the Peninsular Wars. It was erected in 1822.

Prince Albert
The Albert Memorial
Kensington Gore, SW7
Map Ref: 80F
Prince Albert, the consort of Queen Victoria, was the architect of the Great Exhibition of 1851. He is commemorated by an imposing memorial designed by Sir George Gilbert Scott in 1872 and commissioned by Queen Victoria. The sculpture of the prince, made by John Foley, is surrounded by figures representing all the arts, trades, crafts and countries seen at the Exhibition.

Alfred The Great
Trinity Church Square, SE1
Map Ref: 84F
Alfred was the King of Wessex who united the English under one throne. This 14th-century statue of him is the oldest in London and was brought to Southwark from the old Palace of Westminster in 1822.

Queen Anne
Queen Anne's Gate, SW1
Map Ref: 82F
The unfortunate English queen whose life was marred by miscarriages is remembered in this early 18th-century statue moved here from the Church of St Mary-le-Strand.

Queen Boadicea
Westminster Bridge, SW1
Map Ref: 83G
The famous Iceni warrior queen is depicted in her war chariot, accompanied by her daughters. The statue by Thomas Thornycroft was made in 1902.

The Burghers of Calais
Victoria Tower Gardens, SW1
Map Ref: 83GL
This beautiful version of the bronze by Rodin stands in Victoria Tower Gardens close to the Houses of Parliament. It depicts the citizens of Calais who surrendered to Edward III in 1347 to save their town from destruction.

Charles I
Trafalgar Square, SW1
Map Ref: 83C
Charles I was executed in nearby Whitehall. This equestrian statue of him was cast in bronze in 1633 by Hubert Le Sueur and it is regarded as one of London's finest public statues. The statue's original sword was stolen in the 19th century and has been replaced.

Charles II
Soho Square, W1
Map Ref: 76K
A beautiful statue by Cibber. Sadly, it has lost the four large figures representing English rivers that flanked the pedestal.

Sir Winston Churchill
Parliament Square, SW1
Map Ref: 83G
This statue of the greatest statesman of the 20th century is by Ivor Robert Jones and depicts Churchill in typically pugnacious mood staring at the House of Commons.

Eros
Piccadilly Circus, W1
Map Ref: 76P
Commemorating Victorian philanthropist the Earl of Shaftesbury, this is one of London's most famous landmarks. The figure is not as generally thought Eros the Greek hero, but the Angel of Christian Charity.

The Griffin
The Strand, EC4
Map Ref: 77R
This is the unofficial badge of the City of London and marks the entrance to the City where the Strand joins Fleet Street.

Bird's-eye View of London

Where are the best places to gain an over-view of London? Alas, the public galleries of the British Telecom Tower, built in 1965 as a giant aerial to provide improved telecommunication services, are no longer open. The same applies to the viewing gallery of the Shell Centre on the South Bank.

But there are alternatives which give visitors an opportunity to see

London from above the rooftops. First among these must be the Monument near London Bridge. From the wire caged gallery, those who make the effort and climb the 311 steps up the internal staircase may view the jumble of City streets and lanes and the church steeples peeping through from behind the towering office blocks – a stark change from the panorama at the turn of the 17th century. Most prominent on the north side of the Monument is the National Westminster Tower, headquarters of the National Westminster Bank.

Nearer is an extraordinary building, all glass and bands of steel with separate external shafts and pinnacles. Atop each is a blue crane. The whole looks like an outsize Meccano model. It is in fact the new Lloyd's of London, and the external shape is a consequence of the need to provide a large central 'market' room for the underwriters and brokers to transact their business.

For those who are daunted by the thought of a footslog to the top of

The view from the Monument

the Monument, the twin, glass-enclosed walkways of Tower Bridge, 42 metres above the river, provide a lift-accessible alternative. There is a better view of the river itself, with the massive bulk of the World War II cruiser HMS *Belfast* and the Tower of London.

In the City of Westminster is the campanile of Westminster Cathedral. Access to the viewing gallery is by lift situated in the entrance vestibule. From this high point can be seen the Queen Victoria Memorial in front of Buckingham Palace and the line of the Mall. Moving clockwise to the next alcove, one can see in the distance St Paul's Cathedral. Nearer at hand is Westminster Abbey; behind it are the Houses of Parliament.

Views over Kensington and much of the rest of London are provided from the newly-opened Queen's Tower at the centre of the Imperial College campus in Exhibition Road. It is all that remains of the Imperial Institute, built in 1887 to mark Queen Victoria's Golden Jubilee.

There are admission charges for each of these viewing galleries.

James II
Trafalgar Square, WC2
Map Ref: 77Q
James II stands in Roman dress in front of the National Gallery. The statue, by Grinling Gibbons, is regarded as the finest in London.

The Monument
Monument Street, EC3
Map Ref: 79Q
Sir Christopher Wren designed this 202ft fluted Doric column as a memorial of the Great Fire of London, which started exactly 202ft from it in Pudding Lane. (Also see 'Birdseye Views' opposite.)

Lord Nelson
Trafalgar Square, WC2
Map Ref: 83C
The centrepiece of Trafalgar Square, this monument to Britain's greatest naval hero stands 185ft high. There are four identical lions, cast from a single original by Sir Edwin Landseer, at the base of the column.

Peter Pan
Kensington Gardens, W2
Map Ref: 80B
This statue immortalises Sir James Barrie's fictional character who represents eternal youth. It was made by Sir George Frampton in 1911.

Sir Walter Raleigh
Whitehall, SW1
Map Ref: 83C
It was near the spot where this statue stands that Raleigh – seafarer, adventurer, philosopher and poet – was executed in 1618. The statue is short; so was Sir Walter.

Richard I
Old Palace Yard, SW1
Map Ref: 83G
This romantic depiction of the 'Lion Hearted King' was made by Baron Carlo Marochetti in the mid-19th century.

Queen Victoria
Queen Victoria Memorial, The Mall, SW1
Map Ref: 82F
Standing in a dominant position opposite Buckingham Palace, this elegant group of statuary was designed by Sir Aston Webb, and the sculptures were made by Sir Thomas Brock.

The 1st Duke of Wellington
Hyde Park Corner, W1
Map Ref: 81D
Arthur Wellesley, 1st Duke of Wellington, was born in Dublin in 1769. He divided his time between the army and the Irish House of Commons. In the Peninsular War (1808) he demonstrated his military genius and drove the French out of Portugal and Spain and defeated Napoleon's army in 1814. In 1815 he finally defeated Napoleon at the Battle of Waterloo. Subsequently, he turned to politics, becoming Prime Minister in 1828. His beautiful home – designed by Robert Adam – stands at Hyde Park Corner and contains the Wellington Museum. Opposite is a statue of the Duke on Copenhagen, the horse he rode throughout the Battle of Waterloo. It is cast from captured French cannon.

The Whittington Stone
Highgate Hill, N19
Map Ref: 88D9
Dick Whittington, the first Lord Mayor of London, is supposed to have sat on this spot and heard Bow Bells calling to him to 'Turn again, Whittington, thrice Mayor of London'.

Winston Churchill's statue watches over the Houses of Parliament.
Below: Dick Whittington's cat on the Whittington Stone

Duke of York
Carlton House Terrace, SW1
Map Ref: 82B
The 13ft-high statue to the 'Grand Old Duke of York' was made by Sir Richard Westmacott in 1833. The money to pay for it was raised by docking a day's pay from every member of the Army.

The view up Fleet Street towards Ludgate Circus, with St Paul's in the background

STREETS

London is, of course, full of streets. But some have more charm, history or character than others. They range from tiny back alleys, little changed since Victorian times, to teeming thoroughfares very much in the 20th century.

Amen Court, EC1
Map Ref: 78K
The unusual name of this quiet backwater derives from medieval religious ceremonies.

Birdcage Walk, SW1
Map Ref: 82F
It owes its name to the aviary owned by Charles II which was situated here.

Bread Street, EC2
Map Ref: 78K/P
The name comes from medieval times, when it was a bread market. John Milton was born here in 1608.

Carlton House Terrace, SW1
Map Ref: 82B
John Nash designed this terrace as part of his architectural scheme for Regent Street. The Royal Society was formed at No 6 in 1660. No 12 is now The Institute of Contemporary Arts and has an art gallery and a theatre.

Charles Street, W1
Map Ref: 82A
Lovely 18th-century houses, some with their original ironwork, line both sides of this street.

Cheapside, EC2
Map Ref: 78K
This was the original market place of the City. The Anglo-Saxon word 'chepe' meant 'barter'.

Cheyne Walk, SW3
Map Ref: 92B17
This fine row of 18th-century houses stands on the historic site where Henry VIII had a manor house and where Sir Thomas More lived. George Eliot lived at No 4, Dante Gabriel Rossetti at No 16 and Bram Stoker at No 27.

Clink Street, SE1
Map Ref: 85C
Echoes of Victorian London can still be found here with 19th-century warehouses overshadowing cobbled alleyways. Under a railway bridge is a tablet marking the site of the infamous Clink prison.

Downing Street, SW1
Map Ref: 83C
Built in the 17th century by Sir George Downing, who gave No 10 to Sir Robert Walpole. Since then it has been the official residence of the Prime Minister. No 11 is the official residence of the Chancellor of the Exchequer.

Fleet Street, EC4
Map Ref: 78J
Although many national and provincial newspapers have offices in or near Fleet Street, today much of the printing takes place away from central London. The links with the printing trade date back to 1500.

Great Russell Street, WC1
Map Ref: 77L
There are numerous publisher's offices and small bookshops here, although the street is best known as the home of the British Museum. George du Maurier, illustrator for *Punch* and author of *Trilby*, lived here.

Jermyn Street, W1
Map Ref: 82B
Quality shops make this street famous. The original Cavendish Hotel here, owned by Rosa Lewis was the inspiration for the TV series 'Duchess of Duke Street'.

Kings Road, SW3
Map Ref: 80P
During the 17th century this was Charles II's private carriage route between St James's and Hampton Court, and it did not become a public highway until the beginning of the 19th century. The designer Mary Quant opened a boutique here in the 1950s, and ever since the street has been a fashion mecca.

Laurence Pountney Hill, EC4
Map Ref: 79Q
Nos 1 and 2 were built in 1703 and are the finest early 18th-century houses in the City.

Lawrence Street, SW3
Map Ref: 92B17
In the 18th century Chelsea was one of the places renowned for the manufacture of English porcelain; the Chelsea factory was situated at the north end of this street from 1745 to 1784.

10 Downing Street – the official home of the Prime Minister

The Mall, SW1
Map Ref: 82B/F
This grand processional route to Buckingham Palace is flanked by St James's Park on one side and fine Nash buildings on the other.

Paternoster Row, EC1
Map Ref: 78K
Medieval religious tradition is recalled here, as it was part of a processional route along which people told their rosaries. In this street they recited the Lord's Prayer. The street has a long association with the book trade.

Piccadilly, W1
Map Ref: 82A
Its name comes from the 17th-century ruff called 'picadils' once sold here. Today it is famous for luxury shops.

Regent Street, W1
Map Ref: 76J/P
Part of the grand town planning scheme John Nash carried out for the Prince Regent. This is now a fine modern shopping street.

Royal Avenue, SW3
Map Ref: 81Q
This avenue forms part of Sir Christopher Wren's unfinished plan to link the Royal Hospital with Kensington Palace. Many of the present buildings are 19th-century.

St. James's Street, SW1
Map Ref: 82B
Known for gentlemen's clubs – including Boodle's, White's and Brook's – this street also has exclusive shops particularly geared to gentlemen.

Admiralty Arch spans the entrance to the Mall

Savile Row, W1
Map Ref: 76N/P
Today the 'Row' is famed for high-class tailoring. Richard Brinsley Sheridan lived here at No 14.

Seething Lane, EC3
Map Ref: 79R
This is the site of the Navy Office, where Samuel Pepys worked, and the church of St Olave which Pepys called 'Myne owne Church' where he and his wife are buried.

Shaftesbury Avenue, W1
Map Ref: 76P
Laid out in the 19th century to commemorate the Victorian social reformer and champion of the anti-slavery cause Lord Shaftesbury, today this street is famous as the heart of theatreland.

The Strand, WC2
Map Ref: 77Q/R
The oldest road in London, the Strand joins the City of Westminster in the west with the City in the east. Throughout medieval times there were many fine palaces in this 'country area' sloping down to the River Thames.

Villiers Street, WC2
Map Ref: 77Q
A great mansion and gardens belonging to George Villiers, Duke of Buckingham once stood here. Close by, the Adam brothers laid out their famous Adelphi which was pulled down in modern times.

Wine Office Court, EC4
Map Ref: 78J
In this court is the Cheshire Cheese tavern, associated with Dr Johnson and other 17th-century personalities.

The Pall Mall Clubs

Pall Mall, the ancient route linking the City with the Palace of St James, is famed as the home of gentlemen's clubs. These are to be found in the short length of the street from Waterloo Place to St James's Church.

Moving west, the first of these clubs – the United Services – is on the south-east corner of Pall Mall and Waterloo Place. Founded by veterans of the Napoleonic Wars, the building is by John Nash and dates from 1827. It was remodelled by Decimus Burton in the 1850s. In a period of declining membership and financial stringency, there was first a merger with the Royal Aero Club and eventually in 1976 the club closed its doors. Today the building is used as the headquarters of a different kind of club – the Institute of Directors. On the opposite side of Waterloo Place is the Athenaeum, a club founded for 'scientific and literary men and artists'.

Further along Pall Mall are Italian 'palazzo style' buildings. The first is the Travellers' Club dating from 1829; next is the Reform Club of 1841. A condition of membership of the Travellers was that you had travelled out of London, in a straight line, at least 500 miles. This was later increased to 1,000 miles. The Reform Club drew its members from the radical supporters of the Government who had been successful in securing passage of the Reform Bill in 1822. Through the years that radical tradition has been maintained. Still on the south side of Pall Mall is the Royal Automobile Club. The long façade is Edwardian in style. The Oxford and Cambridge University Club at Nos 71-76, built in 1838, reverts to the classical style of architecture. On the north side of Pall Mall, at the entrance to St James's Square, is the new building of the Army and Navy Club, dating from the 1960s.

What is club membership – what do the clubs offer? Originally, they were a home away from home for those who sought good food and wine, a good library and a place to meet for debate and discussion. Occasionally, a club member or a visitor would give talks about his adventures. There was usually a card room and sometimes billiards or backgammon, but gambling and hard drinking had no place in such venues.

Today a club is still special. There is no sign on the door saying what the club is. Number plates were introduced only recently. In winter coal fires burn in the public rooms. Well worn and comfortable leather armchairs provide a haven for the few who have the time to seek rest

The Athenaeum Club, St James's

and read the magazines and papers. The food is good, the wines excellent. There is something unique in being able to entertain your guests in a certain style, and at a certain price.

THE THAMES

One of the best ways to enjoy London is from a boat on the Thames. The river has played a vital role in London's history and development ever since the Romans established their bridgehead here, and a good many of the capital's most important and interesting buildings are close to its banks. The description given here follows the river downstream from Hampton Court to Greenwich, a journey which could comfortably occupy a day.

Information

Boats leave Westminster Pier and Charing Cross Pier for Greenwich, the Thames Barrier and the Tower (all year); from Tower Pier for Westminster and Greenwich (all year); and from Westminster Pier for Kew, Richmond and Hampton Court (summer only). There are also evening cruises from both Westminster and Charing Cross Piers. For information on times and prices, telephone (01) 730 4812.

As the boat moves downstream from **Hampton Court** there is a marvellous view of the **Palace** with its red brick Tudor building and Wren's classical façade. Next comes **Thames Ditton** with its picturesque old houses. Passing under **Kingston Bridge** the town of **Kingston-upon-Thames** is seen on the right. Its written records go back to the 9th century, when it was a crowning place for kings. The crowning stone is preserved outside the Guildhall. **Teddington Weir** and **Teddington Lock** are next passed on the left, while between Teddington and Richmond is **Strawberry Hill**, a riverside house bought in 1747 by Horace Walpole, the son of the then prime minister. It was the first Gothic Revival building in the country and

influenced contemporary architects.

Across the river is **Ham House**, a superb riverside mansion built in 1610. Sixty years later it came into the ownership of the Duke of Lauderdale and became a by-word for luxurious living. It now houses treasures from the Victoria and Albert Museum. On the other side of the river is **Marble Hill House** and **Park**. The house was built for Henrietta Howard, mistress of George II. The little village of **Petersham**, downstream on the right, has considerable character, some interesting 18th-century houses, and boasts Charles Dickens and John Gay among past residents.

The town of **Richmond-upon-Thames** has a long history; it is the site of a royal palace of which little remains today. The town has many notable buildings; Virginia and Leonard Woolf lived here and established the Hogarth Press. **Syon House** is a little further on. Built on the site of a convent founded by Henry V, it came to the Dukes of Northumberland who commissioned the architect Robert Adam to convert the house into a great mansion. Across the river are the **Royal Botanic Gardens** at **Kew**, and **Kew Palace**. The palace was built in 1631 and George II came here to escape the Court life that he detested. The centre of Kew is formed by the Green and there are many splendid Georgian buildings.

Chiswick's river frontage stretches from **Strand-on-the-Green** to **Chiswick Mall**, near **Hammersmith Bridge**. **Chiswick Mall** contains an exceptionally fine group of Georgian houses, one of which was lived in by the Victorian actor-manager Sir Herbert Beerbohm Tree. Close to the Mall is the famous riverside pub called The Dove. It is here that Charles II and Nell Gwynne are said to have met. Sir Joseph Bazalgette designed the fanciful suspension bridge at Hammersmith.

Past Hammersmith Bridge the Thames enters Barn Elms Reach, with warehouses lining the north bank to **Fulham Palace Park**. Previously this area was occupied by market gardens that supplied many of London's vegetable needs. **Fulham Palace** was once the official residence of the Bishop of London. Most of the buildings date from the 18th and 19th centuries and the palace is set in beautiful gardens. From **Putney Bridge**, 18th-century **Hurlingham House**, which is an exclusive tennis, croquet and swimming club can be seen through the trees of the park. The next reach of the river is rather dreary.

Albert Bridge heralds central London. A cantilever and suspension structure resembling a gigantic iron cobweb, it was designed by R M Ordish and opened in 1873. **Chelsea** stretches along the North bank with its houseboats and the Cheyne Walk with its attractive Georgian houses facing the river. On the south bank is **Battersea**, a residential area with a lovely **park** and fine river frontage. **Chelsea Bridge** is a handsome suspension bridge opened in 1937. **Battersea Power Station** is a huge building designed by Sir G G Scott in 1933. Past Battersea is

The Thames Barrier

In the years between the World Wars and again in 1953, serious flooding in the low-lying areas of the Thames estuary led to loss of life and substantial damage to property. A Royal Commission was appointed to make proposals for flood defence. Such defence was made all the more necessary by geological changes: a slow tilting of the British Isles towards the south and east and a sinking of the London clay basin. The combined effects of high spring tides and gale force Easterly winds could well have resulted in a major catastrophe.

The solution proposed was to raise the embankments of the Thames for many miles and to build a barrier at a key point across the river. Woolwich Reach was chosen. At this point the base is of chalk and makes a sound foundation for the barrier, which spans 600 metres of river.

Construction of the barrier began in 1974 and was completed by 1983,

although it was not formally opened by the Queen until May 1984. There are 10 separate movable gates; four of them are 200ft wide and are for navigation. Normally, the gates lie flat in the river bed, but when required to create a barrier they are driven by hydraulic machinery and pivot upwards into a vertical position. Each of the main gates weighs 3,700 tonnes and when raised stands 66ft high. The roofs of the piers, clad in stainless steel, resemble the boat shape of the Sydney Opera House.

There are excellent views of the barrier from the Barrier Buffet and, if the visit has been timed to coincide with high tide, the passage of ships of all kinds on their way into or out of London's inner wharves adds considerable interest. Raising the Barrier in earnest takes 30-45 minutes. To date such occurrences have been rarely necessary. However, during the summer months there are test raisings, perhaps once in every month. Times and dates of such

raisings are set to suit operational requirements. The barrier has become a major tourist attraction with close on half-a-million visitors in the year, and it has a visitor centre with exhibition hall, working models and a dramatic audio visual presentation.

The Thames Barrier floodgates

The walkway of Tower Bridge affords spectacular views over the Thames

Nine Elms, the new Covent Garden Market. Beyond **Vauxhall Bridge**, on the left, is the **Tate Gallery**. In front is **Lambeth Bridge**, with **Lambeth Palace** on the right, the residence of the archbishops of Canterbury for 700 years. Close by is **St Thomas's Hospital**, whose new buildings replace mid 19th-century ones damaged in the blitz. Florence Nightingale founded the Nightingale Training Scheme for Nurses here.

On the north side of the river is the fantastic sight of **The Houses of Parliament** – dominated by **Big Ben** – with **Westminster Abbey** behind them. **Westminster Bridge** is in front and to the right is **The South Bank Complex**, with its stark, modern architecture. Cleopatra's Needle is on the north bank. Mehemet Ali, a viceroy of Egypt presented this famous landmark to Great Britain in 1819.

Beyond **Waterloo Bridge** on the north bank, the gardens of **The Temple** stretch down to the river. On the opposite bank is **Southwark**, almost as old as the City. Travellers to London could not enter the City after dark, and as for centuries the only bridge spanning the river ran from

Southwark to the City, a number of inns and places of amusement grew up in the area. It was here that Chaucer's pilgrims met to travel to Canterbury. **Fishmonger's Hall**, on the north bank was badly damaged during the Blitz, but the hall retains its fine riverside façade. Ahead is **London Bridge**. First built in stone between 1176 and 1209, it was enclosed with shops, a chapel and fortified glass. The present structure was opened in 1973 and its predecessor sold to the USA. **Billingsgate Market**, on the north bank, dates back to AD870. The fish market has now been moved to the Isle of Dogs, but the old building, designed by Sir Horace Jones and built in 1875, remains.

The Tower of London stands proudly on the edge of the City, one of the most important works of Norman and medieval military architecture in Britain. Traitors' Gate can be clearly seen from the river. **Tower Bridge** is by far the most attractive bridge on the Thames. It was built in 1894 and the original machinery for raising and lowering the bridge has been restored. Past the Tower is **St Katharine's Dock**. Thomas Telford, one of the greatest

engineers of the 19th century, designed this superb group of warehouses and basins. The dock was closed in 1968, but has since been restored and been transformed into a yachting marina.

Wapping is on the north bank. Behind the warehouses stretch the vast London Docklands – nearly all being redeveloped. **The Prospect of Whitby** at Wapping is a riverside pub dating from 1520 and one of the oldest pubs on the river. Samuel Pepys was a frequent visitor. Further on is another 16th-century pub, the **Grapes** at Limehouse. It stands at the entrance of the Regent's Canal to the River Thames. Past The Grapes is the tongue of land called **The Isle of Dogs**. Opposite is **Deptford**, an important naval victualling yard from 1513 to the 19th century.

On the south bank is **Greenwich**, a wonderful place to look at British naval history. Here is the **Royal Naval College**, the magnificent 17th-century **Queen's House** and crowning Flamsteed Hill, the **Old Royal Observatory**. Anchored here are the **Cutty Sark**, the only surviving tea-clipper, and **Gipsy Moth IV**, in which Sir Francis Chichester sailed round the world in 1967.

Many of the places listed on these pages are described in greater detail elsewhere in this book. For further information see the index.

Sunset over the City. Inset: Westminster Bridge and Big Ben

THEATRES & CONCERT HALLS

London is the world centre of the performing arts. In addition to the National Theatre and the Royal Shakespeare Company, there are over 40 commercial theatres in the West End, a number of excellent neighbourhood theatres and fringe and pub theatres. Details of current productions can be obtained from weekly entertainment magazines or from the national press. The London Visitor and Convention Bureau produces free literature on current shows.

The Royal Festival Hall, part of the South Bank Complex

Barbican
Barbican, EC2
Map Ref: 78F
The Theatre is part of the huge Barbican complex and the London home of the Royal Shakespeare Company. The company presents new plays and classics of the last century as well as its Shakespeare repertoire. The main auditorium seats 1,160 people while a smaller theatre for experimental plays called The Pit has flexible seating for around 200. The Concert Hall is the home of The London Symphony Orchestra and the Barbican Cinema shows a full range of popular and *avant garde* films. The Barbican Art Gallery shows changing exhibitions. There is a magnificent planted Conservatory and three restaurants.
Nearest Underground: Barbican

Drury Lane
Catherine Street, WC2
Map Ref: 77Q
Situated on one of the oldest theatre sites in London, the theatre here was built in 1663. It was destroyed by fire and replaced by one designed by Sir Christopher Wren, which also burnt down. The present theatre has sumptuous furnishings and a grand entrance. It is usually the venue of lavish musicals such as *Oklahoma, Carousel* and *My Fair Lady.*
Nearest Underground: Covent Garden

The London Coliseum
St Martin's Lane, WC2
Map Ref: 77Q
Built in 1904, the Coliseum was first used as a music hall. It is one of the largest theatres in London, and was the first to install a revolving stage. Sarah Bernhardt, Lillie Langtry and Ellen Terry performed here. Today it is the home of the English National Opera Company.
Nearest Underground: Leicester Square

The London Palladium
Argyll Street, W1
Map Ref: 76J
The Palladium opened in 1910 as a music hall. Among the variety acts which made it popular were the Crazy Gang. Christmas entertainment has now become a feature of the Palladium.
Nearest Underground: Oxford Circus

New London Theatre
Drury Lane, Parker Street, WC2
Map Ref: 77L
This ultra-modern theatre complex stages productions such as *Cats.*
Nearest Underground: Convent Garden

The Old Vic
Waterloo Road, SE1
Map Ref: 83A
Built in the early 19th century, the Old Vic was first known for melodramas. In 1880 Emma Cons bought the premises and started classical plays and opera in the theatre. Her niece Lilian Baylis carried on this tradition and staged excellent Shakespearian productions here. Today its repertoire spans comedy, drama and musicals.
Nearest Underground: Waterloo

Royal Albert Hall
Kensington Gore, SW7
Map Ref: 80F
The foundation stone of this huge, circular building was laid by Queen Victoria in 1867. The auditorium seats 7,000 and contains one of the world's largest organs. It is renowned for the Sir Henry Wood Promenade Concerts, performed daily from mid-July to mid-September. Many other events take place here throughout the year.
Nearest Underground: South Kensington

Royal Court
Sloane Square, SW1
Map Ref: 81M
This has been an experimental theatre since 1870. Many of George Bernard Shaw's and Somerset Maugham's plays were premiered here and John Osborne's *Look Back in Anger* opened here in 1956. Since 1969 the small Theatre Upstairs has specialised in particularly new and experimental work.
Nearest Underground: Sloane Square

Royal Opera House
Covent Garden, WC2
Map Ref: 77Q
Officially opened as an opera house in 1847, opera has flourished here ever since. Thomas Beecham brought ballet to the theatre in 1911. It is now the national home of opera and ballet.
Nearest Underground: Covent Garden

Sadler's Wells
Rosebery Avenue, EC1
Map Ref: 78A
The theatre was noted for its Shakespearian productions during the mid-19th century, and for the performances of Joe Grimaldi, the famous clown. Lilian Baylis campaigned to avoid the closure of the theatre and instigated its renovation. It then became, and remains, famous as a ballet and operatic centre.
Nearest Underground: The Angel

South Bank Centre
South Bank, SE1
Map Ref: 83D
The National Theatre is part of the South Bank Art Centre and actually contains three theatres and three concert halls: the Olivier which seats 1,160 and is open-staged, the Lyttleton, a proscenium theatre which seats 890 and the Cottesloe Theatre, a rectangular theatre with flexible seating, used for experimental and fringe theatre. The Royal Festival Hall was the first permanent building erected on the site for the 1951 Festival of Britain. It is the home of the London Philharmonic Orchestra. There is comfortable seating here for 3,000 people and spacious foyers and fine river views. The Queen Elizabeth Hall seats 1,100 and the Purcell Room seats 400 people; both are concert halls. The Hayward Gallery shows excellent changing exhibitions and the National Film Theatre has three cinemas which show the finest selection of new and classic films in London.
Nearest Underground: Waterloo.

LONDON GUIDE

Atlas

*The maps included here are at a scale of
seven inches to the mile for Central London,
and one inch to the mile for Outer London.
There is a street index on page 116.*

Above: Harrods at night

London Legend

GRID REFERENCE SYSTEM

The map references used in this guide are based on a very simple system.

On the Central London map, a point with a given reference of **82E** will be located on page **82** in grid square **E**

On the London District map, a point with a given reference of **88C2** will be located on page **88** in grid square **C2**

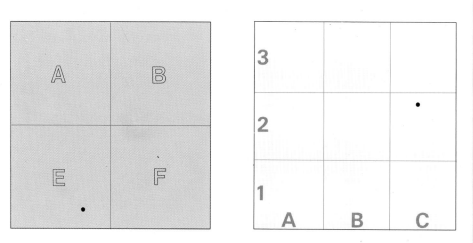

CENTRAL LONDON

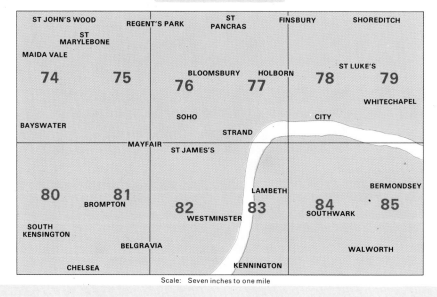

ST JOHN'S WOOD	REGENT'S PARK	ST PANCRAS	FINSBURY	SHOREDITCH
ST MARYLEBONE				
MAIDA VALE			ST LUKE'S	
74	75	BLOOMSBURY 76	HOLBORN 77	78	79
				WHITECHAPEL
BAYSWATER	SOHO	CITY	
	STRAND		
MAYFAIR	ST JAMES'S		

74   75
BLOOMSBURY 76   HOLBORN 77   78   79
WHITECHAPEL
BAYSWATER   SOHO   CITY
STRAND
MAYFAIR   ST JAMES'S
80   81   LAMBETH   BERMONDSEY
BROMPTON   82 WESTMINSTER   83   84 SOUTHWARK   85
SOUTH KENSINGTON
BELGRAVIA   WALWORTH
CHELSEA   KENNINGTON

Scale: Seven inches to one mile

Street Index (Central London)   : See pages 116-118

CENTRAL LEGEND

One-way street	⟵	Police	POL
Banned turn		Post Office	PO
Compulsory turn		Hospital	H
Pedestrians only		Multi-level car park	G
Restricted roads		Official car park	P
Page continuation	75	London Transport station	⊖
AA Centre	AA	British Rail station	▭

LONDON DISTRICT

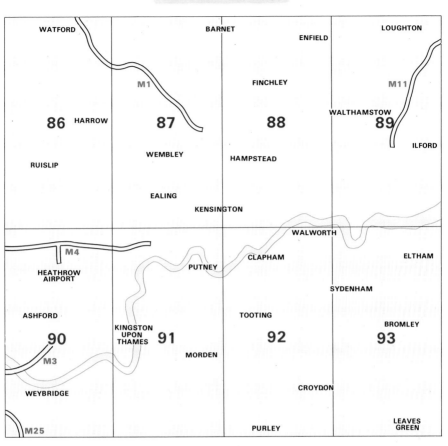

WATFORD	BARNET		LOUGHTON
		ENFIELD	
	M1	FINCHLEY	M11
86 HARROW	87	88	WALTHAMSTOW 89
	WEMBLEY	HAMPSTEAD	ILFORD
RUISLIP			
	EALING		
	KENSINGTON		
		WALWORTH	
M4	PUTNEY	CLAPHAM	ELTHAM
HEATHROW AIRPORT		SYDENHAM	
ASHFORD		TOOTING	BROMLEY
90	KINGSTON UPON THAMES 91	92	93
M3	MORDEN		
WEYBRIDGE		CROYDON	
M25		PURLEY	LEAVES GREEN

Scale: One inch to one mile

DISTRICT LEGEND

Primary Routes	
A road	
B road	
Other road	
Toll	Toll
Level Crossing	L.C.
British Rail Station	●
London Transport Station.	⊖
London Transport & British Rail Station	⊖

Hospital	Ⓗ
Place of Interest	Fenton House ■
Parking at suburban stations	Ⓟ
Garage at surburban stations	Ⓖ
AA Telephone	☎
AA Centre	**AA**
AA Centre (24hr)	AA 24 hour
Road Service Centre	AA 43
Extent of London Central map	

WALKS

Start point of walk	1
Line of walk	
Place of Interest	③
Park	
Water feature	≈
Railway	
Buildings	

TOURS

Motorways	M1
A road	A2213
B road / Other road	B146
Route of tour	→
Featured tour	
Park	
Place of Interest	Charlton House ■

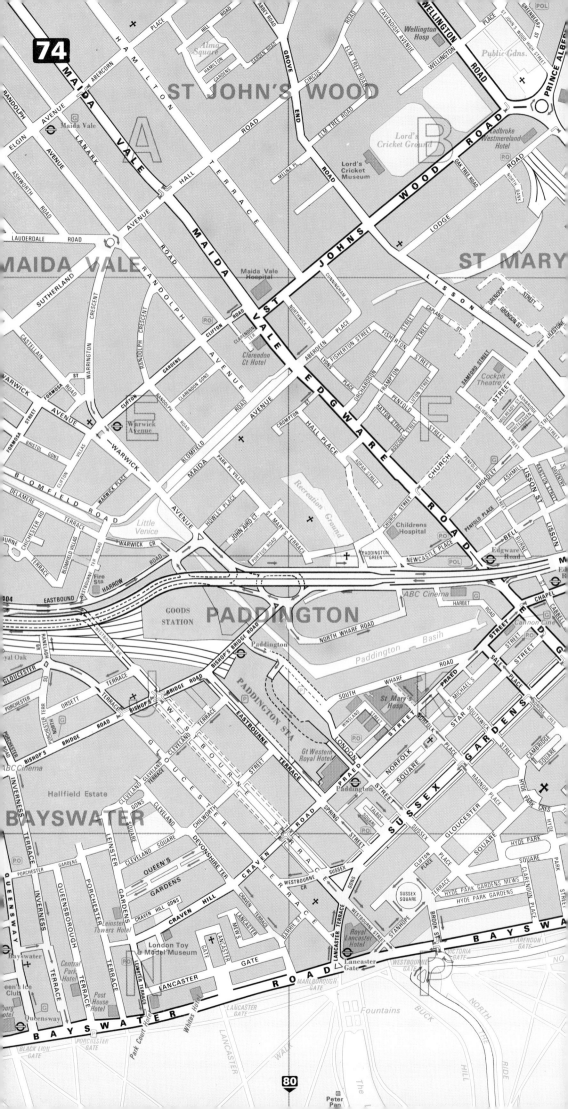

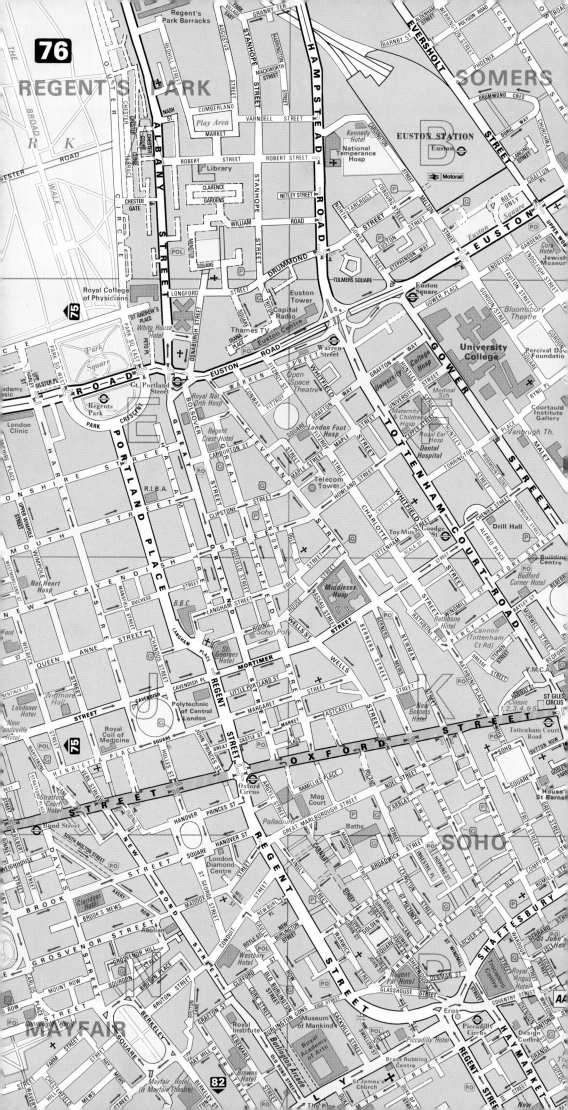

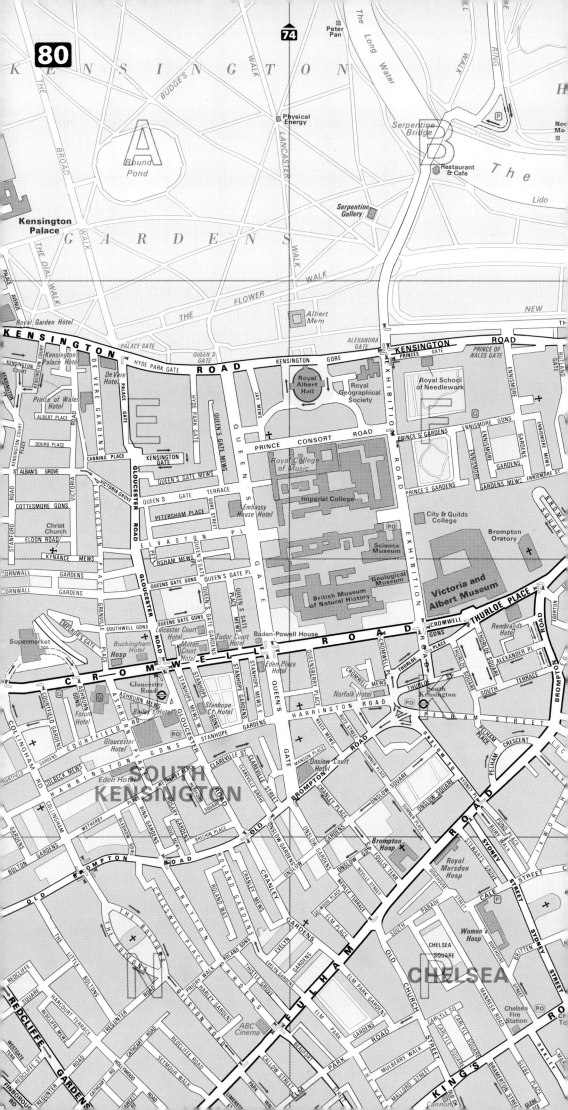

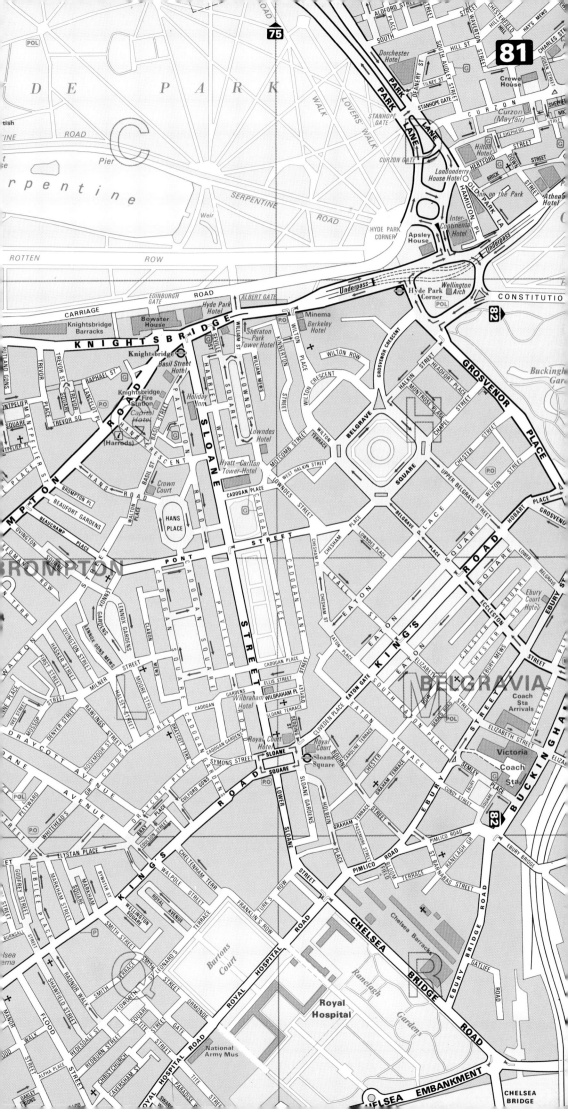

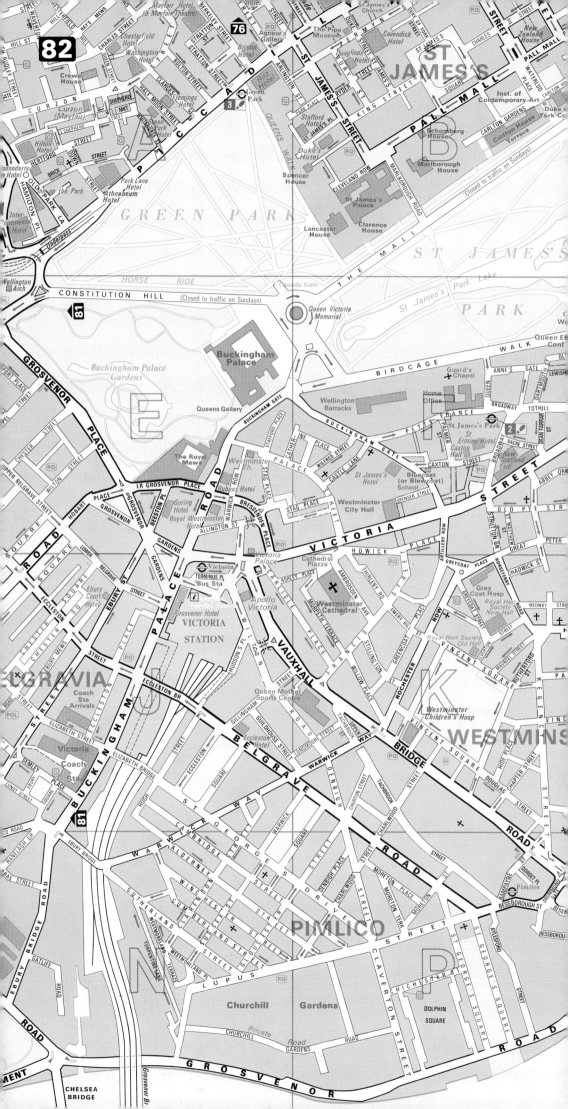

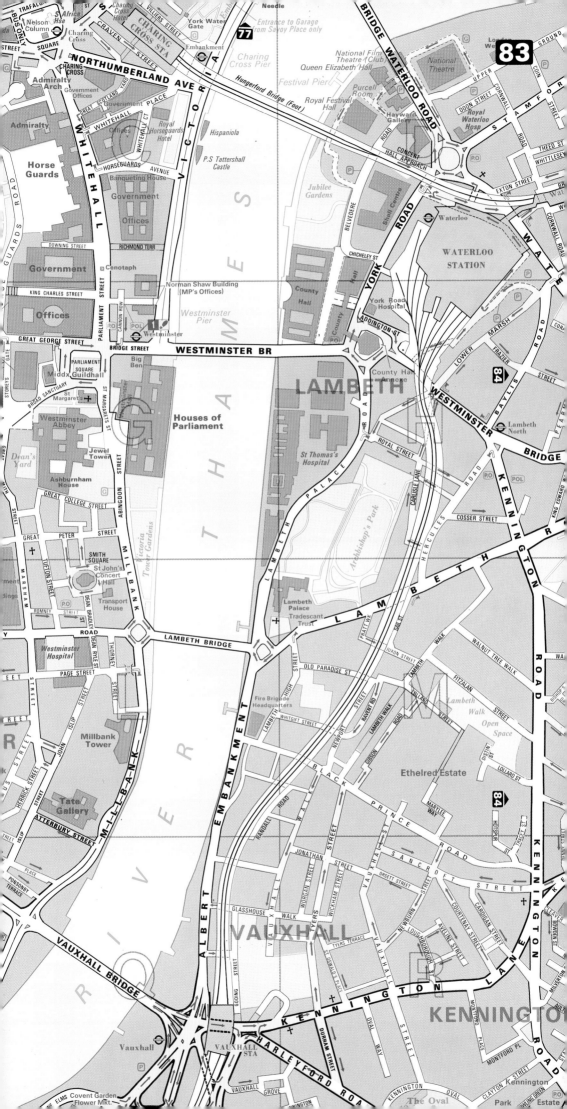

83

NORTHUMBERLAND AVE

WHITEHALL
Nelson Column
CHARING CROSS STA
Admiralty Arch
Africa Hse
Charing Cross Hotel
York Water Gate
Embankment
Charing Cross Pier
Entrance to Garage from Savoy Place only
Needle
National Film Theatre / Club
Queen Elizabeth Hall
Festival Pier
Purcell Room
Royal Festival Hall
Hayward Gallery
National Theatre
BRIDGE
WATERLOO ROAD
London Weekend
GROUND
UPPER GROUND
COIN
CORNWALL
DOON STREET
Royal Waterloo Hosp
THEED ST
WHITTLESEY

Horse Guards
Admiralty
Government Offices
Great Scotland Yard
WHITEHALL
Government Offices
Royal Horseguards Hotel
Hispaniola
P.S Tattershall Castle
Jubilee Gardens
Shell Centre
CONCERT HALL APPROACH
Waterloo
WATERLOO STATION
STAMFORD
EXTON STREET

Banqueting House
HORSEGUARDS AVENUE
WHITEHALL PLACE
WHITEHALL CT
VICTORIA
BELVEDERE ROAD
County Hall
CHICHELEY ST
YORK ROAD
WATER
CORNWALL ROAD

Government
DOWNING STREET
Downing Street
RICHMOND TERR
Norman Shaw Building (MP's Offices)
Westminster Pier
County Hall
York Road Hospital
ADDINGTON ST
MARSH
FRAZIER STREET
84
CORAL

Offices
KING CHARLES STREET
Cenotaph
PARLIAMENT STREET
CANNON ROW
BRIDGE STREET
Westminster
WESTMINSTER BR
County Hall Annexe
WESTMINSTER
Waterloo
LOWER
BAYLIS
Lambeth North

GREAT GEORGE STREET
GATE
PARLIAMENT SQUARE
Midd'x Guildhall
Big Ben
LAMBETH
WESTMINSTER
BRIDGE
KENNINGTON
PEARL
Lambeth North

STOREYS
BROAD SANCTUARY
ST MARGARETS ST
St Margaret's
Westminster
Houses of Parliament
ROYAL STREET
CARLISLE LANE
POL
KING EDWARD STREET

Westminster Abbey
GREAT COLLEGE STREET
ABINGDON STREET
Jewel Tower
St Thomas's Hospital
HERCULES
COSSER STREET

Dean's Yard
Ashburnham House
GREAT PETER STREET
Victoria Tower Gardens
LAMBETH PALACE ROAD
Archbishop's Park
ROAD

MARSHAM
TUFTON STREET
St John's Concert Hall
DEAN BRADLEY ST
Transport House
SMITH SQUARE
Lambeth Palace
Tradescant Trust
LAMBETH
PRATT WK
SAIL ST
JUXON STREET
WALNUT TREE WALK
WA

ROMNEY STREET
DEAN RYLE ST
THORNEY ST
LAMBETH BRIDGE
Old Paradise St
NEWPORT
RAVENT RD
LAMBETH WALK
FITZALAN STREET
Lambeth Walk Open Space

Westminster Hospital
PAGE STREET
JOHN ISLIP STREET
EMBANKMENT
Fire Brigade Headquarters
WHITGIFT STREET
GIBSON ROAD
Lambeth Walk
DISTIN ST
LOLLARD STREET

Millbank Tower
MILLBANK
ALBERT
Ethelred Estate
MARYLEE WAY
84

Tate Gallery
ATTERBURY STREET
ISLIP STREET
BLACK
PRINCE
ROAD
VAUXHALL WALK
MARYLEE WAY
HOTSPUR

HERRICK STREET
PONSONBY TERRACE
JONATHAN STREET
WORGAN STREET
WICKHAM STREET
SANCROFT STREET
ORSETT STREET
COURTENAY STREET
CARDIGAN STREET

VAUXHALL
VAUXHALL BRIDGE
GLASSHOUSE WALK
TYERS STREET
RANDALL ROW
AVELINE STREET
KENNINGTON ROAD

RIVER THAMES
HARLEYFORD ROAD
KENNINGTON
TYERS TERRACE
NEWBURN STREET
LOUGHBOROUGH
KENNINGTON LANE
MONTFORD PL
CLAYTON STREET

Vauxhall
VAUXHALL STA
DURHAM STREET
GOING STREET
VAUXHALL GROVE
Kennington Oval
The Oval
KENNINGTON PARK
BOWLING GREEN
KENNINGTON

Nine Elms Covent Garden Flower Mkt.

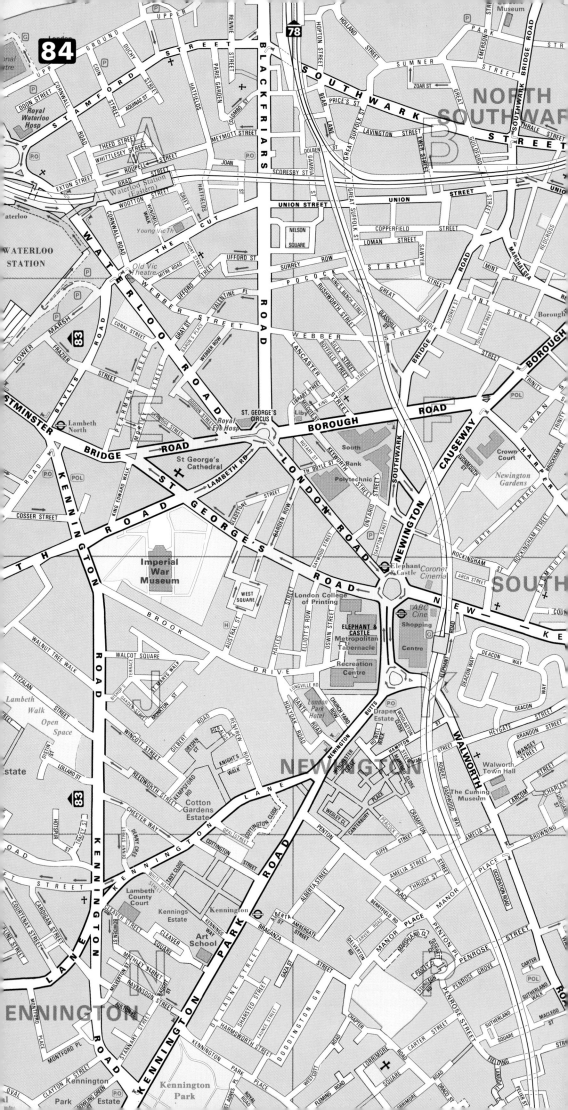

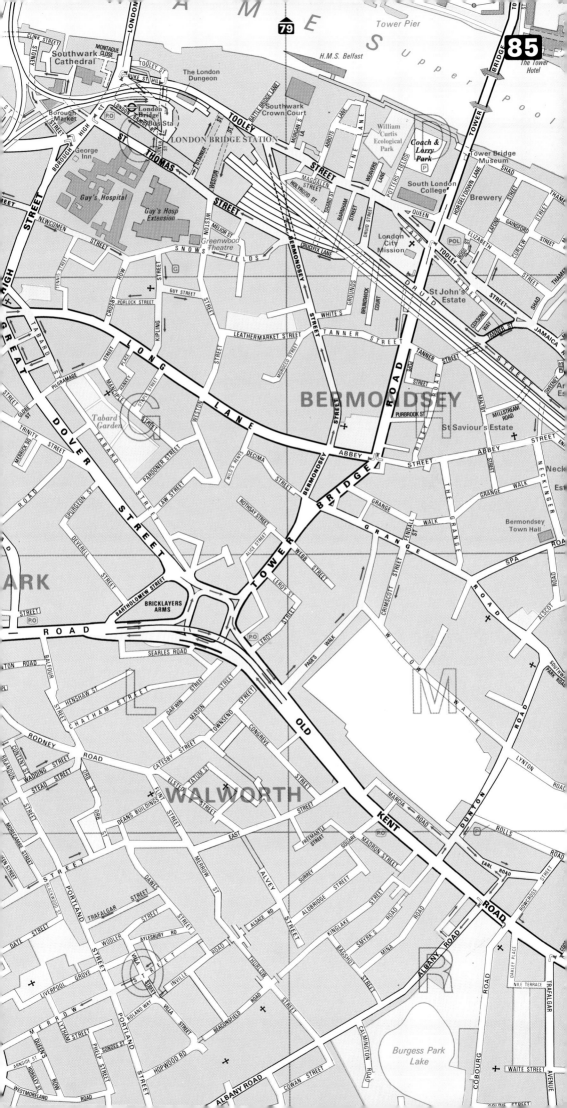

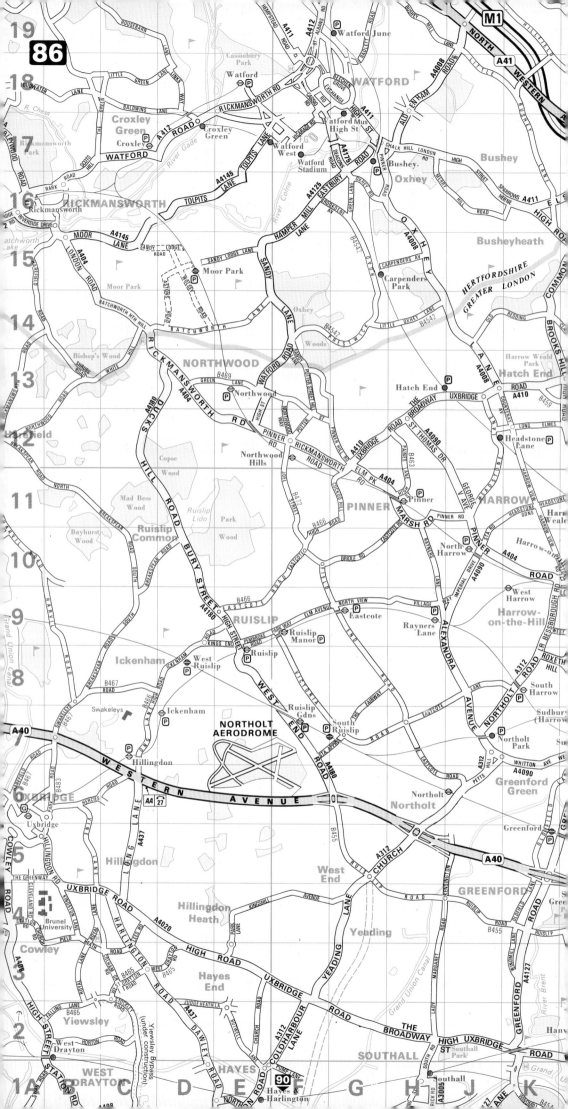

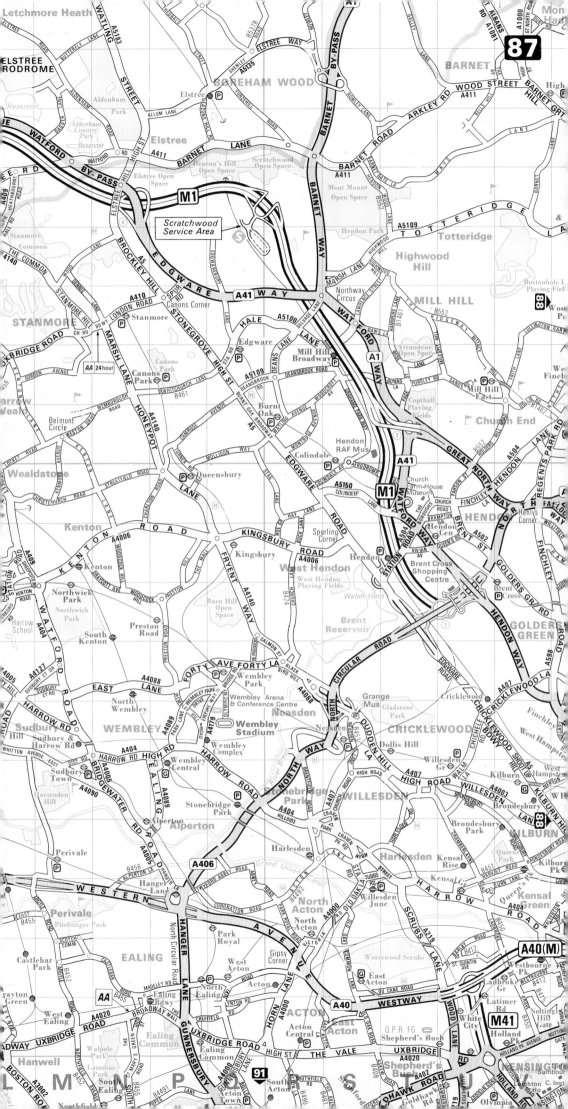

Woolwich Free Ferry
Weekdays 0600-2215h
Sundays 0740-2145 h

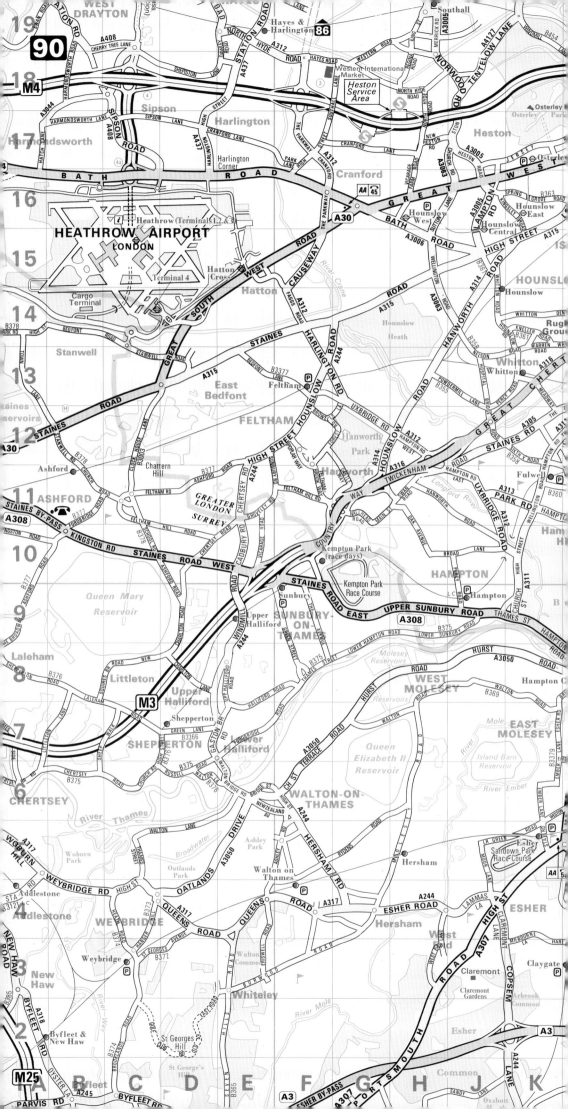

WALK 1
Along Whitehall

This short walk along one of London's most important thoroughfares takes in the seat of Government, memorials to the two world wars, an aspect of the capital's ceremonial and hundreds of years of history.

Allow ¾ hour

Begin at the Bridge Street entrance to Westminster Underground Station. Opposite is 'Big Ben'.

1 'BIG BEN'

The official name of this famous landmark is St Stephen's Clock Tower, but it is always called 'Big Ben', which is actually the enormous bell it contains named after a 19th-century commissioner of Works and Forests. The minute hands on the clock's 23ft-wide dials are each as tall as a double-decker bus. The Latin inscription below the clock's face reads 'Victoria the First'.

Turn right along Bridge Street to reach Parliament Square.

2 PARLIAMENT SQUARE

Before the Palace of Westminster was destroyed by fire in 1834 this area was occupied by mean streets packed with dingy buildings. Sir Charles Barry, one of the architects of the new palace, laid it out as an open square. It was re-designed again after war damage. Today it is best known for its statues – Churchill, Sir Robert Peel, Disraeli, Palmerston, Field-Marshal Smuts, Lord Derby, Lord Canning and Abraham Lincoln.

Cross the square, turn right to reach Great George Street and shortly turn left into Parliament Street.

3 PARLIAMENT STREET

On the left is a large block of Government Offices, built in late Victorian times. Across the roadway are more modest buildings, survivors of private houses which once stood along this street and Whitehall. The two oldest are Nos 43 and 44, which date from about 1753.

Continue along Parliament Street, then turn left into King Charles Street and walk to the end to reach the Cabinet War Rooms.

The Cabinet War Rooms

4 CABINET WAR ROOMS

Something of the siege feeling of World War II can be captured here. The rooms are preserved as they were during the war, and include apartments used by Churchill.

Return to Parliament Street, turn left and reach the Cenotaph.

5 CENOTAPH

Designed by Sir Edwin Lutyens in 1919 as part of the peace celebrations to mark the end of World War I, the Cenotaph remains as a memorial to those killed in both World Wars. It is a deceptively simple structure; but in fact neither vertical nor horizontal lines are employed in its design.

Continue to Downing Street.

6 DOWNING STREET

For security reasons, the public can no longer enter Downing Street, but it is still possible to look up it and see No 10, the residence of the Prime Minister, and No 11 the residence of the Chancellor of the Exchequer. Although the houses look modest enough from the outside, they are in fact very large, stretching back to Horse Guards.

Continue up Whitehall, with the Ministry of Defence opposite.

7 EAST SIDE OF WHITEHALL

Outside the Ministry of Defence Building are statues of Viscount Montgomery, 'Monty' of World War II fame, and Sir Walter Raleigh, who was beheaded in nearby Old Palace Yard. The next building along is Gwydyr House, built in the 18th century and still retaining lamp extinguishers in its wrought-iron railings. Next is the Banqueting House, designed in the 17th century by Inigo Jones and all that remains of Whitehall Palace. Under many of the buildings in the present Whitehall are remains of this palace, built by Henry VIII and largely destroyed by fires late in the 17th century.

Reach Horse Guards.

8 HORSE GUARDS

This is the setting for one of London's colourful daily ceremonies; at 11.00am weekdays and 10.00am on Sundays the Household Cavalry changes guard here. Beyond the archway is London's largest parade ground, the setting for such ceremonies as Trooping the Colour.

Continue along Whitehall, passing the Admiralty Building, to reach Trafalgar Square and the end of the walk.

Around St James's

Set around St James's Park are two royal palaces, two houses that have been or are lived in by royalty and many other lovely or interesting buildings.

Allow 1 hour

Start the walk at St James's Park Underground Station and emerge into Broadway.

1 BROADWAY

The underground station building itself is of interest. The headquarters of London Regional Transport, it was designed by Charles Holden and built in 1929. On its exterior are sculptures and reliefs made by some of the great names in British 20th-century art, including Jacob Epstein, Henry Moore and Eric Gill. Broadway itself was created in 1845, when Victoria Street (to the south) was built. The area had previously been occupied by notorious slums.

Cross Broadway and walk into Queen Anne's Gate.

2 QUEEN ANNE'S GATE

Many of the elegant houses here date from the 18th century, and some have beautiful doorways. The keystones of several of the windows are of Coade stone, an artificial stone whose formula is now lost. The headquarters of the National Trust is in one of the houses on the west side.

Emerge into Birdcage Walk and turn left. Pass the restored Wellington Barracks and the Chapel of the Guards Brigade and reach Buckingham Gate. (A detour can be made here along Buckingham Gate to reach the Queen's Gallery, with its works from the royal collections, and the Royal Mews, where state coaches and their horses can be seen.) Cross the road to reach the front of Buckingham Palace.

The Victoria Memorial in front of Buckingham Palace

3 BUCKINGHAM PALACE

Elizabeth II is the sixth monarch to live in the Palace. The original mansion here, Buckingham House, was built in 1762, but it has been altered and enlarged several times since. The royal standard flies over the palace when royalty are in residence. Changing of the Guard takes place here each day in the summer months and on alternate days in winter. In front of the palace is the Memorial to Queen Victoria, a monumental work weighing 2,300 tons and standing 82ft high. The figure of the Queen is accompanied by statues representing Charity, Truth and Justice, and there are six bronze groups representing Progress, Peace, Manufacture, Agriculture, Painting and Shipbuilding and Architecture. The monument is crowned by a figure of Victory.

From the palace, cross Constitution Hill and turn right to walk along the edge of Green Park. A short way along the Mall is a gateway on the left. Walk through this, and alongside Green Park until Milkmaids Passage is reached (on the right). Walk along this to reach Stable Yard.

4 STABLE YARD

On the south-east side of Stable Yard is Lancaster House, the site of the 18th-century London home of the dukes of York. The present building dates from 1820 and is used as a centre for government hospitality. The range of stable buildings on the north-west side of the yard was designed by Hawksmoor in 1717. On the east side of the yard is part of St James's Palace, with Clarence House, the London home of the Queen Mother, facing St James's Park.

From Stable Yard walk past Clarence House and through the wrought iron gates at the end to enter the Mall. Turn left, and shortly left again into Marlborough Road.

5 MARLBOROUGH ROAD

On the west side of Marlborough Road is St James's Palace, originally built in the 16th century, but largely rebuilt after a fire in the 19th century. It is still the palace of the court, to which foreign ambassadors are accredited when presenting themselves to the Queen. On the east side of the road is the Chapel Royal, standing in the grounds of Marlborough House. The house itself is now the home of the Commonwealth Secretariat. It was built by Sir Christopher Wren for the Duchess of Marlborough.

Return to the Mall, cross the roadway and enter St James's Park.

6 ST JAMES'S PARK

This 93 acres of lawns, lakes and flowerbeds was once an unhealthy swamp prone to flooding from the Tyburn River that flows through it. Henry VIII transformed it into a hunting park in 1532. It was re-designed during the reign of Charles II and by the late 17th century the public had been admitted. Today it is most famous for the wildfowl and other birds in and around the lake. These include ducks, pelicans, geese and swans.

To complete the walk, either make the circuit of the lake or cross the bridge at its centre, to reach Birdcage Walk. Walk along Queen Anne's Gate to return to St James's Park Underground Station.

GREEN PARK

CONSTITUTION HILL

STABLE YARD

Lancaster House

Clarence House

St James's Palace

Marlborough House

MARLBOROUGH RD

THE MALL

Queen Victoria Memorial

Buckingham Palace

ST JAMES'S PARK

St James's Park Lake

Duck Island

SCALE
0 — 110 yds

HORSE GUARDS ROAD

BIRDCAGE WALK

Home Office

Wellington Barracks

QUEEN ANNE'S GATE

BUCKINGHAM GATE

PALACE STREET

Mews

PETTY FRANCE

St James's Park

BROADWAY

TOTHILL STREET

WALK 3
Piccadilly

This is one of the capital's busiest shopping streets. Just off Piccadilly are quieter streets with elegant buildings and fashionable arcades.

Allow ¾ hour

Begin from the Stratton Street side of Green Park Underground Station. Turn left and walk towards the Ritz Hotel, which is on the opposite side of the road.

1 RITZ HOTEL
Although only built in 1906, for the past twenty years the Ritz has been scheduled as a First Class Ancient Monument. It remains one of London's most exclusive establishments, and 'tea at the Ritz' is part of Britain's social high life.
Beyond the entrance to Berkeley Street turn left into Dover Street.

2 DOVER STREET
Once a highly populated street, 'full of the aristocracy', Dover Street now has snob value, hairdressers, and Brown's Hotel, which is still the best place in London to get afternoon tea. At No 40 is the Arts Club, but the only original building from the 17th century is the Duke of Albemarle public house. Across the road from the pub is Ely House, London headquarters of the Oxford University Press. It was designed in the 18th century for the Bishops of Ely in the Palladian style. A bishop's mitre, and bishop's hat form part of the decoration and the area railings have seated lions by Alfred Stevens.
Leave Dover Street by Stafford Street to reach Albemarle Street. (beyond the junction with Albemarle Street, on the left, is the Goat Tavern, complete with life-size model goat.)

3 ALBEMARLE STREET
One of the best houses in this street is No 7, built in 1722 for Admiral Sir John Morris, and for many years the home of the National Book League. Further north can be seen the Royal Arcade, built in 1880, which consists

Fortnum & Mason's – the clock

of twenty shops, and still further up the street is the Royal Institution, founded in 1799 to promote the extension of science and useful knowledge. It looks like one building but in fact it is three houses joined together. Every Christmas the Institution arranges a special series of lectures for children, which are always well attended and over-subscribed. There is also a Faraday Museum here.
Walk northwards along Albemarle Street to reach Grafton Street. Turn right, and shortly right again into New Bond Street.

4 NEW BOND STREET
This is Mayfair's high street, and the smart shopping centre was first built in 1686 by Sir Thomas Bond of Peckham. On the corner is Aspreys, where one should note the iron shafts, and the plate glass on the windows, both of which came here with the company in 1848. On the corner of Burlington Gardens, and at the junction of New and Old Bond Streets, stands 'Atkinson's Building', designed by Vincent Harris in 1926. It is very pleasing to look at, but one wonders why a perfumier (whose building it is) wanted a Gothic gable, and a bell tower complete with a carillon of twenty-three bells!
Shortly, turn left into Burlington Gardens, then right into Burlington Arcade.

5 BURLINGTON ARCADE
Built between 1818 and 1819, according to tradition, to prevent persons from throwing rubbish over the wall here into the grounds of Burlington House, Burlington Arcade is 585ft long, and houses 72 shops, whose original rent was £18 per annum. Until recently it was patrolled by retired members of the 10th Hussars, one of whose duties was to stop people whistling while walking through the arcade, and also from carrying umbrellas. Some of the shops here carry plaques marked 'By Appointment to . . .', meaning they have supplied goods to royalty.
From the arcade emerge into Piccadilly and turn left. On the left is Burlington House.

6 BURLINGTON HOUSE
Best-known as the home of the Royal Academy of Arts and as the location for the famous Summer Exhibition (held May-August), this huge mansion was originally begun in the mid-17th century. It has been extended and re-modelled several times since. As well as the Summer Exhibition, there is also a permanent collection of masterpieces here, including works by such members of the academy as Turner and Gainsborough.
Pass the entrance to Albany Court, with its select chambers for bachelors, and continue to Piccadilly Circus, with the statue called Eros at its centre. Walk back up Piccadilly, this time on the south side. Reach St James's Church.

7 ST JAMES'S CHURCH
Sir Christopher Wren designed this elegant church. It has a font by Grinling Gibbons, with figures of Adam and Eve. Both have 'tummy-buttons', which might seem odd to some since a strict interpretation of the Bible means that neither Adam nor Eve came from the womb. The churchyard here is sometimes the setting for open-air markets, and the church crypt is a brass-rubbing centre.
Continue to Fortnum and Mason's.

8 FORTNUM AND MASON'S
High-quality provisions and gifts are the hallmark of Fortnum and Mason's style. The exterior of the emporium is enlivened by a clock with moving figures of Mr Fortnum and Mr Mason.
Pass the Piccadilly Arcade and cross the junction with St James's Street (with St James's Palace at the bottom) to return to Green Park Underground Station.

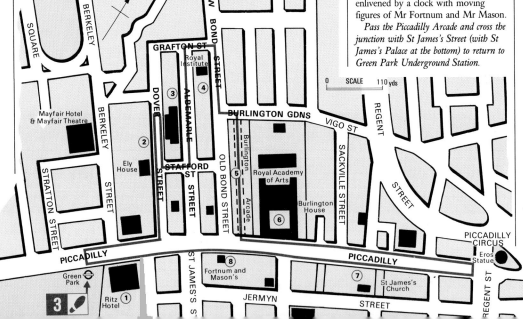

On the Trail of Sherlock Holmes

The story of Sherlock Holmes' London is the story of Victorian London, with horse-drawn hackney carriages and dark foggy streets. Through the dense fog can be seen two familiar figures – Mr Sherlock Holmes and his ever-patient assistant, Doctor Watson, MD.

Allow 1 hour

Begin the walk at Baker Street Underground Station and leave by the Marylebone Road exit. Turn left and shortly will be seen the Planetarium with, immediately beyond, Madame Tussaud's.

1 MADAME TUSSAUD'S

Perhaps the most famous waxworks in the world, this extraordinary establishment was of use to Holmes in the case of the mysterious marksman who tried to shoot him. For more clues see 61 Baker Street.

Turn into Allsop Place, beside the Planetarium, and follow it round to Baker Street. Walk down the street, and shortly reach, on the right-hand side, the headquarters of the Abbey National Building Society.

2 221 BAKER STREET

The headquarters of the building society is the 221 Baker Street of today. However, in Holmes' time that portion of the street was known as York Place, and there was no such number as 221 in the whole of the street. Today people who still write to Holmes get a reply from this address.

Continue along Baker Street to the post office.

3 111 BAKER STREET

This is now a post office, but it is not *the* office that Holmes sent Watson out to telegraph messages from in his day. However, this building and the one to the side give a firm impression of the type of building in which they lived.

Continue along Baker Street, passing Curtis the Chemist, where Dr Watson used to obtain cocaine for Holmes. Reach the headquarters of Marks and Spencer.

4 61 (or is it the real 221) BAKER STREET

Today this is the headquarters building of Marks and Spencer. One of the reasons given for siting *the* house here is that it is in direct line with Kendal Mews from which in the *Empty House* Holmes is shot at one evening. But having heard of the possibility in advance, he borrowed a plaster cast head from Madame Tussaud's, placed it in the window – and went out for the evening!

From Marks and Spencer cross Baker Street and enter Blandford Street. Shortly, on the right, is Kendal Mews, mysteriously now called Kendal Place. At the end of Blandford Street turn right into Manchester Street. Reach the junction with George Street where, a short way down on the left is Durrant's Hotel.

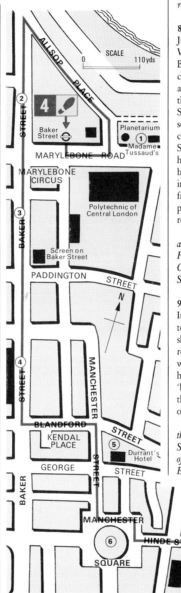

5 DURRANT'S HOTEL

This hotel was one of Holmes' places for interviewing clients.

Continue along Manchester Street to Manchester Square.

6 MANCHESTER SQUARE

This square, laid out in the latter half of the 18th century, is dominated by Hertford House, now the Wallace Collection. Here can be found paintings by Claude Joseph Vernet, and, as the story of the *Greek Interpreter* shows, he was Holmes' grandmother's brother on his mother's side.

Leave the square by Hinde Street and continue forward into Bentinck Street. Reach the junction with Welbeck Street.

7 JUNCTION OF BENTINCK AND WELBECK STREETS

Holmes received a nasty shock here one day, as retold in the *Final Problem*. While standing here, waiting to cross the road, he was nearly run down by a horse-drawn van that made off in the direction of Marylebone Lane.

Turn right along Welbeck Street and reach Wigmore Street.

8 WIGMORE STREET

Just to the west of the junction with Welbeck Street can still be seen John Bell and Croyden, the 'all-night chemist' where Watson used to come and buy larger quantities of cocaine than he could from Curtis's of Baker Street. In *The Sign of Four* Holmes sent Watson to the post office and he chose to go to the one in Wigmore Street, and on his return Holmes told him that he knew he had been there by the reddish earth he had on the instep of his shoes. Holmes knew from a visit there himself just previously that workmen were doing repairs next to the post office.

Cross Wigmore Street and continue along Welbeck Street, then turn left into Henrietta Place. Shortly, by the lovely Church of St Peter, turn right into Vere Street.

9 VERE STREET

It was while walking along here, as told in *The Final Problem*, that some slates and bricks fell from a nearby roof, narrowly missing Holmes as he walked past. 'I called the police and had the place examined,' he recalled, 'but they would have me believe that they had toppled over in the wind . . . of course I know better.'

Walk to the end of Vere Street, and then turn right into Oxford Street. Bond Street Underground Station and the end of the walk is a short distance away. Elementary.

WALK 5
Temple Precincts

Sandwiched between the City of London and the City of Westminster is a precinct whose history goes back to the 12th century, and which is almost as private today as it was all those centuries ago – it is The Temple. Here are the Inner Temple and the Middle Temple; the Outer Temple has since been built over and the site is now occupied by the Royal Courts of Justice.

Vanity Fair caricatures in the window of the long-established Wig and Pen Club, Fleet Street

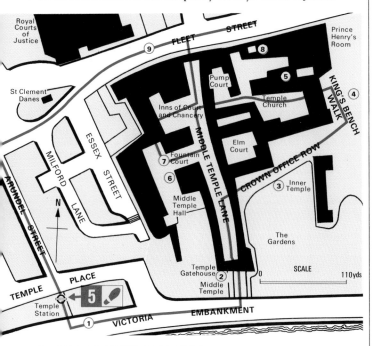

Allow 1 hour

Start at Temple Underground Station (note: trains do not stop here on Sundays). Turn right at the booking hall entrance and walk down to the Victoria Embankment. Turn left.

1 VICTORIA EMBANKMENT
It is hard to imagine the Thames without its embankments, but they are comparatively modern, having been built by Sir Joseph Bazalgette in the 19th century. Although they serve as marvellous promenades, their function is purely practical; they hold back the river, and they contain important underground services, including immense sewers. On this stretch of the Embankment are moored three ships – HQS *Wellington*, the floating headquarters of the Master Mariners Company, and two RNVR ships, HMS *Chrysanthemum* and HMS *President*.

Cross Temple Place and pass the boundary of the City of London, with its dragon holding the arms of the City. Turn left through a gateway in the railings to reach Middle Temple Lane and the Temple precincts. Reach the Gatehouse.

2 TEMPLE GATEHOUSE
This 19th-century gatehouse looks formidable, perhaps to deter undesirables from entering the precincts. On the exterior are the Flying Horse, indicating the property of the Middle Temple, and the Agnus Dei (Lamb of God) signifying the Inner Temple.

Pass through the Gatehouse, and shortly turn right through an archway to enter the Inner Temple. On the right are Inner Temple Gardens.

3 INNER TEMPLE GARDENS
Only Temple members and their guests are allowed to walk in these gardens. At the far side is a fountain which is a memorial to Charles Lamb, who was born in a house behind here. The wrought iron gates were erected in the 18th century, while the roses are said to be the descendants of the red and white ones that were plucked and thrown down in challenge between the Yorkists (white) and Lancastrians (red) at the start of the Wars of the Roses.

Continue ahead to King's Bench Walk.

4 KING'S BENCH WALK
This is the largest of the courts of the Temple. Here can be seen the handsome 17th-century houses that replaced those destroyed in the Great Fire, as well as later buildings.

At the top end of the Walk there is an archway that leads into Church Court, with the Master of the Temple's house on the right-hand side. Beyond this is the Temple Church.

5 TEMPLE CHURCH
Consecrated in 1185, this is one of only four round churches in Britain. The long rectangular nave was added in the 13th century. It was after the disbandment of the Knights Templars in the 14th century that the 'men of law and their students' came to live here, and have been here ever since.

From the south porch of the church

turn right and walk through Pump Court to Middle Temple Lane. Turn left and shortly reach Middle Temple Hall.*

6 MIDDLE TEMPLE HALL
Built in 1547, this is a gem of Tudor architecture, and is where the Benchers, members of the Middle Temple, dine regularly, being summoned by blasts on a horn. The Hall is open to the public, but first check to make sure that it is not being used by the Benchers.

From the Hall walk across to Fountain Court.

7 FOUNTAIN COURT
With its fountain and goldfish in its pond this is an altogether charming spot. Here Ruth Pinch and John Westlock in Charles Dickens' *Martin Chuzzlewit* found their own 'little Eden'.

From the Court walk up a short flight of steps on the north side, turn right through the passageway and emerge in Essex and Brick Court. This leads, once again, to Middle Temple Lane. Turn left and walk up the lane noting at the far end the 16th-century houses that abut onto the Gatehouse that guards the entrance to Fleet Street. Turn right to reach Prince Henry's Room.

8 PRINCE HENRY'S ROOM
This 17th-century building bestrides an entrance, by way of Inner Temple Lane, to The Temple. On the first floor there is an interesting exhibition of Samuel Pepys and his times arranged by the Samuel Pepys Club of London. The room has a superb ceiling and lovely panelling. You may need to knock to gain admittance.

From Prince Henry's Room return down Fleet Street.

9 FLEET STREET
In the middle of the roadway in this part of Fleet Street is the Temple Bar Monument, marking the boundary between the Cities of London and Westminster. A little further towards St Clement Danes, on the left, is the Wig and Pen Club, a famous wining and dining club that is housed in two early 17th-century houses. Also on the left is a branch of Lloyds Bank, housed in a building with superb tiled decoration. Across the road are the Royal Courts of Justice – the Law Courts – built in 1882 to the designs of architect G E Street.

Continue past St Clement Danes on the island site in the Strand and shortly turn left into Arundel Street to return to Temple Underground Station.

Covent Garden

Although the famous flower, fruit and vegetable market has moved from Covent Garden, the area is still full of life and interest. Indeed, there are many who would say there is now more for the visitor to see and do. George Bernard Shaw's *Pygmalion* and its musical successor *My Fair Lady* are in parts a theatrical celebration of Covent Garden, and London's theatreland is only a few steps to the west.

Allow ¾ hour

Start at Leicester Square Underground Station by the side of Wyndhams Theatre. Walk past the front of the theatre and turn left into St Martin's Court.

1 ST MARTIN'S COURT

Lined with small shops, this court is one of several pedestrian walkways in the area. At the far end is the Salisbury, one of London's most opulent Victorian pubs. Its position at the heart of theatreland guarantees it a theatrical clientele.

Turn right into St Martin's Lane.

2 ST MARTIN'S LANE

On the right is the Albery Theatre, opened in 1903. It has the peculiar distinction of being the only London theatre to have staged a play about a dictator written by another dictator – in 1932 Mussolini's *Napoleon* was staged here.

Opposite, and a little to the right of the Salisbury, is an archway reached up two or three steps. This leads to Godwin's Court.

3 GODWIN'S COURT

The unassuming archway leads to one of London's many surprises – a row of Regency shopfronts complete with bow-fronted windows.

Walk through the court and emerge into Bedfordbury. Turn right.

4 BEDFORDBURY

On the left of this street is one of a number of Peabody Estates which are scattered through the capital. They were founded by George Peabody – a successful businessman on the Stock Exchange – who aimed to provide living accommodation for workers near to their place of work.

Continue past the back of the Coliseum and then turn left into Chandos Place.

5 CHANDOS PLACE

At the end of this street, on the right, is a recently renovated building in rubbed brick which bears a blue plaque recording this as the site of the blacking factory where Charles Dickens first worked in London.

Reach Bedford Street and turn left into

Craftwork sellers, good shops and places to eat ensure a lively crowd in the market

it. Shortly pass Henrietta Street and find, on the right, wrought iron gates which lead to Inigo Place and St Paul's Covent Garden. The lamps lining the walkway here are still lit by gas.

6 ST PAUL'S COVENT GARDEN

The commission which Inigo Jones received for building this church included the statement that it should not be much larger than a barn. To this Jones replied: 'You shall have the handsomest barn in Christendom'. Needless to say he achieved that and more besides. It was under the portico of the church that Samuel Pepys saw the first performance in England of 'Punch and Judy', and the same portico is one of the settings in Shaw's *Pygmalion*.

On leaving the church turn left, go through an archway and turn left again into Henrietta Street. Walk forward into Covent Garden.

7 COVENT GARDEN

Originally planned by Inigo Jones as an open piazza surrounded by elegant houses, Covent Garden soon became a market centre as traders made use of the open area and the covered walkways in front of the buildings. The first specially-built market buildings were erected on the site in 1830. In 1974 the market was moved out to Nine Elms, as the site was congested and inconvenient for modern traffic. Today the market buildings are occupied by dozens of shops of all sorts, and street musicians and entertainers are usually on hand to enliven proceedings. In the south-east corner is the London Transport Museum.

To finish the walk, leave by James Street, on the square's north side, and reach Covent Garden Underground Station in Long Acre.

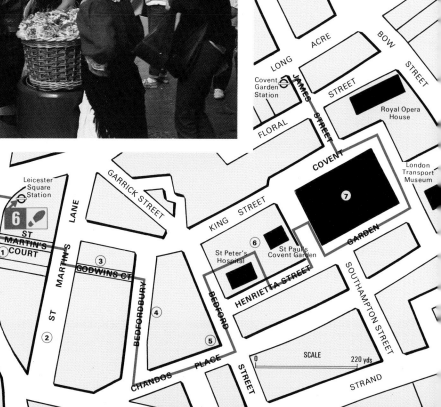

WALK 7
St Paul's Precincts

In the shadow of St Paul's is a network of streets and alleys where Company halls rub shoulders with ancient pubs and where churches stand close to places where riotous plays were once staged.

Allow 1½ hours

Begin the walk at St Paul's Underground Station, near to the new office precinct of Paternoster Square. Go through the archway of St Paul's Shopping Precinct, with a short flight of stairs. Half way up is the curious figure of the Panyer Boy. Continue to Paternoster Square, with its Christopher Wren pub and Elisabeth Frink sculpture. Cross the square and leave by a sloping ramp to reach Warwick Lane. Turn right to reach the Hall of the Worshipful Company of Cutlers.

1 HALL OF THE WORSHIPFUL COMPANY OF CUTLERS

This is the Cutlers' fourth hall, opened in 1887. The frieze on the outside of the building shows the various stages of the cutlers' craft. The elephant crest is a reminder that in former days the tusks of elephants were used for handles of cutlery.

Return down Warwick Lane, passing the entrance to Warwick Square, with its private door for the Lord Mayor into the Central Criminal Court. Reach Amen Court.

2 AMEN COURT

Here live the Dean and Chapter of St Paul's Cathedral in houses which range in date from the 17th to the 19th century, a good deal restored in the present century. The whole range of buildings abuts the City wall.

Warwick Lane now becomes Ave Maria Lane, its name a reminder that in pre-Reformation days this was part of a processional route round the cathedral precincts along which the rosary was recited. Turn right into a small courtyard behind the next office block to reach Stationers' Hall.

3 STATIONERS' HALL

The Stationers first petitioned the Corporation for recognition in 1403, when they were described as being 'writers of text, lynmers (illustrators), bookbinders and booksellers'. It was not until 1553 that they received their Charter and became one of the livery companies of the City. Until the Copyright Act of 1911 books registered with the Company were entitled to have 'Entered at Stationers' Hall, London' printed on the title page, as a form of copyright registration. The coat of arms of the Company is to be seen on the railings, at the side of the public footpath which leads to Ludgate Hill.

From Stationers' Hall take the footpath to Ludgate Hill. Turn right to reach the Church of St Martin Ludgate.

4 ST MARTIN LUDGATE

There has been a church here since about the year 600, according to a 13th-century chronicler. Today's church was designed by Sir Christopher Wren and contains much fine woodwork which is attributed to Grinling Gibbons.

Opposite the church is Pilgrim Street. Walk along it for a short distance, then turn left into Ludgate Broadway. Shortly turn left into Carter Lane, then go through an archway on the right into Church Entry. Pass a notice on railings marking the site of Blackfriars Monastery. Reach Playhouse Yard.

5 PLAYHOUSE YARD

In the late 16th and early 17th centuries the first indoor theatres in London were to be found here. Here William Shakespeare and others played. There were constant complaints about the behaviour of the theatre-goers that included the wearing of sweaty night-caps!

From Playhouse Yard walk east into Ireland Yard, where there are slight remains of Blackfriars, and where Shakespeare set up home, having bought a house for £100. Reach St Andrew's Hill and turn right by the Cockpit pub. Reach the Church of St Andrew by the Wardrobe.

6 ST ANDREW BY THE WARDROBE

Rebuilt after the Great Fire by Wren, and since then restored after war damage, inside this church are several interesting pieces of furniture including a font that came from St

Matthew Friday Street and a Royal Stuart coat of arms from St Olave Old Jewry. The whole church is lit by two 18th-century chandeliers.

Return up St Andrew's Hill to Carter Lane and turn right into it. Shortly, on the right, is an archway leading to Wardrobe Place.

7 WARDROBE PLACE

Until the Great Fire of 1666 this was the site of the monarch's wardrobe, which explains the enigmatic name of the spot and of the nearby church. Today it is a quiet oasis among the City bustle.

Return to Carter Lane, with the former St Paul's Cathedral Choir School opposite, and turn right to pass the entry to Dean's Court, where the former Deanery of St Paul's is situated. Just past Addle Hill, on the right of Carter Lane, is a plaque commemorating Shakespeare. Reach Godliman Street, turn right and reach Knightrider Street, once the longest street in the City. Turn left to reach the Horn pub.

8 THE HORN

A former Dickensian house – he mentions the 'Horn' in Pickwick Papers – there is a bust of the great man in the public bar. However, the first mention of the 'Horn' is in 1687, when officers from the nearby College of Arms used it to discuss the rebuilding of their premises after the Great Fire of 1666. The street name sign on the side of the public house is Sermon Lane, reminding present day visitors that here a sermon was often preached in medieval times at the end of the walk around the precincts of St Paul's.

Turn left by the pub, cross Carter Lane, then go through an alley to reach St Paul's Churchyard. Cross the road, turn right, and reach a gateway into the gardens around St Paul's. Walk round the east end of the cathedral, passing the site of St Paul's Cross, and keep ahead to end the walk at St Paul's Underground Station.

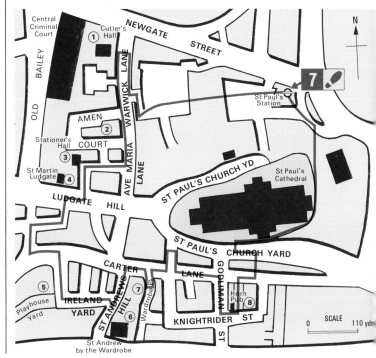

Samuel Pepys Walk

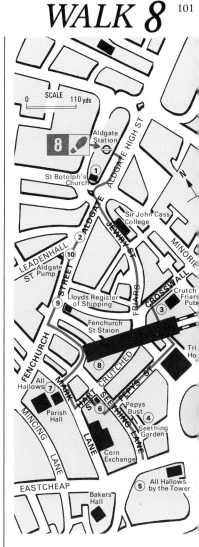

Pepys, perhaps best known as the author of a diary that recorded his everyday life for nearly ten years, should also be remembered as being the Secretary to the Navy Office at a time of reorganisation for which later historians have dubbed him the 'Saviour of the Navy'. Born in 1632/3 in Salisbury Court off Fleet Street, and baptised in St Bride's Church, he was educated at St Paul's School, London, and took a Bachelor of Arts degree at Cambridge at Magdalene College. It was to the college that he left his extensive library, which is still there today. As a civil servant, he rose to become Secretary to the Navy office in 1673. While in office he lived in Seething Lane, and attended the nearby church of St Olave, where he is buried alongside his wife Elizabeth. This walk follows in Pepy's footsteps through a part of London he knew well.

Allow 1½ hours

Begin at Aldgate Underground Station. Turn right to reach St Botolph's Church.

1   ST BOTOLPH'S CHURCH
Although there has been a church on this site since Saxon days, the present building was erected between 1741 and 1744 to the designs of George Dance the Elder.

Cross Aldgate High Street by way of the traffic island and reach the blue plaque marking the site of Aldgate.

2   ALDGATE
This was one of the Roman gates into the city. It was demolished in the 18th century to make more room for traffic entering and leaving the city.

From the Aldgate plaque walk west to Jewry Street, and turn into it. Go past Sir John Cass's College (on the left) and just before a railway arch is reached, turn left into Crosswall to reach the Crutched Friars pub.

3   CRUTCHED FRIARS PUB
The name and inn-sign of this pub are reminders that this area in Pre-Reformation days was inhabited by the Order of the Holy Cross, who wore a large, leather cross on their robes. Hence the crossed or crutched friars, as they became known during their 300 years here.

Return to the street called Crutched Friars, go under the railway arch, and turn left into Coopers Row. Reach Pepys Street and turn right. Walk to its junction with Seething Lane and turn left to find Seething Garden.

4   SEETHING GARDEN
In the garden can be seen a stone monument containing a blue plaque commemorating the site of the Navy Office until its destruction by fire in the 17th century.

Continue along Seething Lane to reach the Church of All Hallows by the Tower.

5   ALL HALLOWS BY THE TOWER
It was from this church's tower that Pepys watched some of the progress of the Great Fire of 1666. In the crypt are remains of a Roman villa and a model of Roman London.

Walk back along Seething Lane to reach the entrance gateway to the churchyard of St Olave, Hart Street.

Gateway to St Olave's

---

6   ST OLAVE, HART STREET
Before entering the churchyard look up at the entrance gateway, a memorial to members of the parish who died in a plague in the early 17th century. On entering the churchyard note on the south wall of the church a blocked doorway at window level. This marks the entrance to the Navy Office pew, in the former gallery of the church, and which was regularly used by Pepys when he attended worship here. There are strong ties with Norway, whose flag hangs in the church, and to King Olaf (or Olave) to whom the church is dedicated. Both Samuel and Elizabeth Pepys lie buried 'near ye holie table', in unmarked tombs, while Elizabeth's memorial, high up on the north wall of the chancel, looks straight down into the site of the former Navy Pew.

Leave the church by way of the north-west door and turn left into Hart Street, then right into Mark Lane. Reach, on the left, the Parish Hall of St Olave's, to the side of which is All Hallows Church.

7   ALL HALLOWS CHURCH
Under the ruins of this church (demolished in 1870) is an 11th-century crypt which was brought here in the 19th century when St James's on the Wall Church, Monkwell Square, was pulled down. It is a fine, rare example of the Norman style of architecture. The notice on the door explains from whom the key may be obtained in order to visit the crypt.

Opposite the church site is London Street, take this to reach Railway Place and Fenchurch Street Station.

8   FENCHURCH STREET STATION
Built in 1836 for the London and Blackwall Railway Company, the station made for easy access to the East and West India Docks. However, its stationary engines, used to pull the carriages into the City, were constantly breaking down and had to be replaced by moving steam engines

– much to the annoyance of the residents of the City at that time.

Continue round Railway Place until Fenchurch Street is reached and turn right. Shortly, on the right, reach Lloyds Register of Shipping.

9   LLOYD'S REGISTER OF SHIPPING
This building houses the organisation that registers shipping for insurance. To be 'A1' at Lloyd's is all that any ship owner wants to be said about his ships.

Continue along Fenchurch Street to reach the Aldgate Pump.

10   ALDGATE PUMP
Citizens have been able to draw water from here since medieval times. But the strangest story concerning the pump comes from the earliest part of this century. Passers-by drinking from the pump were apt to remark that it tasted 'different', more like an aerated water than ordinary tap water. After much searching, the source of supply was traced through a hidden river. The cause of the taste was also found. At one stage of its journey, from the northern hills of London, it ran underground through a graveyard, and the calcium of the bones being 'washed' by the water gave it that 'different' taste. Today the supply is pure Thames Water Authority water.

Walk along Aldgate High Street to reach Aldgate Underground Station and the end of the walk.

WALK 9
Cheapside Stroll

Cheapside, stretching eastwards from St Paul's Cathedral, was the City's market place in medieval times. Now it is a teeming thoroughfare with side streets and alleys where something of the atmosphere of old London can still be captured.

Allow 1 hour

Begin at St Paul's Underground Station, and walk towards St Paul's Churchyard to reach the site of St Paul's Cross.

1 ST PAUL'S CROSS
A monument erected in 1910 marks the site of this preaching cross, which had a roofed pulpit. It was removed in 1642. Edicts from the Pope were read from here, as were other proclamations affecting the citizens of London. Sermons were also preached, and the quarterly folk moots – the general assembly of the citizens – were summoned by 'Great Paul', the largest of the cathedral bells.
Leave the churchyard, and crosss New Change and then Cheapside to reach Foster Lane and the Church of St Vedast.

2 ST VEDAST
Only two other churches in England are dedicated to this saint – one at Norwich, the other at Tathwell in Lincolnshire. It is not known why the church should be named after a 6th-century Bishop of Arras in France. The medieval church here was destroyed in the Great Fire and rebuilt by Sir Christopher Wren. It now contains furnishings from other Wren churches. Among these are the pulpit from All Hallows, Bread Street and a 17th-century hour glass from St Alban, Wood Street.
Return to Cheapside, and walk towards the Church of St Mary le Bow, whose tall tower and spire can be seen on the opposite side of the road. Pass Gutter Lane, where the Worshipful Company of Saddlers have had their hall since the 14th century (the present building is 20th-century). Continue to Wood Street, and turn left into it.

3 WOOD STREET
On the left, near the corner, are the railings of the former St Peter's Church West Clepe. On the railings is a figure of St Peter with the keys of heaven in his hands. Further along Wood Street, on the right, is Compter House. Beyond the archway here is a courtyard occupied by a debtor's prison until 1791. Below the courtyard are the dungeons, now used as a wine store.
Return to Cheapside.

4 CHEAPSIDE
At the junction of Wood Street and Cheapside, until the 17th century, stood one of the Eleanor Crosses erected by Edward I to commemorate places where the body of his Queen was rested overnight on its way from Lincoln to burial in Westminster Abbey. When it was destroyed, William Laud, then Archbishop of Canterbury, wrote that 'the cross in Cheapside was taken down to cleanse that great street of superstition'. All the small side streets off the main Cheapside reflect in some way or other the occupations of the inhabitants in former times. Friday Street, where once the Friday Fish Market was held, now runs under the modern buildings on the site. Its neighbour is Bread Street, where the bakers used to make, bake and sell their bread. Across the way is Milk Street, where in 1478 Thomas More was born, and where as a child he would have watched the dairymaids selling their wares 'fresh from the kine'.
Continue, and cross Cheapside, to reach St Mary le Bow.

5 ST MARY LE BOW
By tradition, all those born within the sound of Bow Bells are true Cockneys. Built on 'bows', arches erected in Pre-Conquest times, the church has been rebuilt several times since then. Today's church is largely a reconstruction after severe war damage. Suspended over the altar steps is a hanging rood – the crucifixion scene complete with Mary, the Mother of Jesus and St John – the gift of the German Church as an act of reparation after the end of World War II. Like many other City churches it functions only during the weekdays to the thousands of people who work in the City, but return to their homes every evening.
From the church, turn left into Bow churchyard, then left again to reach Bow Lane. Turn right into it.

6 BOW LANE
Bow Lane takes its name from the shape of a longbow whose pattern it follows on its journey from Cheapside to Cannon Street. Halfway down is Groveland Court, where is to be found Williamson's tavern. Tradition says that this was the site of the original Mansion House of the lord mayors of London. This is probably based on the fact that one lord mayor in the late 17th century entertained William and Mary to dinner here. They presented their host with a pair of wrought iron gates which can be seen at the end of the alleyway.
At the junction with Watling Street is Ye Olde Watling, one of the City's most venerable public houses. Return to Cheapside and turn right. Cross over to King Street, and walk up it to the Guildhall and St Lawrence Jewry.

7 GUILDHALL AND ST LAWRENCE JEWRY
Parts of the Guildhall date back to the 15th century. The outstanding part of the complex is undoubtedly the splendid Great Hall, where the Court of Common Council, governing body of the City, meets. Across Guildhall Yard is the church of St Lawrence Jewry (its entrance is in Gresham Street). It is the official Church of the City. The north-east chapel is dedicated to the Commonwealth. Within can be seen a unique collection of alms-bags showing the coats of arms of the various livery guilds who use the church for their services, together with the banner of the Worshipful Company of Parish Clerks of the City of London, which shows St Nicholas, their patron saint.
Return to Cheapside and turn left. Continue to Ironmonger Lane, in which is the Hall of the Company of Mercers.

8 HALL OF THE WORSHIPFUL COMPANY OF MERCERS
The Company of Mercers is the 'number one' company in order of precedence of all the ninety-six Companies today. The hall is built on the site of the house in which Thomas à Becket was born in 1118, and where a hospital was built in his memory by his sister in 1190. At the Dissolution of the Monasteries in the 16th century the chapel was granted to the Mercers Company, and it was in this chapel's floor after its destruction in the blitz of 1940 that a 14th-century figure of Christ was found buried.
Return to Cheapside. From this point onwards to Bank Underground Station the street changes its name and becomes Poultry – indicating its prime function as a poultry market in medieval times. On the wall of the Midland Bank at the junction of Poultry and Princes Street is a reminder of those times – carvings of a small boy holding a goose. Finish the walk at Bank Underground Station.

London Wall

It was not until late in the 2nd century that the Romans enclosed Londinium with a wall, and so made it the third largest city in the Roman Empire. The wall stretched from where the Tower of London now stands in a crude half-circle to where in the Middle Ages the Blackfriars monastery was to be found. Later the two ends were joined together with the erection of the riverside length of the wall. Its total length was over three miles, and while much of it has been pulled down, or has fallen down over the last few hundred years, it makes a pleasant route to follow in modern-day London.

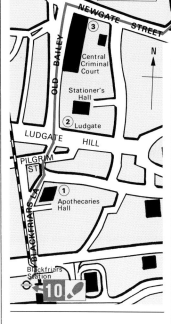

Allow 2 hours

Begin at Blackfriars Underground Station on the Queen Victoria Street side of the Station. (To the left, under the railway arch, is the ornate exterior of the Blackfriars pub.) Cross the roadway and walk up Blackfriars Lane. On the right is an archway leading to Apothecaries' Hall.

1 APOTHECARIES' HALL

Charmingly set round a courtyard complete with clock on the wall facing the archway, Apothecaries' Hall was built in the 17th century.

Continue up Blackfriars Lane into Ludgate Broadway, cross Pilgrim Street into Ludgate Court, which runs alongside a site where bomb damage from World War II has still to be cleared, and reach Ludgate. Cross the roadway, turn right towards St Paul's and walk up the hill until a blue plaque is found on the wall just past Ye Olde London pub.

2 LUDGATE

The blue plaque marks the site of Ludgate, which was a postern gate into the walled city; that is it was used by pedestrians only.

Retrace the route back to Old Bailey and turn right into it to reach the Central Criminal Courts.

3 CENTRAL CRIMINAL COURTS

Popularly known as the Old Bailey, the courts stand on a site that was once an open area in front of the wall. On the Newgate side of the building is a blue plaque recording the site of Newgate, which despite the name, was one of the original Roman gates into the City.

Turn right along Newgate and reach the ruins of Christ Church. Turn left into King Edward Street, and shortly past a post office (which is on the left) turn right into Postman's Park.

4. POSTMAN'S PARK

This charming park is especially interesting for its little memorials commemorating heroic deeds by ordinary people. In the north-east corner of the park is the church of St Botolph Without, which was founded in 1291 but rebuilt during the 18th century. Its brick tower is particularly attractive.

Emerge into Aldersgate Street and turn right. Across the street is a tablet marking the site of Aldersgate. Shortly turn left into Gresham Street, then left again into Noble Street, passing the Church of St Anne and St Agnes.

5 NOBLE STREET

In this street is one of the best surviving stretches of the wall. It has been excavated in recent years, and it is easy to distinguish the Roman, medieval and later masonry. The southernmost stretch here formed the watchtower and wall of Cripplegate Fort, built by the Romans before the city wall. One of its features is a small archway where a stream passed through the wall.

At the end of Noble Street reach the roadway called London Wall. A diversion can be made here to visit the Museum of London. The wall continues under the roadway, where can be seen the West Gate of the fort (open weekdays only), and reappears in the gardens opposite. Cross London Wall and find the entrance to the gardens by walking under the raised walkway and following signs for Bastion House; the gardens are on the right as you go down.

One of the memorials to heroic people in Postman's Park

6 BARBICAN GARDENS

Laid out in the heart of the Barbican complex, these secluded gardens come as a quiet surprise after the rushing traffic along London Wall. The city wall here is particularly well preserved, and at the far end of this stretch is Cripplegate Bastion, its masonry reflected in the waters of a large pool complete with water lilies and goldfish.

Return to London Wall and climb the stairs onto the raised walkway. Walk away from the Museum of London to the Podium pub. Descend more steps and turn right into Wood Street.

7 WOOD STREET

At the end of the street is Roman House, with a blue plaque marking the site of Cripplegate. The word 'cripple' in this instance comes from the Saxon word 'crefel'; literally translated it means 'a den or lair'. Used here it refers to the underground passage that enabled anybody locked out of the City after curfew had rung to be let in. In the reception area of Roman House, is a painting, by the late Alan Sorrell, of London in Roman times with the city wall clearly visible.

Return along Roman House and turn left into St Alphage Garden.

8 ST ALPHAGE GARDEN

In this garden is one of the finest portions of the wall still visible today. There are stairs down to the wall, and there is another flight of stairs at the end of the roadway that will give an almost aerial view of the wall. Both are well worth using to get the best possible idea of the strength and size of the wall in its heyday.

Ascend the stairs at the far end of the garden, turn right, then almost immediately left and walk to the Plough pub. Bear left and continue to where the walkway overlooks Moorfields, then turn left to reach the escalator which takes you down to street level. Turn left for Moorgate Underground Station and the end of the walk.

WALK 11
Moorgate

The area around Moorgate is full of banks, insurance companies, and a livery company hall or two. Its side streets and alleyways are a veritable maze. When the traveller surfaces at Moorgate Underground Station he is faced with tall office buildings, and a few shops. Long since have the 'moor fields' disappeared to have their place taken by the buildings. It is hard to imagine the washerwomen and bleachers of earlier times making use of the River Walbrook which flowed near here.

The Nat West Tower

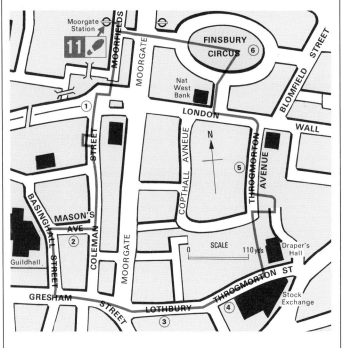

Allow 1 hour

Leave the main entrance of Moorgate Underground Station by way of the street called Moorfields, turn right and walk towards the City. On the right, at the junction with London Wall, is Moor House, on which is a plaque commemorating Sir Ebenezer Howard, the founder of the garden city movement. Cross London Wall and enter Coleman Street.

1 COLEMAN STREET
At the junction of Coleman Street and London Wall is the hall of the Worshipful Company of Armourers and Braziers. The Company has been here since the 15th century, although the present building dates only from the 19th century. Particularly attractive is the coat of arms on the parapet. Almost opposite, in Basinghall Avenue, is the hall of the Worshipful Company of Girdlers. Like many other livery companies, they maintain a close connection with their trade and at times of coronations have the privilege of making the girdle and stole for the monarch to wear. Continue along the street, which takes its name from its 18th-century builder, looking out for the coat of arms of the Worshipful Company of Merchant Taylors who are landlords of some of the present buildings.
Reach Mason's Avenue, on the right, and turn into it.

2 MASON'S AVENUE
On the left of this avenue is Doctor Butler's Head, a pub with an ornate façade. Opened in 1616 by the 'good doctor' it offered beer as a cure for sciatica when James I contracted the malaise. History does not record whether he was cured or not. The black and white building opposite the tavern was built as an hotel, but is now used for offices.
Reach Basinghall Street, with part of the Guildhall (decorated with stone dragons) opposite. Turn left and walk to Gresham Street, and turn left into it. Cross Coleman Street and Moorgate to reach Lothbury.

3 LOTHBURY
The whole of the south side of this street is dominated by the Bank of England. It was founded in 1694 to provide funds for the war against Louis XIV of France, but did not become the Government's Banker until much later. Opposite is the church of St Margaret's, designed by Sir Christopher Wren. Inside is a Post-Reformation rarity, a rood screen that was originally designed for All Hallows-the-Great Church in Upper Thames Street, and a font attributed to Grinling Gibbons. Next to the church is No 7 Lothbury, one of the most ornate buildings in the City. At the side of the building is Tokenhouse Yard, which takes its name from the tokens made here prior to the reign of James I – a sort of 'mini-mint'.
Continue into Throgmorton Street.

4 THROGMORTON STREET
On the right of the street is the Stock Exchange, which has a visitors' gallery. Here can be seen one of the City's most famous mottos 'My word is my bond'. Opposite is the hall of the Worshipful Company of Drapers. Founded in 1364, they purchased this site from Henry VIII in 1541. The present hall is their fourth here and dates from 1870, and is a splendid example of the classical revival style of the period.
On the left side of Drapers' Hall is the entrance to Throgmorton Avenue, guarded by two heavy wrought iron gates. Go through the archway into the avenue.

5 THROGMORTON AVENUE
This is a private road, as is indicated by the absence of yellow lines, and is the responsibility of the Drapers' Company and the Carpenters' Company rather than that of the City Corporation. In the gardens of the Drapers' Hall are a number of mulberry trees, the fruits of which were once put into pies for company members. Just past the garden's railings a right turn can be made to Austin Friars. Founded in 1253 the Augustinian monastery here became one of the most important religious houses in England. The church was one of the great sights of medieval London, which at the Reformation was handed over to the Dutch Reform Church for their own services – it is still in their hands today, although the present building dates only from 1957. Towering above the church, to the east, is the National Westminster Tower. Return to Throgmorton Avenue and walk to Carpenters' Hall. The Carpenters have been here since 1428, although successive halls were destroyed in the Great Fire and the Blitz.
At the far end of Throgmorton Avenue turn left into London Wall. Shortly, cross the road and enter Circus Place, with a National Westminster Bank on the left corner. A blue plaque on this building marks the site of Bethlehem Hospital, the lunatic asylum which was moved to Lambeth in 1815. Enter Finsbury Circus.

6 FINSBURY CIRCUS
Originally laid out after 1815, the circus provides a pleasant green oasis in this part of the city. It has a bowling green, and a small restaurant. Of the buildings which surround it, one of the most notable is No 16, designed by Sir Edwin Lutyens.
Leave Finsbury Circus on the west side to reach Moorgate and the underground station.

Ten City Churches

Churches remain a vital component of the City scene, even though many are dwarfed by huge modern buildings. This walk visits ten of them via streets and alleys that have much else of interest.

Allow 1½ hours

Start at Bank Underground Station, leaving by the exit to the Royal Exchange. From the Exchange cross Cornhill, and walk through Pope's Head Alley – noting the Pope's head on one of the keystones of the second archway. Emerge into Lombard Street, with St Mary Woolnoth opposite.

1 ST MARY WOOLNOTH

Perhaps Nicholas Hawksmoor's most distinctive church, this severe building was completed in 1727. Its massive stone walls were designed to keep out the noise of 18th-century London, and still do a remarkable job today. Inside, the church is light and airy, with the pulpit the dominant feature. Memorials here include one to John Newton. He had once been a pirate, but went on to become rector of this church and a noted hymn writer. Another memorial is to Edward Lloyd, in whose coffee house in Lombard Street Lloyds of London was founded.

Leave the church and walk along Lombard Street – one of the world's leading financial centres. Several of the banking institutions in the street are still identified by decorative signs; one of the most distinctive is a golden grasshopper. Beyond Birchin Lane, on the left, reach St Edmund, King and Martyr.

2 ST EDMUND, KING AND MARTYR

The tower of this church, designed by Sir Christopher Wren, looks like a medieval lighthouse, and one of the parishes incorporated in the present parish is St Nicholas who, amongst other titles, is patron saint of lighthouse keepers. Inside can be seen a tablet to Charles Melville Hays, who drowned in the *Titanic* disaster in 1912. The east window depicts legends associated with St Nicholas.

From the church turn left into George Yard, go through the archway at the far side, passing the ancient George and Vulture Tavern, and walk along St Michael's Alley. On the right here is a blue plaque marking the site of the first coffee house (1652). Reach St Michael-upon-Cornhill.

3 ST MICHAEL-UPON-CORNHILL

This church has one of the finest peals of bells in the City. All but the tower was rebuilt by Wren after the Great Fire, but much of the Wren interior was altered in the late 19th century. Especially interesting here is a large wooden pelican, made in 1775 as part of the altar piece.

Turn right along Cornhill and reach St Peter-upon Cornhill.

4 ST PETER-UPON-CORNHILL

This church was designed by Wren, and still contains much of the original woodwork installed by him. Mendelssohn composed a piece of music here when he visited the church in 1840. The keyboard on which he played is preserved in the vestry.

From the church, cross the Church Street/Bishopsgate junction into Leadenhall Street. On the right is Leadenhall market. Also here is a viewing gallery for the excavations of Roman London's Basilica. Towering over the whole area is the new Lloyds Building – looking rather like an up-market gas works. At the junction of Leadenhall Street and St Mary Axe is the Church of St Andrew Undershaft.

5 ST ANDREW UNDERSHAFT

In pre-Reformation days a huge may-pole was erected outside this 16th-century church on May Day, which explains the last part of the church's name. There is much of interest inside, including a memorial to 16th-century historian John Stow. Stow's bust holds a real quill pen, which is replaced in an annual ceremony.

Cross St Mary Axe to the open area opposite. Walk diagonally across, with the Commercial Union block on the right, to reach St Helen Bishopsgate.

6 ST HELEN BISHOPSGATE

This church is unique in the City in having a double nave and a double chancel. This was once two adjoining churches, one for Benedictine nuns and one for the parishioners. At the Dissolution the dividing wall was removed. Inside are a large number of tombs and memorials to former parishioners. Among these are several brasses dating from the 15th and early 16th centuries.

Leave the church, walk forward into Bishopsgate and turn right to reach St Ethelburga Bishopsgate.

7 ST ETHELBURGA BISHOPSGATE

Tucked between tall buildings, this unassuming little church has a history going back to the 12th century. It was here that Henry Hudson received communion before sailing to search for America's north-west passage. The church is now a centre for healing, and is not always open.

Continue along Bishopsgate and beyond the junction of Wormwood Street and Camomile Street is St Botolph's Bishopsgate.

8 ST BOTOLPH'S BISHOPSGATE

In the churchyard here is a 19th-century parish hall which functioned as a charity school. On its front are two statues of a boy and girl dressed in 'school uniform'. The church itself was rebuilt in 1729.

Return to Wormwood Street and turn right. Shortly, on the right, reach All Hallows London Wall.

9 ALL HALLOWS LONDON WALL

George Dance the Younger designed this elegant, classical-style church, which was completed in 1767. Today it is a Guild Church, with quarterly services. The nave houses the library of the Council for the Care of Churches. The vestry is built on the foundations of one of the bastions of the City Wall and is semi-circular.

On leaving the church, cross the road and turn right along London Wall. Reach Carpenter's Hall and turn left into Throgmorton Avenue (see walk 11). Reach Throgmorton Street, turn right and then keep forward into Lothbury to reach St Margared Lothbury.

10 ST MARGARET LOTHBURY

Rebuilt by Wren, this church contains furniture from other Wren churches that have been demolished. The church is now responsible for seven former parishes from earlier times, in addition to its own.

From the church cross Lothbury and walk alongside the Bank of England to return to Bank Underground Station.

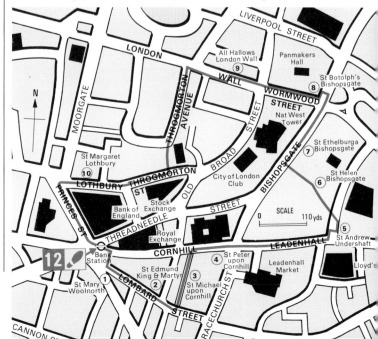

WALK 13
Jack the Ripper Walk

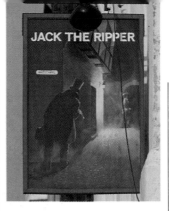

Of all the murders, solved and unsolved, that have come to the attention of the public, none has caught the imagination more than a short series of brutal attacks that took place between August and November 1888. They were the Jack the Ripper murders. Perhaps the public would have forgotten them had not the American author, Jack London, come to London to research for a book. That book, called *The People of the Abyss*, was to arouse the public interest in the East End, and to bring to light once more this brutal series of unsolved crimes.

Allow 2 hours

Start the walk at Whitechapel Station. The building to the left of the station was the Whitechapel Working Lads Institute and was used for the inquest on Jack the Ripper's first victim. From the station turn right and walk along Whitechapel Road. Shortly, reach a passageway on the right which leads to Winthrop Street. Turn left to reach Durward Street.

1 DURWARD STREET
Known at the time as Bucks Row, this was the scene of the first murder. Like all the others, the victim, Mary Anne Nichols, was a prostitute, in her 40s. Her body, covered by a tarpaulin, was discovered on 31 August 1888.

At the end of Durward Street turn right into Vallance Road, then turn left into Old Montague Street. Reach Brick Lane and turn right. Continue to Hanbury Street and turn left into it.

2 HANBURY STREET
In this street is a brewery, then a courtyard, where Annie Chapman was murdered on the morning of 8 September 1888.

Continue along Hanbury Street, then turn left into Commercial Street to reach the Jack the Ripper pub.

3 JACK THE RIPPER PUB
At the time of the murders this pub was called the Ten Bells. It was here that Annie Chapman met her killer. Her usual fee, for services rendered, was fourpence, so that she could have a bed with breakfast in the nearby convent. This sad little fact says much about the pathetic nature of the victims and about the underside of London life.

On the next corner is Christ Church, Spitalfields, designed by Nicholas Hawksmoor. Shortly past the church cross the road and enter a private road between a building and a multi-storey car park. This was once called Dorset Street.

4 DORSET STREET
Along here, in 1888, was to be found Miller's Court, where the fifth murder took place on 9 November. It was the only one of Jack the Ripper's crimes to be committed indoors.

Continue to Crispin Street and turn left. Across the road is the convent where Annie Chapman was able to get bed and breakfast. From here to Mitre Square, the next murder site, the route passes through some of the drabbest and most run-down areas of the East End, and it is not hard to imagine this same area a hundred years ago. After leaving the convent walk down Bell Lane, where many of the dwellings are still much as they were in the last century. Look into one or two of the courtyards, now mercifully empty of inhabitants, and realise how easy it would have been to harbour a felon here in the 1880s. Turn right into Wentworth Street and at the end turn right into Middlesex Street, better known for its Sunday market as Petticoat Lane. Turn left into Harrow Place, walk to the end, turn left into White Kennett Street, and then right into Stoney Lane. Cross Houndsditch into Creechurch Lane, and then left again into Duke's Place, cross the roadway, and walk along to St James's Passage to the side of the Sir John Cass School, and at the end is Mitre Square.

5 MITRE SQUARE
In the early hours of 30 September Catherine Eddowes was walking home, having been arrested earlier in the evening for being drunk in Bishopsgate. The Ripper killed her here.

Turn left into Mitre Street, reach Aldgate and turn left again. Follow the road until Commercial Road is reached. Walk down it until Henriques Street is reached.

6 HENRIQUES STREET
Elizabeth Stride was killed here on the same night as Catherine Eddowes was murdered. After November the killing stopped. To this day no one knows who the murderer was, although there have been many theories. Many would say the murders are best forgotten, but it is possible that similar horrors can be prevented if people recall that ignorance and poverty certainly aided Jack the Ripper.

Return along Commercial Road to reach Aldgate East Underground Station.

SCALE
0   110 yds

13
Whitechapel Station

Richmond

Known originally as Sheen, from the shining river, the earliest record of a town here comes from the 8th-century Anglo-Saxon Chronicle, since which time the small township has grown to become one of the outer suburbs of London. Here may be found the remains of a royal palace, a green surrounded by elegant houses, and marvellous views of the Thames. The walk can be extended to include Richmond Hill and the green expanses of Richmond Park.

Allow 1½ hours

Start at the railway station. Cross the road and turn left along the Quadrant. Shortly turn right into Duke Street to reach Greenside. To the right is Richmond Theatre, built in 1899, and, across the road, Little Green, given to the town by Charles II as a bowling green. Ahead is Richmond Green.

1 RICHMOND GREEN
The Green itself is one of the finest in the London area. It is surrounded by buildings of various styles, with the 'Cricketers' pub signboard showing a

19th-century cricket match in progress. Cricket is still regularly played on the Green in the summer. The west side of the Green is dominated by a terrace of houses known as Maids of Honour Row, built by command of George I in 1724 to accommodate ladies of the Court. At the end of the Row are the remains of the Tudor royal palace. Walk through the archway and enter the courtyard of the palace.
Leave the Green by Old Palace Yard, passing Trumpeter's Court, whose riverside frontage is a superb example of Georgian architecture, reach Old Palace Lane and turn left. Reach Asgill House.

2 ASGILL HOUSE
This grand 18th-century house was built for Sir Charles Asgill, Lord Mayor of London in 1758.
Reach Cholmondeley Walk with Twickenham Bridge to the right. Walk under the bridge to Richmond Lock.

3 RICHMOND LOCK
This is a half-tide lock, used to hold the flow of water above the lock, making the river tidal up to Teddington for four-hour periods.
Return to Cholmondeley Walk, and continue towards Richmond Bridge, with Richmond Ait (or Island) in the river to the right (during high spring and autumn tides the river overflows along this path). Reach Richmond Bridge.

4 RICHMOND BRIDGE
Originally built in the 18th century as a toll bridge, this bridge became free in 1859. It was widened in 1937, and the newer stonework can clearly be made out. Attached to the side of the bridge is an 18th-century milestone.
Ascend to road level by walking up the steps of the bridge. Walk up Bridge Street to Hill Street and turn left to pass the town hall with its vine. Continue along Hill Street and shortly turn right into Red Lion Street, which becomes Paradise Road. Reach the parish church of St Mary Magdalene.

5 PARISH CHURCH
Most of the church dates from about 1750, but the tower remains from the 15th century building which stood here. Among the monuments inside is a brass to Robert Cotton, Officer to the Wardrobe at Richmond Palace, who died in 1591. There are also several dramatic 18th-century memorials.
From the north side of the church turn left into Sheen Road. At the end turn right into the Quadrant for the return to the railway station.

Detour
No visit to Richmond would be complete without seeing the view from Richmond Hill and visiting the Park. From the church return along Paradise Road and Red Lion Street to Hill Street. Turn left and walk up Richmond Hill. One of the best views over the Thames is from the Roebuck pub. Walk on past the Star and Garter Home to enter the park at Richmond Gate.

Richmond Park – over 2,000 acres of trees, grass and flowers

6 RICHMOND PARK
It was Charles I who first enclosed some 2,500 acres here to form a deer hunting park, and for the next 200 years it was a popular hunting place. Within the park today are to be found over two dozen ponds (the most famous of which are the Pen Ponds, which teem with a variety of fish), two 18th-century houses – the White Lodge (1727-29), now the Royal Ballet School, and the Thatched House Lodge, built by Sir Robert Walpole in 1727. The Park has much to offer (including deer) and many hours can be spent there.
Retrace the route to the railway station.

WALK 15
Hampstead

Standing high on a hill overlooking London, Hampstead still retains much of its village atmosphere. It is an atmosphere that has attracted men of letters and the arts for many generations, as is evidenced by the number of commemorative plaques to be seen throughout this walk.

Allow 2 hours

Begin the walk from Hampstead Underground Station (having ascended 192ft from the platform!) Turn left outside the station and walk down Hampstead High Street for a short distance before turning left into Flask Walk.

1 FLASK WALK

The Flask pub is noted for its mural of a 19th-century soldier courting a nursery maid. Flask Walk runs out of Well Walk, which takes its name from the wells which made Hampstead a fashionable spa in the 18th century. In Flask Walk itself are the Victorian Flask Walk Baths (now closed). Next to them is an attractive group of restored Georgian artisans' cottages.

At the end of Flask Walk turn left into New End Square.

2 NEW END SQUARE

On the right is Burgh House, a handsome Queen Anne building which houses the Hampstead Museum of Local History. Further along, also on the right, is Ye Olde White Bear pub, built at the beginning of the 18th century. The views across London from here are excellent.

Walk along New End Square to steps on the right leading to Christ Church.

3 CHRIST CHURCH

Built in 1852, this church has a gallery added by Sir Gilbert Scott in 1860. One of the leading architects of his day, Sir Gilbert lived in Hampstead and was a member of the congregation here.

From the church emerge into Hampstead Square and turn left (No 1 dates from the latter part of the 17th century). Follow the square round to Elm Row, with its pleasant 18th-century houses. At the end of the Row reach Heath Street and turn left. Just beyond the Baptist church cross the road and ascend a flight of steps. On the left is Golden Yard, a tiny picturesque square. Continue up the steps. At the top, on the left, is a private house that was once a chapel where John Wesley preached in the 18th century. Turn right, passing the 17th-century Holly Bush pub. Keep right to enter Hampstead Grove.

4 HAMPSTEAD GROVE

This is a street of pleasant houses of various dates, set back from the road. Close to Holly Bush Hill, on the right, is a house that was the home of painter George Romney. On the left is Fenton House, a mansion of about 1693 with a walled garden. It contains a collection of furniture, porcelain, and keyboard instruments, including a harpsichord of 1612 played by Handel. The house belongs to the National Trust and is open to the public. Further along on the right, at No 28, is New Grove House, from 1874 to 1895 the home of George du Maurier, the Punch cartoonist better known for his novel *Trilby* (1894) in which he created the character of Svengali.

Halfway along the Grove a detour can be made to the left into Admiral's Walk.

5 ADMIRAL'S WALK

Two of the houses in Admiral's Walk are especially interesting because of their former residents: Admiral's House, home in the 18th century of an admiral who converted the roof into a quarter deck and fired cannons from it, and also home, in the 19th century, of the architect Sir George Gilbert Scott; and Grove Lodge, where the novelist John Galsworthy, author of *The Forsyte Saga*, lived from 1918 until his death in 1933.

Continue up Hampstead Grove to Whitestone Pond. Just beyond are Jack Straw's Castle pub and the highest point of the Heath. Cross Heath Street, and turn right, then left to reach East Heath Road. Walk along the road, with the heath stretching away to the left. This road merges into South End Road. With a post office ahead, turn right into Keats Grove. On the left is Keats' House Museum.

Keats House was the home of the poet from 1818 to 1820

6 KEATS' HOUSE MUSEUM

Two lovely semi-detached cottages here are now one house and are where the poet John Keats spent a large portion of his working life. The house is now a museum and contains books, manuscripts and memorabilia relating to his life.

Continue along Keats Grove to Downshire Hill. Turn left along Downshire Hill.

7 DOWNSHIRE HILL

This attractive thoroughfare has been the home of several distinguished figures. They include the painter John Constable, who stayed at Nos 25-6, the poet Edwin Muir (1889-1959), who lived at No 7, and the famous art historian, Roland Penrose, who lived at No 21.

At the end of Downshire Hill turn right into Hampstead High Street. Continue until Hampstead Underground Station is reached.

Greenwich

In medieval times Greenwich was a fishing village. Today it has some of London's most elegant buildings, including a royal palace and an observatory. It also has superb views of the Thames, and the best way to taste the delights of Greenwich is to arrive by river.

Allow 1½ hours

From the pier (where the Cutty Sark and Francis Chichester's Gypsy Moth IV can be seen) walk up King William Walk to the gateway into the Royal Naval College. (This entrance is only open from 2.30pm to 4.45pm; when it is closed walk along the Embankment from the pier to reach Trafalgar Tavern).

1 ROYAL NAVAL COLLEGE

Founded in 1694 by William and Mary as a hospital for seamen, this is now the university of the Royal Navy. The main rooms of interest are the Painted Hall, with its walls and ceilings painted by Sir James Thornhill, and the Chapel, with its late 18th-century painting by the American artist Benjamin West, showing the preservation of St Paul after his shipwreck on Malta. Much of the architecture here is by Sir Christopher Wren, but Nicholas Hawksmoor, Vanbrugh and several others also worked on the buildings.

Walk through the Royal Naval College and emerge through gates into Park Row. Turn left to reach Trafalgar Tavern and Crane Street.

The Cutty Sark was one of the swift tea clippers which vied for the fastest time along the tea trade route in the 19th century. Beautifully preserved, she can now be visited in dry dock on Greenwich Pier

2 TRAFALGAR TAVERN AND CRANE STREET

At the end of Park Row is the Trafalgar Tavern. Built in 1837, it has served as a place of refreshment, as homes for aged sailors, living quarters for men of the Royal Navy, and as a men's club. In Crane Street is the Yacht public house, over 300 years old, from which one can watch the river, and also the Trinity Almshouses, founded in 1613 for 12 men from Greenwich and eight from Shottisham, in Surrey.

Return along Park Row to the junction of Trafalgar and Romney roads. Cross over to the entrance to the National Maritime Museum.

3 NATIONAL MARITIME MUSEUM

Opened by George VI in 1937, this museum illustrates the maritime history of Great Britain. It has since been extended and now includes the Queen's House, with which it is linked by an arcade. The museum contains paintings, boats, uniforms, navigational instruments, models and much else besides. The Queen's House, perhaps the first true example of Palladian architecture in the country, was begun during the reign of James I, but not completed until the reign of Charles I.

Walk through the museum complex, and leave by the exit into Romney Road. Reach King William Walk and turn left to reach the Avenue and Greenwich Park.

4 GREENWICH PARK

The park covers over 200 acres, and owes its existence to Duke Humphrey, who enclosed the land and stocked it with deer for royal hunting in the 15th century. The park was opened to the public in the 18th century. At the high point of the park are Flamsteed House and the Old Royal Observatory, with the Greenwich meridian line. Here too can be seen a statue of General Wolfe, the hero of the battle on the Heights of Abraham at Quebec in Canada.

Leave the park by the Avenue and return to Nelson and Romney Roads. Turn left and cross Greenwich Road to reach the Church of St Alphege.

5 ST ALPHEGE

Nicholas Hawksmoor designed the present church in the 18th century as part of the New Churches Act of 1711, which allowed a number of new, or rebuilt, churches to be erected in and around London. It contains an organ keyboard dating back to the 16th century, and the grave of General Wolfe. The whole interior was redesigned after war damage, but the carvings by Grinling Gibbons and the altar rails, in wrought iron, by Jean Tijou, survived.

From the church, there are two ways to complete the walk. Either turn right and go along Greenwich Road to reach Greenwich railway station, or walk along Greenwich Church Street to reach the pier and river transport.

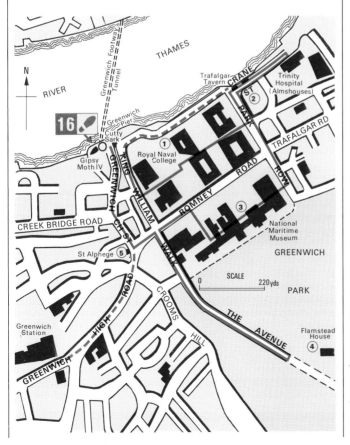

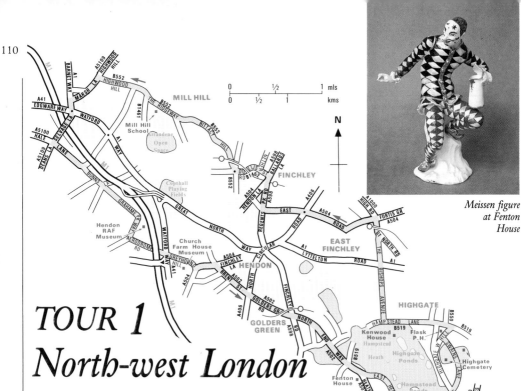

Meissen figure at Fenton House

TOUR 1
North-west London

Hampstead, Hendon and Highgate are included in this drive through north-west London. Regent's Park is the suggested starting place, but the route can be joined or left at any point.

A life mask of the poet at Keats' House

REGENT'S PARK
Formerly a hunting park, Regent's Park achieved its present appearance early in the 19th century, when it was laid out by John Nash. As well as hundreds of acres of trees and grass, it also has many recreational facilities. In the north-east corner is London Zoo.

THE ROUND HOUSE
Robert Stephenson built this monument to the industrial revolution in 1847 to house steam locomotives.

KEATS HOUSE, HAMPSTEAD
Now a museum devoted to poet John Keats, this house (then two cottages) was where he lived and wrote some of his finest poetry.

FENTON HOUSE, HAMPSTEAD
Built in 1693, this mansion houses notable collections of oriental, continental and English china, needlework and furniture, along with the Benton Fletcher collection of early musical instruments.

HAMPSTEAD HEATH
Some of the finest views over London can be had from the Heath's 790 acres. There are extensive tracts of open grassland dotted with ancient trees, and formal areas originally set out in the Regency period. Two of London's rivers – the Fleet and the Westbourne – rise on the Heath. Fairs have long been part of the Heath's attractions, and these are still held on bank holidays.

CHURCH FARM HOUSE MUSEUM, HENDON
This gabled house of about 1660 is now the setting for a museum of local interest. The working kitchen is furnished in late 18th-century style.

RAF MUSEUM, HENDON
Among the aeroplanes on display in this complex are aircraft from the Battle of Britain, bombers such as the Lancaster, Wellington and Vulcan, and many others, from the earliest days of flying to the present day.

THE FLASK, HIGHGATE
Set in one of London's prettiest villages, the Flask dates from 1663, although a tavern has stood here since the 15th century.

KENWOOD HOUSE
This classical-style house is largely the work of Robert Adam. It contains a superb collection of paintings by artists such as Rembrandt and Vermeer.

HIGHGATE CEMETERY
Tombs of the famous and the unknown can be seen here, many of them almost disappearing in a luxuriant growth of trees and shrubs. Karl Marx has the best-known memorial.

Several of the places on the route of this drive are described elsewhere in this book; for further details see the index. There is a walk in Hampstead, described on page 108.

TOUR 2
South-west London

This drive takes in some of the most historic and scenic parts of south-west London. The suggested starting place is Putney Bridge, but the route can be joined or left at any point.

The west front of Hampton Court Palace

FULHAM PALACE
Most of the buildings which make up the palace today date from the 18th and 19th centuries, but the great quadrangle was built in the early 16th century. Between the palace and the Thames is Bishop's Park, a wooded public open space.

PUTNEY BRIDGE
This 19th-century bridge is the starting point of the Oxford and Cambridge boat race.

RICHMOND PARK
Wildest of London's royal parks, this huge expanse of woodland, glades and grassland also has many ponds as well as more formal garden areas. The deer are its most prominent animal inhabitants, but there are also badgers, foxes and many species of breeding birds.

HAM HOUSE
Built in 1610, this mansion now houses treasures from the Victoria and Albert Museum.

HAMPTON COURT PALACE
One of the finest mansions in Britain, this great palace has architectural features from the 16th to the 19th century and contains a wealth of treasures. Its gardens and grounds have tremendous variety – ranging from formal, walled gardens under the lee of the palace, to the charming wilderness dell, and from the magnificent 17th-century Long Water to the famous maze.

BUSHY PARK
Deer-grazed grasslands and huge old trees are the dominant features of this park, but it also has the Longford River (created by Charles I), Waterhouse Plantation, with its arrays of shrubs and flowers, and recreation areas. Chestnut Avenue was the creation of Sir Christopher Wren.

MARBLE HILL HOUSE
This Palladian-style house was built for Henrietta Howard, mistress of George II. Mrs Fitzherbert, mistress and secret wife of the Prince Regent (later George IV) was a later occupant.

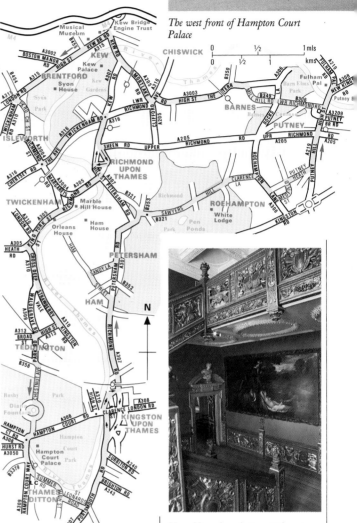

Ham House has glorious 17th-century interiors

SYON HOUSE AND PARK
Robert Adam transformed the former convent here into a magnificent mansion in the 18th century. The interior shows Adam's craftsmanship at its best. Syon Park was laid out by Capability Brown. Many rare shrubs and trees can be seen here, and the Great Conservatory has a splendid collection of tropical plants. Also here is the London Butterfly House.

KEW GARDENS
Plants from all over the world are gathered here. There are glasshouses, formal areas, water gardens, woodland areas and miles of delightful walks. In the gardens is Kew Palace, built in 1631. It was later the private retreat of George III.

KEW BRIDGE ENGINES TRUST
Steam engines, beam engines and traction engines are among the exhibits here. Many are in working order. There is also a museum of London's water supply, with original buildings and equipment.

MUSICAL MUSEUM
Working musical instruments are shown here. Many are played during tours of the museum.

Several of the places on the route of this drive are described elsewhere in this book; for further details see the index. There is a walk in Richmond, described on page 107.

TOUR 3
South-east London

Greenwich excepted, south-east London is not as visited as perhaps it should be. It does have several excellent museums, as this drive illustrates, and a character of its own. The suggested starting place of this drive is Greenwich, but the route can be joined or left at any point.

The Meridian Line at Greenwich

Although the Thames Barrier has a purely practical function, it looks like sculpture

Sir Christopher Wren designed the Old Royal Observatory at Greenwich

GREENWICH

It would be worth visiting Greenwich for its views of the Thames alone. However, it also has the *Cutty Sark*, last of the lovely clipper ships, Sir Francis Chichester's *Gypsy Moth IV*, in which he sailed round the world, the Royal Naval College and the National Maritime Museum, an unrivalled collection of sea-craft, artefacts, documents and paintings, set in buildings of great beauty. In Greenwich Park are the Old Royal Observatory and the Rangers' House, an 18th-century mansion containing Jacobean and Stuart portraits.

THAMES BARRIER CENTRE

Built to save London from flooding in the event of abnormally high tides, the Thames Barrier is a third of a mile long, and is an engineering feat of considerable beauty as well as practical genius. An exhibition tells its story by way of an audio-visual programme.

MUSEUM OF ARTILLERY IN THE ROTUNDA, WOOLWICH

John Nash designed this extraordinary circular structure which stood at one time in St James's Park. It contains a collection of artillery.

HORNIMAN MUSEUM, FOREST HILL

The building here is almost as interesting as the objects it contains. It was designed in a striking *art-nouveau* style in 1901. Rising above the building is an unmistakable tower. The objects gathered here live up to the building, however, being a remarkably diverse collection spanning natural history, musical instruments, tribal artefacts and much else.

DULWICH COLLEGE

This charitable institution was founded by Edward Alleyn, a contemporary of Shakespeare and one of the great actors of his day.

He established the almshouses here in 1613. Parts of the range of buildings still serve as almshouses, and Alleyn's tomb can be seen in the chapel.

DULWICH PICTURE GALLERY

England's first public picture gallery, this gallery has works by Rubens, Raphael, Rembrandt and many others. The building was designed by Sir John Soane.

SOUTH LONDON ART GALLERY, CAMBERWELL

Works on display here include Victorian paintings and drawings, a small collection of modern British art and 20th-century prints. There are also paintings of local subjects.

Several of the places on the route of this drive are described elsewhere in this book; for further details see the index. There is a walk in Greenwich, described on page 109.

Directory

Hotels, restaurants and guesthouses

Given below are the names and addresses of all AA recommended hotels, restaurants and guesthouses in the London postal district. They are arranged in postal district order. For full details of these establishments see the range of AA Annual Guides.

AA CLASSIFICATIONS

Hotels

1-star   Good hotels and inns, generally of small scale and with good furnishings and facilities.

2-star   Hotels with a higher standard of accommodation. There should be 20% private bathrooms or showers.

3-star   Well-appointed hotels. Two thirds of the bedrooms should have private bathrooms or showers.

4-star   Exceptionally well-appointed hotels offering high standards of comfort and service. All bedrooms should have private bathrooms or showers.

5-star   Luxury hotels offering the highest international standards.

Hotels often satisfy *some* of the requirements for higher classifications than that awarded.

Red-star   Red stars denote hotels which are considered to be of outstanding merit within their classification.

Country   A hotel where a relaxed informal
House   atmosphere prevails. Some of the
Hotel   facilities may differ from those at urban hotels of the same classification.

Restaurants

1 fork   Modest but good restaurant

2 forks   Restaurant offering a higher standard of comfort than above

3 forks   Well-appointed restaurant

4 forks   Exceptionally well-appointed restaurant

5 forks   Luxury restaurant

Rosettes

Hotels and restaurants where, in the opinion of our inspectors, the food is of a particularly high standard are awarded rosettes.

1 rosette   Hotel or restaurant where the food is of a higher standard than expected for its classification.

2 rosettes   Hotel or restaurant offering excellent food and service, irrespective of classification.

3 rosettes   Hotel or restaurant offering outstanding food and service, irrespective of classification.

E1 STEPNEY *and east of the Tower of London*
Hotel **Tower Thistle**, St Katherine's Way, 4-star *tel* 01-488 4134
Restaurant **Blooms**, 90 Whitechapel High St, 1-fork *tel* 01-247 6001

E14 POPLAR
Restaurant **Good Friends**, 139-141 Salmon Ln, 1-fork *tel* 01-987 5541

E18 SOUTH WOODFORD
Guesthouse **Grove Hill Hotel**, 38 Grove Hill *tel* 01-989 3344

EC1 CITY OF LONDON *Barbican, Clerkenwell, Farringdon*
Restaurants **La Bastille**, 116 Newgate St, 1-fork *tel* 01-600 1134

Three Compasses, 66 Cowcross St, 1-fork *tel* 01-253 3368

EC2 CITY OF LONDON, *Bank of England, Liverpool Street Station*
Restaurants **Le Poulbot**, 45 Cheapside, 3-forks, 1-rosette *tel* 01-236 4379
Baron of Beef, Gutter Ln, Gresham St, 3-forks *tel* 01-606 9415

EC3 CITY OF LONDON, *Monument, Tower of London*
Restaurant **Shares**, 12-13 Lime St, 2-forks *tel* 01-623 1843

EC4 CITY OF LONDON. *Blackfriars, Cannon Street and Fleet Street*
Restaurants **Le Gamin**, 32 Old Bailey, 1-fork *tel* 01-236 7931
Ginnan, 5 Cathedral Pl, 1-fork *tel* 01-236 4120

N1 ISLINGTON
Restaurants **Fredericks**, Camden Passage, 2-forks *tel* 01-359 2888
Annas Place, 90 Mildmay Park, 1-fork, 1-rosette *tel* 01-249 9379
Mr Bumbles, 23 Islington Grn, 1-fork *tel* 01-354 1952
M'sieur Frog, 31a Essex Rd, 1-fork *tel* 01-226 3495
Portofino, 39 Camden Passage, 1-fork *tel* 01-226 0884

N6 HIGHGATE
Restaurants **Bayleaf Tandoori**, 2 North Hill, 2-forks *tel* 01-340-1719
San Cario, 2 High St, 2-forks *tel* 01-340 5823
China Garden, 12 Shepherds Hill, 1-fork *tel* 01-348 8606

N8 HORNSEY
Restaurant **M'Sieur Frog**, 36 The High St, 1-fork *tel* 01-340 2116
Guesthouse **Aber Hotel**, 89 Crouch Hill *tel* 01-340 2847

N14 SOUTHGATE
Restaurant **L'Oiseau Noir**, 163 Bramley Rd, 1-fork *tel* 01-367 1100

N16 STOKE NEWINGTON
Restaurant **Eleganza**, 70 High St, 1-fork *tel* 01-254 1950

NW1 REGENT'S PARK *Baker Street, Euston and King's Cross Stations*
Restaurants **Viceroy of India**, 3-5 Glentworth St, 2-forks *tel* 01-486 3401
Asuka, Berkeley Arcade, 209a Baker St, 1-fork *tel* 01-486 5026
One-Legged Goose, 17 Princess Rd, Regents Park, 1-fork *tel* 01-722 9665
Sagarmatha, 339 Euston Rd, 1-fork *tel* 01-387 6531

NW2 CRICKLEWOOD, WILLESDEN
Restaurant **Quincy's '84'**, 675 Finchley Rd, 1-fork *tel* 01-794 8499
Guesthouses **Clearview House**, 161 Fordwych Rd, *tel* 01-452 9773
Garth Hotel, 70-76 Hendon Way, *tel* 01-455 4742

NW3 HAMPSTEAD
Hotel **Holiday Inn Swiss Cottage**, King Henry's Rd, 4-star *tel* 01-722 7711
Charles Bernard, 5 Frognal, 3-star *tel* 01-794 0101
Post House, Haverstock Hill, 3-star *tel* 01-794 8121
Swiss Cottage, 4 Adamson Rd, 3-star *tel* 01-722 2281
Restaurants **Bunny's**, 9 Pond St, 2-forks *tel* 01-435 1541

Keats, 3 Downshire Hill, 2-forks 1-rosette, *tel* 01-435 3544
Finches, 250 Finchley Rd, 1-fork 01-435 8622
Green Cottage II, 122a Finchley Rd, 1-fork *tel* 01-794 3833
Hawelli Tandoori, 102 Heath St, 1-fork *tel* 01-431 0172
Peachey's, 205 Haverstock Hill, 1-fork *tel* 01-435 6744
Wakaba, 31 College Cres, 1-fork 01-586 7960
Guesthouse **Frognal Lodge Hotel**, 14 Frognal Gdns, *tel* 01-435 8238

NW4 HENDON
Hotel **Hendon Hall**, Ashley Ln, 3-star *tel* 01-203 3341
Guesthouse **Peacehaven Hotel**, 94 Audley Rd, *tel* 01-202 9758

NW6 KILBURN
Restaurants **La Frimousse**, 75 Fairfax Rd, 1-fork *tel* 01-624 3880
Peters Bistro, 63 Fairfax Rd, 1-fork *tel* 01-624 5142
Sheridan's, 351 West End Ln, 1-fork *tel* 01-794 3234
Vijay, 49 Willesden Ln, 1-fork *tel* 01-328 1087

NW7 MILL HILL
Hotel **Travelodge**, M1 Scratchwood Service Area (Access from Motorway only) 2-star *tel* 01-906 0611
Restaurant **Good Earth**, 143-145 Broadway, Mill Hill, 2-forks *tel* 01-959 7011

NW8 ST JOHN'S WOOD
Hotel **Ladbroke Westmoreland**, 18 Lodge Rd, 4-star *tel* 01-722 7722
Restaurants **Lords Rendezvous**, 24 Finchley Rd, 2-forks *tel* 01-722 4750
Oslo Court, Prince Albert Rd, 2-forks *tel* 01-722 8795
L'Aventure, 3 Blenheim Ter, 1-fork *tel* 01-624 6232
Fortuna Garden, 128 Allitsen Rd, 1-fork *tel* 01-586 2391

NW10 HARLESDEN, WILLESDEN
Restaurants **Khas Tandoori**, 39 Chamberlayne Rd, 1-fork *tel* 01-969 2537
Kuo Yuan, 217 High Rd, 1-fork 01-459 2297

NW11 GOLDERS GREEN
Restaurant **Luigis**, 1-4 Belmont Pde, Finchley Rd, 2-forks *tel* 01-455 0210
Guesthouses **Central Hotel**, 35 Hoop Ln *tel* 01-458 5636
Croft Court Hotel, 44-46 Ravenscourt Ave *tel* 01-458 3331

SE1 SOUTHWARK, WATERLOO
Restaurants **RSJ's**, 13a Coin St, 1-fork *tel* 01-928 4554
South of the Border, Joan St, 1-fork *tel* 01-928 6374

SE3 BLACKHEATH
Guesthouses **Bardon Lodge Hotel**, 15 Stratheden Rd *tel* 01-853 4051
Stonewall House, 35-37 Westcombe Park Rd *tel* 01-858 8706

SE9 ELTHAM
Guesthouse **Yardley Court Private Hotel**, 18 Court Rd *tel* 01-850 1850

SE10 GREENWICH
Restaurants **Mean Time**, 47-49 Greenwich Church St, 2-forks *tel* 01-858 8705
Spread Eagle, 2 Stockwell St, 2-forks *tel* 01-853 2333
Le Papillon, 57 Greenwich Church St, 1-fork *tel* 01-858 2668
Mr Chung, 166 Trafalgar Rd, 1-fork *tel* 01-858 4245

SE11 KENNINGTON
Hotel **London Park**, Brook Dr, 2-star *tel* 01-735 9191

SE13 LEWISHAM
Restaurant **Curry Centre**, 37 Lee High Rd, 1-fork *tel* 01-852 6544

SE19 NORWOOD
Guesthouse **Crystal Palace Tower Hotel**, 114 Church Rd *tel* 01-653 0176

SE23 FOREST HILL
Guesthouse **Rutz**, 16 Vancouver Rd
tel 01-699 3071

SW1 WESTMINSTER *St James Park,
Victoria Station, Knightsbridge, Lower Regent St*
Hotels **Berkeley**, Wilton Pl, 5-star
tel 01-235 6000
Hyatt Carlton Tower, Cadogan Pl, 5-star
tel 01-235 5411
Hyde Park, Knightsbridge, 5-star 01-235 2000
Sheraton Park Tower, 101 Knightsbridge,
5-star *tel* 01-235 8050
Cavendish, Jermyn St, 4-star *tel* 01-930 2111
Duke's, St James's Pl, 4-star, 1-rosette
tel 01-491 4840
Goring, Beeston Pl, Grosvenor Gdns, 4-star
tel 01-834 8211
Holiday Inn Chelsea, 17-25 Sloane St, 4-star
tel 01-235 4377
Royal Westminster Thistle, 49 Buckingham
Palace Rd, 4-star *tel* 01-834 1821
Stafford, 16-18 St James's Pl, 4-star
tel 01-493 0111
Lowndes Thistle, 19 Lowndes St, 3-star
tel 01-235 6020
Royal Horseguards Thistle, Whitehall Court,
3-star *tel* 01-839 3400
Rubens, Buckingham Palace Rd, 3-star
tel 01-834 6600
Ebury Court, 26 Ebury St, 1-star 01-730 8147
Restaurants **Auberge De Provence**,
Buckingham Gate, 3-forks *tel* 01-834 6655
Dolphin Brasserie, Rodney House,
Dolphin Sq, 3-forks *tel* 01-828 3207
L'Amico, 44 Horseferry Rd, 2-forks
tel 01-222 4680
Le Caprice, Arlington House, Arlington St,
2-forks *tel* 01-629 2239
Gavvers, 61 Lower Sloane St, 2-forks,
1-rosette *tel* 01-730 5983
Ken Lo's Memories of China, 67 Ebury St,
2-forks, 1-rosette *tel* 01-730 7734
Le Mazarin, 30 Winchester St, 2-forks,
1-rosette *tel* 01-828 3366
Mijanou, 143 Ebury St, 2-forks, 1-rosette
tel 01-730 4099
Pomegranates, 94 Grosvenor Rd, 2-forks
tel 01-828 6560
Saloos, 62-64 Kinnerton St, 2-forks,
1-rosette *tel* 01-235 4444
Tate Gallery, Millbank Embankment,
2-forks *tel* 01-834 6754
Ciboure, 21 Eccleston St, 1-fork, 1-rosette
tel 01-730 2505
Eatons, 49 Elizabeth St, 1-fork *tel* 01-730 0074
La Fantaisie Brasserie, 14 Knightsbridge Gn,
1-fork *tel* 01-589 0509
Le Poule au Pot, 231 Ebury St, 1-fork
tel 01-730 7763
Tent, 15 Eccleston St, 1-fork *tel* 01-730 6922
Le Trou Normand, 27 Motcomb St, 1-fork
tel 01-235 1668
Guesthouses **Arden House**, 12 St Georges Dr
tel 01-834 2988
Chesham House, 64-66 Ebury St
tel 01-730 8513
Elizabeth Hotel, 37 Eccleston Sq 01-828 6812
Hanover Hotel, 30 St Georges Dr
tel 01-834 0134
Willet Hotel, 32 Sloane Gdns, Sloane Sq
tel 01-824 8415
Windermere Hotel, 142 Warwick Way
tel 01-834 5163

SW3 CHELSEA
Hotels **The Capital**, Basil St, 4 Red-star,
1-rosette *tel* 01-589 5171
Basil Street, Basil St, 3-star *tel* 01-581 3311
Restaurants **Waltons**, 121 Walton St,
4-forks, 1-rosette *tel* 01-584 0204
Zen Chinese, Chelsea Cloisters, Sloane Ave,
3-forks *tel* 01-589 1781
Avoirdupois, 334 Kings Rd, 2-forks
tel 01-352 6151
Daphnes, 112 Draycott Ave, 2-forks
tel 01-589 4257
English Garden, 10 Lincoln St, 2-forks,
1-rosette *tel* 01-584 7272
English House, 3 Milner St, 2-forks,
1-rosette *tel* 01-584 3002
Le Francais, 259 Fulham Rd, 2-forks
tel 01-352 4748
Good Earth, 233 Brompton Rd, 2-forks
tel 01-584 3658
Good Earth, 91 Kings Rd, 2-forks
tel 01-352 9321

Mario, 260-262a Brompton Rd, 2-forks
tel 01-584 1724
Menage a Trois, 15 Beauchamp Pl, 2-forks
tel 01-589 4252
Meridiana, 169 Fulham Rd, 2-forks
tel 01-589 8815
St Quentin, 243 Brompton Rd, 2-forks
tel 01-589 8005
San Frediano, 62 Fulham Rd, 2-forks
tel 01-584 8375
Tandoori, 153 Fulham Rd, 2-forks
tel 01-589 7749
Tante Claire, 68 Royal Hospital Rd,
2-forks, 2-rosettes *tel* 01-352 6045
Choy's, 172 Kings Rd, 1-fork, *tel* 01-352 9085
Dans, 119 Sydney St, 1-fork, 1-rosette
tel 01-352 2718
Dumpling House, 9 Beauchamp Pl, 1-fork
tel 01-589 8240
Ma Cuisine, 113 Walton St, 1-fork,
1-rosette *tel* 01-584 7585
Mes Amis, 31 Basil St, 1-fork *tel* 01-584 4484
Poissonnerie, 82 Sloane Ave, 1-fork
tel 01-589 2457
Le Suquet, 104 Draycott Ave, 1-fork
tel 01-581 1785
Guesthouses **Eden House Hotel**, 111 Old
Church St 01-352 3403
Garden House Hotel, 44-46 Egerton Gdns
tel 01-584 2990
Knightsbridge Hotel, 10 Beaufort Gdns
tel 01-589 9271

SW4 CLAPHAM
Restaurant **Maharani Indian**, 117 Clapham
High St, 1-fork *tel* 01-622 2530

SW5 EARLS COURT
Hotels **London International**, 147
Cromwell Rd, 3-star *tel* 01-370 4200
Hogarth, Hogarth Rd, 2-star *tel* 01-370 6831
Restaurants **Pontevecchio**, 256 Old
Brompton Rd, 2-forks *tel* 01-373 9082
Tiger Lee, 251 Old Brompton Rd, 2-forks
tel 01-370 2323
L'Aquitaine, 158 Old Brompton Rd, 1-fork
tel 01-373 9918
L'Artiste Affame, 243 Old Brompton Rd,
1-fork *tel* 01-373 1659
New Lotus Garden, 257 Old Brompton Rd,
1-fork *tel* 01-370 4450
Reads, 152 Old Brompton Rd, 1-fork,
1-rosette *tel* 01-373 2445

SW6 FULHAM
Restaurants **Gastronome One**, 311-313 New
Kings Rd, 2-forks, 1-rosette *tel* 01-731 6381
Hippocampe, 131a Munster Rd, 1-fork,
1-rosette *tel* 01-736 5588
Mao Tai Szechuan, 58 New Kings Rd,
1-fork *tel* 01-731 2520
Perfumed Conservatory, 182 Wandsworth
Bridge Rd, 1-fork, 1-rosette *tel* 01-731 0732
Trencherman, 271 New Kings Rd, 1-fork
tel 01-736 4988

SW7 SOUTH KENSINGTON
Hotels **Gloucester**, 4-18 Harrington Gdns,
4-star *tel* 01-373 5842
Rembrandt, Thurloe Pl, 3-star *tel* 01-589 8100
Restaurants **Bombay Brasserie**. Courtfield
Close, Gloucester Rd, 3-forks *tel* 01-370 4040
Hilaire, 68 Old Brompton Rd, 2-forks,
1-rosette *tel* 01-584 8993
Montpeliano, 13 Montpelier St, 1-fork
tel 01-589 0032
Zen Too, 53 Old Brompton Rd, 1-fork
tel 01-225 1609
Guesthouse **Number Eight Hotel**,
8 Emperors Gate *tel* 01-370 7516

SW8 BATTERSEA
Restaurants **L'Arlequin**, 123 Queenstown Rd,
2-forks, 2-rosettes *tel* 01-622 0555
Chez Nico, 129 Queenstown Rd, 2-forks,
1-rosette *tel* 01-720 6960
Lampwicks, 24 Queenstown Rd, 2-forks
tel 01-622 7800

SW10 WEST BROMPTON
Restaurants **Brinkleys**, 47 Holywood Rd,
2-forks *tel* 01-01-351 1683
Nikitas, 65 Ifield Rd, 2-forks *tel* 01-352 6326
L'Olivier, 116 Finborough Rd, 2-forks
tel 01-370 4183
September, 457 Fulham Rd, 2-forks
tel 01-352 0206

Bagatelle, 5 Langton St, 1-fork 01-351 4185
Chelsea Wharf, Lots Rd, 1-fork 01-351 0861
La Croisette, 168 Ifield Rd, 1-fork 01-373 3694
Jake's, 14 Hollywood Rd, 1-fork 01-352 8692
Van B's, 360b Fulham Rd, 1-fork 01-351 0863

SW11 BATTERSEA
Restaurants **Ormes**, 245 Lavender Hill,
1-fork *tel* 01-228 9824
Pollyanna's, 2 Battersea Rise, 1-fork
tel 01-228 0316

SW13 BARNES
Restaurant **Barnaby's**, 39b High St, Barnes,
1-fork *tel* 01-878 4750

SW14 EAST SHEEN
Restaurants **Crowthers**, 481 Upper
Richmond Rd, West East Sheen, 1-fork
tel 01-876 6372
Janine's, 505 Upper Richmond Rd,
West East Sheen, 1-fork *tel* 01-876 5075

SW15 PUTNEY
Restaurants **Annia's**, 349 Upper Richmond
Rd, 2-fork *tel* 01-876 4456
Bert's, 34 Upper Richmond Rd, 1-fork
tel 01-874 8839
Buzkash Afghan, 4 Chelverton Rd, 1-fork
tel 01-788 0599
Samratt, 18 Lacy Rd, 1-fork *tel* 01-788 9110
Wild Thyme, 96 Felsham Rd, 1-fork
tel 01-789 3323

SW16 NORBURY
Restaurants **Malean**, 1585 London Rd,
Norbury, 1-fork *tel* 01-764 2336

SW19 WIMBLEDON
Restaurant **Les Amoureux**, 156 Merton
Hall Road, 1-fork *tel* 01-543 0567
Guesthouses **Trochee Hotel**, 21 Malcolm Rd,
Wimbledon *tel* 01-946 1579 & 3924
Wimbledon Hotel, 78 Warple Rd,
Wimbledon *tel* 01-946 9265
Worcester House, 38 Alwyne Rd 01-946 1300

W1 WEST END *Piccadilly Circus, Soho, St
Marylebone and Mayfair*
Hotels **Claridge's**, Brook St, 5 red-star
tel 01-629 8860
The Connaught, Carlos Pl, 5 red-star,
2-rosette 01-499 7070
Churchill, Portman Sq, 5-star *tel* 01-486 5800
Grosvenor House, Park Ln, 5-star
tel 01-499 6363
Inn on the Park, Hamilton Pl, Park Ln,
5-star *tel* 01-499 0888
Inter-Continental, 1 Hamilton Pl, Hyde Park
Corner, 5 red-star, 2-rosette 01-409 3131
London Hilton, 22 Park Ln, 5-star
tel 01-493 8000
Mayfair Inter-Continental, Stratton St,
5-star *tel* 01-629 7777
Ritz, Piccadilly, 5-star *tel* 01-493 8181
The Dorchester, 53 Park Ln, 5 red-star,
1-rosette *tel* 01-629 8888
The Athanaeum, Piccadilly, 4 red-star
tel 01-499 3464
Britannia, Grosvenor Sq, 4-star
tel 01-629 9400
Cumberland, Marble Arch, 4-star
tel 01-262 1234
Holiday Inn, Marble Arch, 123 George St,
4-star *tel* 01-723 1277
London Marriot, Grosvenor Sq, 4-star
tel 01-493 1232
Brown's, Dover St, Albemarle St, 4 red-star
tel 01-493 6020
Montcalm, Great Cumberland Pl, 4-star
tel 01-402 4288
Park Lane, Piccadilly, 4-star, 1-rosette
tel 01-499 6321
Portman Inter-Continental, 22 Portman Sq,
4-star *tel* 01-486 5844
St George's, Langham Pl, 4-star 01-580 0111
Selfridge, Orchard St, 4-star 01-408 2080
Westbury, New Bond St, 4-star 01-629 7755
Berners, Berners St, 3-star *tel* 01-636 1629
Chesterfield, 35 Charles St, 3-star *tel* 01-491 2622
Clifton-Ford, 47 Welbeck St, 3-star
tel 01-486 6600
Mandeville, Mandeville Pl, 3-star 01-935 5599
Mount Royal, Bryanston St, Marble Arch,
3-star *tel* 01-629 8040
Stratford Court, 350 Oxford St, 3-star
tel 01-629 7474

Bryanston Court, 56-60 Great Cumberland Pl, 2-star *tel* 01-262 3141
Regent Palace, Glasshouse St, Piccadilly, 2-star *tel* 01-734 7000
Restaurants **Cafe Royal**, 68 Regent St, 5-fork *tel* 01-439 6320
Ninety Park Ln, 90 Park Ln, 5-fork *tel* 01-409 1290
Le Gavroche, 43 Upper Brook St, 4-fork, 3-rosette *tel* 01-408 0881
London Hilton Hotel, Park Ln, 4-fork *tel* 01-493 7586
Greenhouse, 27a Hay's Mews, 3-fork *tel* 01-499 3331
Masako, 6-8 St Christopher Pl, 3-fork *tel* 01-935 1579
Princess Garden of Mayfair, 8-10 North Audley St, 3-fork *tel* 01-493 3223
Tandoori of Mayfair, 37a Curzon St, 3-fork *tel* 01-629 0600
Au Jardin Des Gourmets, 5 Greek St, 2-fork, 1-rosette *tel* 01-437 1816
Chambell, 12 Great Castle St, 2-fork *tel* 01-636 0662
Chessa, 10 Wardour St, 2-fork 01-734 1291
La Cucaracha, 12 Greek St, 2-fork *tel* 01-734 2253
Gallery Rendezvous, 53 Beak St, 2-fork *tel* 01-734 0445
Gay Hussar, 2 Greek St, 2-fork, 1-rosette *tel* 01-437 0973
Lai Qila, Tottenham Court Rd, 2-fork *tel* 01-387 4570
Langan's Brasserie, Stratton St, 2-fork *tel* 01-491 8822
Library, 115 Mount St, 2-fork *tel* 01-499 1745
Mr Kai of Mayfair, 65 South Audley St, 2-fork *tel* 01-493 8988
Odin's, 27 Devonshire St, 2-fork, 1-rosette *tel* 01-935 7296
Red Fort, 77 Dean St, 2-fork *tel* 01-437 2525
Rue St Jacques, 5 Charlotte St, 2-fork, 2-rosette *tel* 01-637 0222
Sawasdee, 26-28 Whitfield St, 2-fork *tel* 01-631 0289
Yumi, 110 George St, 2-fork *tel* 01-935 8320
Alastair Little, 49 Frith St, 1-fork 01-734 5183
Arirang, 31-32 Poland St, 1-fork *tel* 01-437 6633
Aunties, 126 Cleveland St, 1-fork 01-387 1548
D'Artagnan, 19 Blandford St, 1-fork *tel* 01-935 1023
Desaru, 60-62 Old Compton St, 1-fork *tel* 01-734 4379
Frith's, 14 Frith St, 1-fork *tel* 01-439 3370
Fuji Japanese, 36-40 Brewer St, 1-fork *tel* 01-734 0957
Gaylord, 79 Mortimer St, 1-fork 01-580 3615
Ho Ho Chinese, 29 Maddox St, 1-fork *tel* 01-493 1228
Kerzenstuber, 9 St Christopher's Pl, 1-fork *tel* 01-486 3196
Lee Ho Fook, 15 Gerrard St, 1-fork *tel* 01-734 9578
Little Akropolis, 10 Charlotte St, 1-fork *tel* 01-636 8198
Mayflower, 66-70 Shaftesbury Av, 1-fork *tel* 01-734 9027
New World, 1 Gerrard Pl, 1-fork *tel* 01-734 0677
Regent Tandoori, 10 Denman St, 1-fork *tel* 01-434 1134
Relais Des Amis, 17b Curzon St, 1-fork *tel* 01-499 7595
Sav's, 53 Cleveland St, 1-fork *tel* 01-580 7608
Yung's, 23 Wardour St, 1-fork, 1-rosette *tel* 01-437 4986
Guesthouses **Hotel Concorde**, 50 Great Cumberland Pl *tel* 01-402 6169
Georgian House Hotel, 87 Gloucester Pl, Baker St *tel* 01-935 2211
Hart House Hotel, 51 Gloucester Pl, Portman Sq *tel* 01-935 2288
Montagu House, 3 Montagu Pl *tel* 01-935 4632

W2 BAYSWATER, PADDINGTON
Hotels **Royal Lancaster**, Lancaster Ter, 4-star *tel* 01-262 6737
Central Park, Queensborough Ter, 3-star *tel* 01-229 2424
Hospitality Inn, 104/105 Bayswater Rd, 3-star *tel* 01-262 4461
London Embassy, 150 Bayswater Rd, 3-star *tel* 01-229 2623
Park Court, 75 Lancaster Gate, 3-star *tel* 01-402 4272
White's, Lancaster Gate, 3-star *tel* 01-262 2711

Restaurants **Bombay Palace**, 2 Hyde Park Sq, 3-fork *tel* 01-723 8855
Bali, 101 Edgware Rd, 2-fork *tel* 01-723 3303
Trat-West, 143 Edgware Rd, 2-fork *tel* 01-723 8203
Ajimura Japanese, 51-53 Shelton St, 1-fork *tel* 01-240 0178
Al-Khayam Tandoori, 27-29 Westbourne Gv, 1-fork *tel* 01-727 5154
Ganges, 101 Praed St, 1-fork *tel* 01-723 4096
Green Jade, 29-31 Portchester Rd, 1-fork *tel* 01-229 7221
Kalamara's, 76-78 Inverness Mews, 1-fork *tel* 01-727 9122
Le Mange Tout, 34 Sussex Pl, 1-fork *tel* 01-723 1199
Veronica's Chez Franco, 3 Hereford Rd, 1-fork *tel* 01-229 5079
Guesthouses **Ashley Hotel**, 15 Norfolk Sq, Hyde Park *tel* 01-723 3375
Camelot Hotel, 45 Norfolk Sq, Hyde Park *tel* 723 9118
Dylan Hotel, 14 Devonshire Ter, Lancaster Gate *tel* 01-723 3280
Garden Court Hotel, 30-31 Kensington Gardens Sq *tel* 01-727 8304
Nayland Hotel, 134 Sussex Gdns *tel* 01-723 3380
Pembridge Court Hotel, 34 Pembridge Gdns *tel* 01-229 9977
Slavia Hotel, 2 Pembridge Sq *tel* 01-727 1316

W4 CHISWICK
Guesthouse **Chiswick Hotel**, 73 Chiswick High Rd *tel* 01-994 1712

W5 EALING
Hotel **Carnarvon**, Ealing Common, 3-star *tel* 01-992 5399

W6 HAMMERSMITH
Hotel **Novotel London**, 1 Shortlands, 3-star *tel* 01-741 1555
Restaurants **Anarkall**, 303 King St, 1-fork *tel* 01-748 1760
Aziz, 116 King St, 1-fork *tel* 01-748 1826
Light of Nepal, 268 King St, 1-fork *tel* 01-748 3586

W8 KENSINGTON
Hotels **Royal Garden**, Kensington High St, 5-star *tel* 01-937 8000
Kensington Palace Thistle, De Vere Gardens, 4-star *tel* 01-937 8121
London Tara, Scarsdale Pl, off Wright Ln, 4-star *tel* 01-937 7211
Kensington Close, Wrights Ln, 3-star *tel* 01-937 8170
Hotel Lexham, 32-38 Lexham Gdns, 2-star *tel* 01-373 6471
Restaurants **Belvedere**, Holland House, Holland Park, 3-fork *tel* 01-602 1238
Le Crocodile, 38c&d Kensington Church St, 2-fork *tel* 01-938 2501
Kensington Tandoori, 1 Abingdon Rd, 2-fork *tel* 01-937 6182
Le Ruelle, 14 Wrights Ln, 2-fork, 1-rosette *tel* 01-937 8525
Sailing Junk, 59 Melrose Rd, 2-fork *tel* 01-937 2589
Ark, 35 Kensington High St, 1-fork *tel* 01-937 4294
Il Barbino, 32 Kensington Church St, 1-fork *tel* 01-937 8752
Maggie Jones, 6 Old Court Pl, Church St, 1-fork *tel* 01-937 6462
Michel, 343 Kensington High St, 1-fork *tel* 01-603 3613
Siam, 12 St Alban's Grove, 1-fork *tel* 01-937 8765
Guesthouses **Apollo Hotel**, 18-22 Lexham Gdns *tel* 01-373 3236
Atlas Hotel, 24-30 Lexham Gdns *tel* 01-373 7873

W9 MAIDA VALE
Restaurant **Didier**, 5 Warwick Pl *tel* 01-286 7484

W11 HOLLAND PARK, NOTTING HILL
Hotel **Hilton International Kensington**, Holland Park Av, 3-star *tel* 01-603 3355
Restaurants **Leiths**, 92 Kensington Park Rd, 3-fork *tel* 01-229 4481
Chez Moi, 1 Addison Av, 2-fork *tel* 01-603 8267

La Pomme d'Amour, 128 Holland Park Av, 2-fork *tel* 01-229 8532
Cap's, 64 Pembridge Rd, 1-fork *tel* 01-229 5177
La Residence, 148 Holland Park Av, 1-fork *tel* 01-221 6090
Restaurant 192, 192 Kensington Park Rd, 1-fork *tel* 01-229 0482

W12 SHEPHERDS BUSH
Restaurant **Shireen**, 270 Uxbridge Rd, 1-fork *tel* 01-749 5927

W13 EALING (NORTHFIELDS)
Restaurant **Maxim Chinese**, 153-155 Northfield Av, 1-fork *tel* 01-567 1719

W14 WEST KENSINGTON
Guesthouse **Avonmore Hotel**, 66 Avonmore Rd *tel* 01-603 4296

WC1 BLOOMSBURY, HOLBORN
Hotels **Marlborough Crest**, Bloomsbury St, 4-star *tel* 01-636 5601
Hotel Russell, Russell Sq, 4-star 01-837 6470
Bloomsbury Crest, Coram St, 3-star *tel* 01-837 1200
London Ryan, Gwynne Pl, King's Cross Rd, 3-star *tel* 01-278 2480
Restaurants **Mr Kai of Russell Square**, 50 Woburn Pl, 2-fork *tel* 01-580 1188
Winston's Eating House, 24 Coptic St, 2-fork *tel* 01-580 3422
Les Hailes, 57 Theobolds Rd, 1-fork *tel* 01-242 6761
Guesthouse **Mentone Hotel**, 54-55 Cartwright Gdns *tel* 01-387 3927

WC2 COVENT GARDEN, *Leicester Square, Strand and Kingsway*
Hotels **Savoy**, Strand, 5 red-star, 1-rosette *tel* 01-836 4343
Waldorf, Aldwych, 4-star *tel* 01-836 2400
Drury Lane Moat House, 10 Drury Ln, 3-star *tel* 01-836 6666
Royal Trafalgar Thistle, Whitcomb St, 3-star *tel* 01-930 4477
Strand Palace, Strand, 3-star *tel* 01-836 8080
Restaurants **Savoy Hotel Grill**, Embankment Gdns, 5-fork *tel* 01-836 4343
Inigo Jones, 14 Garrick St, 4-fork, 1-rosette *tel* 01-836 6456
Boulestin, 1a Henrietta St, Covent Garden, 3-fork, 1-rosette *tel* 01-836 3819
P S Hispaniola, Victoria Embankment, River Thames, 3-fork *tel* 01-839 3011
Neal Street, 26 Neal St, 3-fork *tel* 01-836 8368
L'Opera, 32 Great Queen Street, 3-fork *tel* 01-405 9020
Rules, 35 Maiden Ln, Strand, 3-fork *tel* 01-836 2559
Chez Solange, 35 Cranbourne St, 2-fork *tel* 01-836 0542
Interlude de Tabaillau, 7-8 Bow St, 2-fork *tel* 01-379 6473
Poons of Covent Garden, 41 King St, 2-fork, 1-rosette *tel* 01-240 1743
Thomas de Quincey's, 36 Tavistock St, 2-fork *tel* 01-240 3972
Tourment d'Amour, 19 New Row, 2-fork, 1-rosette *tel* 01-240 5348
Bates English, 11 Henrietta St, 1-fork *tel* 01-240 7600
Le Cafe des Amis du Vin, 11-14 Hanover Pl, 1-fork *tel* 01-379 3444
Le Cafe du Jardin, 28 Wellington St, 1-fork *tel* 01-836 8769
Cafe Pelican, 45 St Martins Ln, 1-fork *tel* 01-379 0309
La Coree Korean, 56 St Giles High St, 1-fork *tel* 01-836 7235
Happy Wok, 52 Floral St, 1-fork *tel* 01-836 3696
Last Days of the Raj, 22 Drury Ln, 1-fork *tel* 01-836 1628
Il Passetto, 230 Shaftesbury Av, 1-fork *tel* 01-836 9391
Plummers, 33 King St, 1-fork *tel* 01-240 2534
Poon's, 4 Leicester St, 1-fork, 1-rosette *tel* 01-437 1528
La Provence, 8 Mays Court, 1-fork *tel* 01-836 9180
Sheekey's, 29-31 St Martin's Court, 1-fork *tel* 01-240 2565
Taste of India, 25 Catherine St, 1-fork *tel* 01-836 6591

Street Index

TO INNER LONDON MAPS

The map employs an arbitrary system of grid reference. Pages are identified by numbers and divided into eight squares. Each square contains a black letter; all references give the page number first, followed by the letter of the square in which a particular street can be found. Reference for Exhibition Road is 80F, meaning that the relevant map is on page 80 and that the street appears in the square designated F.

A

Abbey Orchard St SW1 *82F*
Abbey Rd NW8 *74A*
Abbey St SE1 *85H*
Abbots Lane SE1 *85D*
Abchurch Lane EC4 *79Q*
Abercorn Pl NW8 *74A*
Aberdeen Pl NW8 *74F*
Abingdon St SW1 *83G*
Acton St WC1 *77D*
Adam St WC2 *77Q*
Adam's Row W1 *75R*
Addington St SE1 *83H*
Addle St EC2 *78K*
Adelaide St WC2 *77Q*
Adeline Pl WC1 *76K*
Adpar St WC2 *74F*
Agar St WC2 *77Q*
Agdon St EC1 *78A*
Albany Rd SE5 *85Q*
Albany St NW1 *76A*
Albermarle St W1 *76N*
Albert Enbankment SE1/SE11 *83Q*
Albert Pl W8 *80E*
Alberta St SE17 *84N*
Albion Pl EC1 *78E*
Albion St W2 *75Q*
Aldbridge St SE17 *85R*
Aldenham St NW1 *76B*
Aldermanbury EC2 *78K*
Alderney St SW1 *82N*
Aldersgate St EC1 *78F*
Alford St W1 *75R*
Aldgate EC3 *79M*
Aldgate High St EC3 *79M*
Aldwych WC2 *77R*
Alexander Pl SW7 *80K*
Alfred Pl WC1 *76F*
Alice St SE *85G*
Alie St E1 *79M*
Allington St SW1 *82E*
Allsop Pl NW1 *75G*
Alpha Pl SW3 *81Q*
Alsace Rd SE17 *85Q*
Alscot Rd SE1 *85M*
Alvey St SE17 *85Q*
Ambergate St SE17 *84P*
Ambrosden Av SW1 *82K*
Amelia St SE17 *84P*
Ampton St WC1 *77D*
Amwell St EC1 *78A*
Angel St EC1 *78K*
Appold St EC2 *79H*
Aquinas St SE1 *84A*
Arch St SE1 *84K*
Archer St W1 *76P*
Argyle St WC1 *77C*
Argyle Sq WC1 *77C*
Argyll St W1 *76J*
Arlington St SW1 *82A*
Arlington Way EC1 *78A*
Arne St WC2 *77L*
Arnold Circus E2 *79D*
Arnside St SE17 *85Q*
Arthur St EC4 *79Q*
Artillery Ln E1 *79M*
Artillery Row SW1 *82K*
Arundel St WC2 *77R*
Ashbridge St NW8 *74F*
Ashburn Gdns SW7 *80J*
Ashburn Mews SW7 *80J*
Ashburn Pl SW7 *80J*
Ashby St EC1 *78B*
Ashley Pl SW1 *82J*
Ashmill St NW1 *74F*
Ashworth Rd W9 *74A*
Astell St SW3 *81Q*
Atterbury St SW1 *83L*
Attneave St WC1 *77D*
Augustus St NW1 *76A*
Aulton Pl SE11 *84N*
Austin St E2 *79D*
Austral St SE11 *84J*
Aveline St SE11 *83R*
Ave Maria Lane EC4 *78K*
Avonmouth St SE1 *84F*
Avery Row W1 *76N*
Aybrook St W1 *75M*
Aylesbury Rd SE17 *85Q*
Aylesbury St EC1 *78E*
Aylesford St SW1 *82P*

B

Baches St N1 *79C*
Back Hill EC1 *78E*
Bacon St E2 *79H*
Bagshot St SE17 *85R*
Baker St W1/NW1 *75G*
Baker's Row EC1 *78E*
Balcombe St NW1 *75G*
Balderton St W1 *75R*
Baldwin's Gdns EC1 *77H*
Balfour St SE17 *85L*
Baltic St EC1 *78F*
Bankend SE1 *85C*
Bankside SE1 *78P*
Banner St EC1 *78F*
Barnby St NW1 *76B*
Barnham St SE1 *85D*
Baron's Pl SE1 *84E*
Baroness Rd E2 *79D*
Barrett St W1 *75M*
Barrie St W2 *74N*
Barter St WC1 *77L*
Bartholomew Cl EC1 *78K*
Bartholomew Ln EC2 *79L*
Bartholomew St SE1 *85L*
Basil St SW3 *81G*
Basinghall Av EC2 *79L*
Basinghall St EC2 *79L*
Bastwick St EC1 *78F*
Bateman's Row EC2 *79D*
Bath St EC1 *79C*
Bath Ter SE1 *84F*
Battle Bridge Ln SE1 *85C*
Bayley St WC1 *76K*
Baylis Rd SE1 *83H*
Bayswater Rd W2 *74N*
Beaconsfield Rd SE17 *85Q*
Beak St W1 *76P*
Bear Ln SE1 *84B*
Beauchamp Pl SW3 *81G*
Beaufort Gdns SW3 *81G*
Beaufort St SW3 *80P*
Beaumont St W1 *75H*
Beckway St SE17 *80L*
Bedford Av WC1 *76K*
Bedfordbury WC2 *77Q*
Bedford Pl WC1 *77G*
Bedford Row WC1 *77H*
Bedford Sq WC1 *76K*
Bedford St WC2 *77Q*
Bedford Way WC1 *77G*
Beech St EC2 *78F*
Beeston Pl SW1 *82E*
Belgrave Pl SW1 *81H*
Belgrave Rd SW1 *82J*
Belgrave Sq SW1 *81H*
Belgrove St WC *77C*
Bell Ln E1 *79M*
Bell St NW1 *74F*
Bell Yd WC2 *77M*
Belvedere Rd SE1 *83D*
Benjamin St EC1 *78E*
Bentinck St W1 *75M*
Berkeley Sq W1 *76N*
Berkeley St W1 *76N*
Bermondsey St SE1 *85H*
Bernard St WC1 *77G*
Berners Mews W1 *76K*
Berners St W1 *76K*
Berry St EC1 *78F*
Berryfield Rd SE17 *84P*
Berwick St W1 *76K*
Bessborough Gdns SW1 *82P*
Bessborough Pl SW1 *82P*
Bessborough St SW1 *82P*
Bethnal Gn Rd E1 *79H*
Betterton St WC2 *77L*
Bevenden St N1 *79C*
Bevis Marks EC3 *79M*
Bickenhall St W1 *75G*
Bidborough St WC1 *77C*
Billiter St EC3 *79M*
Bina Gdns SW5 *80J*
Binney St W1 *75R*
Birchin Ln EC3 *79Q*
Bird St W1 *75M*
Birdcage Walk SW1 *82F*
Birkenhead St WC1 *77C*
Bishop's Br Rd W2 *74J*
Bishopsgate EC2 *79L*
Bishop's Ter SE11 *84J*
Blackfriars Br SE1 *78N*
Blackfriars Rd SE1 *84A*
Black Prince Rd SE11 *83M*
Blackwood St SE17 *85Q*
Blandford St W1 *75L*
Blomfield Rd W9 *74E*
Blomfield St EC2 *79L*
Blomfield Villas W2 *74J*
Bloomfield Ter SW1 *81R*
Bloomsbury Sq WC1 *77L*
Bloomsbury St WC1 *77L*
Bloomsbury Way WC1 *77L*
Bolsover St W1 *76E*
Boltons The SW10 *80N*
Bolton Gdns SW5 *80N*
Bolton St W1 *82A*
Bonhill St EC2 *79G*
Bonnington Sq SE11 *83R*
Boot St N1 *79C*
Borough High St SE1 *84E*
Borough Rd SE1 *84F*
Borrett Cl SE17 *84P*
Boscobel St NW8 *74F*
Boss St SE1 *85D*
Boston Pl NW1 *75G*
Boswell St WC1 *77G*
Botolph Ln EC3 *79Q*
Boundary St E2 *79D*
Bourdon St W1 *76N*
Bourne St SW1 *81M*
Bourne Ter W2 *74E*
Bouverie St EC4 *78J*
Bow Ln EC4 *78P*
Bow St WC2 *77L*
Bowden St SE11 *84N*
Bowling Gn Ln EC1 *78E*
Bowling Green St SE11 *84N*
Bowling Gn Walk N1 *79C*
Boyfield St SE1 *84F*
Boyle St W1 *76N*
Brad St SE1 *84A*
Braganza St SE17 *84N*
Bramerton St SW3 *80P*
Brandon St SE17 *84K*
Bray Pl SW3 *81L*
Bread St EC4 *78P*
Bream's Buildings EC4 *77M*
Brechin Pl SW7 *80N*
Brendon St W1 *75L*
Bressenden Pl SW1 *82E*
Brewer St W1 *76P*
Brick Ln E1/E2 *79D*
Brick St W1 *81D*
Bridge St SW1 *83G*
Bridle Ln W1 *76P*
Briset St EC1 *78E*
Bristol Gdns W9 *74E*
Britannia St WC1 *77C*
Britannia Walk N1 *79C*
Britten St SW3 *80P*
Britton St EC1 *78E*
Broad Ct WC2 *77L*
Broadley St NW8 *74F*
Broadley Ter NW1 *74F*
Broad Sanctuary SW1 *83G*
Broadway SW1 *82F*
Broadwick St W1 *76P*
Brockham St SE1 *84F*
Brompton Pl SW3 *81G*
Brompton Rd SW3 *80K*
Brompton Sq SW3 *80F*
Brook Dr SE11 *84J*
Brook St W2 *74P*
Brook St W1 *75R*
Brooke St EC1 *78J*
Brook's Mews W1 *76N*
Brown St W1 *75L*
Browning St SE17 *84P*
Brownlow Mews WC1 *77H*
Brune St E1 *79M*
Brunswick Ct SE1 *85H*
Brunswick Pl N1 *79C*
Brunswick Sq WC1 *77G*
Brushfield St E1 *79H*
Bruton Ln W1 *76N*
Bruton Pl W1 *76N*
Bruton St W1 *76N*
Bryanston Pl W1 *75L*
Bryanston Sq W1 *75L*
Bryanston St W1 *75Q*
Buckingham Gate SW1 *82E*
Buckingham Palace Rd SW1 *82J*
Bucknall St WC2 *77L*
Bulstrode St W1 *75M*
Bunhill Row EC1 *79G*
Burlington Arcade W1 *76N*
Burlington Gdns W1 *76N*
Burne St NW1 *74F*
Burnsall St SW3 *81Q*
Burton St WC1 *77C*
Bury Pl WC1 *77L*
Bury St EC3 *79M*
Bury St SW1 *82B*
Bury Walk SW3 *80K*
Bush Ln EC4 *79Q*
Bute St SW7 *80K*
Byng Pl WC1 *76F*
Byward St EC3 *79R*
Bywater St SW3 *81Q*

C

Cabbell St NW1 *74K*
Cadiz St SE5 *84P*
Cadogan Gdns SW3 *81L*
Cadogan Ln SW1 *81M*
Cadogan Pl SW1 *81G*
Cadogan Sq SW1 *81L*
Cadogan St SW3 *81L*
Cale St SW3 *80P*
Callow St SE5 *80N*
Calmington Rd SE5 *85R*
Calthorpe St WC1 *77H*
Calvert Av E2 *79D*
Calvin St E1 *79H*
Cambridge Circus WC2 *77Q*
Cambridge Sq W2 *74K*
Cambridge St SW1 *82J*
Camlet St E2 *79D*
Camomile St EC3 *79M*
Canning Pl W8 *80E*
Cannon Row SW1 *83G*
Cannon St EC4 *78P*
Canterbury Pl SE17 *84K*
Capland St NW8 *74F*
Capper St WC1 *76F*
Carburton St W1 *76E*
Cardigan St SE11 *83R*
Cardington St NW11 *76B*
Carey St WC2 *77M*
Carlisle Ln SE1 *83H*
Carlisle Pl SW1 *82J*
Carlos Pl W1 *75R*
Carlton Gdns SW1 *82B*
Carlton House Ter SW1 *82B*
Carlyle Sq SW3 *80P*
Carmelite St EC4 *78N*
Carnaby St W1 *76P*
Caroline Ter SW1 *81M*
Carriage Rd, The SW1 *80F*
Carter Ln EC4 *78P*
Carter Pl SE17 *84P*
Carter St SE17 *84P*
Carting Ln WC2 *77Q*
Cartwright Gdns WC1 *77C*
Castellain Rd W9 *74E*
Castle Baynard St EC4 *78P*
Castle Ln SW1 *82F*
Catesby St SE17 *85L*
Cathcart Rd SW10 *80N*
Catherine Pl SW1 *82E*
Catherine St WC2 *77Q*
Causton St SW1 *82K*
Cavendish Ave NW8 *74B*
Cavendish Pl W1 *76J*
Cavendish Sq W1 *76J*
Caversham St SW3 *81Q*
Caxton St SW1 *82F*
Cayton St EC1 *79C*
Cecil Ct WC2 *77Q*
Central St EC1 *78B*
Chadwell St EC1 *78A*
Chadwick St SW1 *82K*
Chagford St NW1 *75G*
Chalton St NW1 *76B*
Chambord St E2 *79D*
Chance St E2 *79H*
Chancery Ln WC2 *77M*
Chandos Pl WC2 *77Q*
Chandos St W1 *76J*
Chapel St NW1 *74K*
Chapel St SW1 *81H*
Chapter Rd SE17 *84P*
Chapter St SW1 *82K*
Charing Cross SW1 *83C*
Charing Cross Rd WC2 *76K*
Charles Sq N1 *79C*
Charles St W1 *82A*
Charles II St SW1 *82B*
Charleston St SE17 *84K*
Charlotte Rd EC2 *79D*
Charlotte St W1 *76F*
Charlwood St SW1 *82P*
Chart St N1 *79C*
Charterhouse Sq EC1 *78F*
Charterhouse St EC1 *78J*
Chatham St SE17 *85L*
Cheapside EC2 *78K*
Chelsea Br Rd SW1 *81R*
Chelsea Embankment SW1 *81R*
Chelsea Manor St SW3 *80P*
Chelsea Sq SW3 *80P*
Cheltenham Ter SW3 *81Q*
Chenies St WC1 *76F*
Chequer St EC1 *78F*
Chesham Pl SW1 *81H*
Chesham St SW1 *81M*
Chester Cl W1 *76A*
Chester Ct W1 *76A*
Chester Gate W1 *76A*
Chester Rd NW1 *75D*
Chester Row SW1 *81M*
Chester Sq SW1 *81M*
Chester St SW1 *81H*
Chester Ter NW1 *76A*
Chester Way SE11 *84J*
Chesterfield Hill W1 *75R*
Cheval Pl SW7 *80F*
Chicheley St SE1 *83D*
Chichester Rd W2 *74E*
Chichester St SW1 *82P*
Chiltern St W1 *75H*
Chilworth St W2 *74J*
Chiswell St EC1 *79G*
Chitty St W1 *76F*
Christchurch St SW3 *81Q*
Christopher St EC2 *79G*
Church St NW8/W2 *74F*
Church Yard Row SE11 *84K*
Churchill Gdns Rd SW1 *82N*
Churchway NW1 *76B*
Churton St SW1 *82K*
Circus Rd NW8 *74B*
City Rd EC1 *78A*
City Garden Row EC1 *78B*
Clabon Mews SW1 *81L*
Claremont Cl EC1 *78A*
Claremont Sq EC1 *78A*
Clarence Gdns NW1 *76A*
Clarendon Gdns W9 *74E*
Clarendon Pl W2 *74P*
Clarendon St SW1 *82N*
Clarendon Ter W9 *74E*
Clareville Gv SW7 *80J*
Clareville St SW7 *80J*
Clarges St W1 *82A*
Claverton St SW1 *82P*
Clayton St SE11 *83R*
Cleaver Sq SE11 *84N*
Cleaver St SE11 *84N*
Clere St EC2 *79G*
Clerkenwell Cl EC1 *78E*
Clerkenwell Gn EC1 *78E*
Clerkenwell Rd EC1 *77H*
Cleveland Gdns W2 *74J*
Cleveland Row SW1 *82B*
Cleveland Sq W2 *74J*
Cleveland St W1 *76E*
Cleveland Ter W2 *74J*
Clifford St W1 *76N*
Clifton Gdns W9 *74E*
Clifton Pl W2 *74P*
Clifton Rd W9 *74E*
Clifton St EC2 *79G*
Clifton Villas W9 *74E*
Clink St SE1 *85C*
Clipstone St W1 *76E*
Cliveden Pl SW1 *81M*
Cloak Ln EC4 *79Q*
Cloth Fair EC1 *78K*
Club Row E1/2 *79D*
Cobb St E1 *79M*
Cobourg Rd SE5 *85R*
Cobourg St NW1 *76B*
Cock Ln EC1 *78K*
Cockspur St SW1 *82B*
Coin St SE1 *84A*
Colbeck Mews SW7 *80J*
Cole St SE1 *84F*
Coleman St EC2 *79L*
Coley St WC1 *77H*
Collingham Gdns SW5 *80J*
Collingham Rd SW5 *80J*
Colombo St SE1 *84A*
Columbia Rd E2 *79D*
Commercial St E1 *79H*
Compton St EC1 *78F*
Concert Hall Approach SE1 *83D*
Conduit St W1 *76N*
Congreve St SE17 *85L*
Connaught Pl W2 *75Q*
Connaught Sq W2 *75L*
Connaught St W2 *74P*
Constitution Hill SW1 *81H*
Content St SE17 *85L*
Conway St W1 *76E*
Cooper's Rd SE1 *85R*
Cooper's Row EC3 *79R*
Copperfield St SE1 *84B*
Copthall Av EC2 *79L*
Coptic St WC1 *77L*
Coral St SE1 *84E*
Coram St WC1 *77G*
Cork St W1 *76N*
Cornhill EC3 *79L*
Cornwall Gdns SW7 *80J*
Cornwall Rd SE1 *83D*
Coronet St N1 *79C*
Corporation Row EC1 *78E*
Corsham St N1 *79C*
Cosser St SE1 *83H*
Cosway St NW1 *75G*
Cotham St SE17 *84K*
Cottesmore Gdns W8 *80E*
Cottington Cl SE11 *84N*
Cottington St SE11 *84N*
Coulson St SW3 *81Q*
County St SE1 *84K*
Courtenay St SE11 *83R*
Courtfield Gdns SW5 *80J*
Courtfield Rd SW7 *80J*
Coventry St W1 *76P*
Cowan St SE17 *85Q*
Cowcross St EC1 *78E*
Cowper St EC2 *79C*
Coxsons Way SE1 *85H*
Cramer St W1 *75M*
Crampton St SE17 *84K*
Cranbourn St WC2 *77Q*
Cranley Gdns SW7 *80N*
Cranley Mews SW7 *80N*
Cranley Pl SW7 *80K*
Cranwood St EC1 *79C*
Craven Hill W2 *74N*
Craven Hill Gdns W2 *74N*
Craven Rd W2 *74N*
Craven St WC2 *83C*
Craven Ter W2 *74N*
Crawford Pl W1 *75L*
Crawford St W1 *75L*
Cremer St E2 *79D*
Cresswell Pl SW10 *80N*
Crestfield St WC1 *77C*
Crimscott St SE1 *85M*
Cromer St WC1 *77C*
Cromptons St W2 *74E*
Cromwell Gdns SW7 *80K*
Cromwell Mews SW7 *80K*
Cromwell Pl SW7 *80K*
Cromwell Rd SW5/SW7 *80J*
Crosby Row SE1 *85G*
Crosswall EC3 *79R*
Crucifix Ln SE1 *85D*
Cruikshank St WC1 *77D*
Crutched Friars EC3 *79R*
Cubitt St WC1 *77D*
Culford Gdns SW3 *81L*
Culross St W1 *75R*
Cullum St EC3 *79Q*
Cumberland Mkt NW1 *76A*
Cumberland St SW1 *82N*
Cundy St SW1 *81M*
Cunningham Pl NW8 *74F*
Cureton St SW1 *82K*
Curlew St SE1 *85D*
Cursitor St EC4 *77M*
Curtain Rd EC2 *79H*
Curzon St W1 *81D*
Cut, The SE1 *84A*
Cutler St E1 *79M*
Cygnet St E1 *79H*
Cyrus St EC1 *78B*

D

Dacre St SW1 *82F*
Dallington St EC1 *78F*
Dante Rd SE11 *84K*
D'Arblay St W1 *76K*
Dartmouth St SW1 *82F*
Darwin St SE17 *85L*
Date St SE5 *85Q*
Daventry St NW1 *74F*
Davies St W1 *75R*
Dawes St SE17 *85Q*
Deacon Way SE17 *84K*
Dean St W1 *76K*
Dean's Bldgs SE17 *85L*
Dean Bradley St SW1 *83L*
Dean Farrar St SW1 *82F*
Dean Ryle St SW1 *83L*
Deanery St W1 *81D*
Decima St SE1 *85G*
Delamere Ter W2 *74E*
Delverton Rd SE17 *84P*
De Laune St SE17 *84N*
Denbigh Pl SW1 *82P*
Denbigh St SW1 *82K*
Denman St W1 *76P*
Denmark St WC2 *77L*
Denny Cres SE11 *84J*
Denny St SE11 *84N*
Denyer St SW3 *81L*
Dering St W1 *76J*
De Vere Gdns W8 *80E*
Deverell St SE1 *85G*
Devonshire Pl W1 *75H*
Devonshire St W1 *75H*
Devonshire Ter W2 *74N*
Diana Pl NW1 *76E*
Dickens Sq SE1 *84F*
Dingley Rd EC1 *78B*
Diss St E2 *79D*
Distin St SE11 *83M*
Doddington Gv SE17 *84N*
Dodson St SE1 *84E*
Dolben St SE1 *84B*
Dolphin Sq SW1 *82P*
Dominion St EC2 *79G*
Donne Pl SW3 *81L*
Doon St SE1 *83D*
Doric Way NW1 *76B*
Dorset Pl SW1 *82P*
Dorset Rise EC43 *78J*
Dorset Sq NW *75G*
Dorset St W1 *75L*
Doughty Mews WC1 *77H*
Doughty St WC1 *77H*
Douglas St SW1 *82K*
Douro Pl W8 *80E*
Dovehouse St SW3 *80P*
Dove Mews SW5 *80J*
Dover St W1 *76N*
Dowgate Hill EC4 *79Q*
Down St W1 *82A*
Downing St SW1 *83C*
D'Oyley St SW1 *81M*
Draco St SE17 *84P*
Draycott Av SW3 *81L*
Draycott Pl SW3 *81L*
Draycott Ter SW3 *81L*
Drayton Gdns SW10 *80N*
Druid St SE1 *85H*
Drummond Cres NW1 *76B*
Drummond Gt SW1 *82P*
Drummond St NW1 *76A*
Drury Ln WC2 *77L*
Dryden Ct SE11 *84J*
Dryden St WC2 *77L*
Drysdale St N1 *79D*
Duchess St W1 *76J*
Duchy St SE1 *84A*
Dufferin St EC1 *79G*
Duke St W1 *75M*
Duke St Hill SE1 *85C*
Duke St. St James's SW1 *82B*
Duke of York St SW1 *76P*
Duke's Pl EC3 *79M*
Duke's Rd WC1 *76B*
Duncannon St WC2 *77Q*
Dunraven St W1 *75Q*
Dunton Rd SE1 *85M*
Durham St SE11 *83R*
Dyott St WC1 *77L*
Dysart St EC2 *79G*

E

Eagle St WC1 *77M*
Earl Rd SE1 *85R*
Earl St EC2 *79G*
Earlham St WC2 *77Q*
Earnshaw St WC2 *77L*
East Rd N1 *79C*
East St SE17 *84P*
East Harding St EC4 *78J*
Eastbourne Ter WC2 *74J*
Eastcastle St W1 *76K*
Eastcheap EC3 *79Q*
Easton St WC1 *77D*
East Smithfield E1 *79R*
Eaton Gt SW1 *81M*
Eaton Pl SW1 *81M*
Eaton Sq SW1 *81M*
Eaton Ter SW1 *81M*
Ebenezer St N1 *79C*
Ebor St E2 *79H*
Ebury Br SW1 *82N*
Ebury Br Rd SW1 *81R*
Ebury Mews SW1 *81M*
Ebury Sq SW1 *81M*
Ebury St SW1 *81M*
Eccleston Br SW1 *82J*
Eccleston Pl SW1 *82J*
Eccleston Sq SW1 *82J*
Eccleston St SW1 *81M*
Edgware Rd W2 *74F*
Egerton Cres SW3 *80K*
Egerton Gdns SW3 *80K*
Egerton Ter SW3 *80K*
Elba Pl SE17 *84K*
Elder St E1 *79H*
Eldon Rd W8 *80E*
Eldon St EC2 *79L*
Elephant Rd SE17 *84K*
Elgin Av W9 *74A*
Elizabeth Br SW1 *82J*
Elizabeth St SW1 *81M*
Elliott's Row SE11 *84K*
Ellis St SW1 *81L*

Street Index

CONTINUED

Index

Acknowledgements

The Automobile Association wishes to thank the following photographers, organisations and libraries for material reproduced in this book. Many of the photographs are the copyright of the AA Picture Library.

M Adelman 46 RAF Museum, 64 Golden Square, 70 Festival Hall; *BBC Hulton* 28 Sir Joseph William Bazalgette, 29 Edwin Lutyens, 29 Sir Norman Shaw; *Imperial War Museum* 12 Blitz; *London Wildlife Trust* 14 Kidbrooke Rly Station, 19 Sydenham Hill Wood; *Mansell Collection* 6/7 Panorama Vischer Print, 7 Tower of London, 8 Globe, 8/9 Panorama Vischer Print, 9 Coats of Arms, 10 Plague, 10/11 Panorama Vischer, 10/11 Panorama Vischer, 11 Vauxhall Gardens, 12 Gt Exhibition; *Mary Evans Picture Library* 23 Inigo Jones, 24 Christopher Wren, 28 George Gilbert Scott; *S & O Mathews* Cover, Tower Bridge, 15 View from Richmond Hill, 21 Richmond Park Deer, 21 Highgate Cemetary, 23 Queens House, Greenwich, 25 Horse-guards, 29 Battersea Power Station, 36 St Paul's Dome, 37 Southwark Cathedral, 39 Coat of Arms Group, 47 V & A Museum, 48 Hampton Court Beast, 49 Tower of London, 51 Yeoman – Tower of London, 53 Holland Park Flower Garden, 55 Kew Palm House, 59 Petticoat Lane, 60 New Court Garden, 63 Trafalgar Square, 63 Churchill Statue, 65 Dick Whittington's Cat, 66 10 Downing Street, 71 Harrods, 75 Victoria Memorial, 96 Clock at Fortnum & Masons, 103 Pageant, 107 Richmond, 110 Fenton House, 111 Hampton Court; *Museum of London* 11 Fire of London; *National Gallery* 41 Mr & Mrs Andrews; *National Portrait Gallery* 40 Lady Diana; *Nature Photographs* 15 Small Tortoiseshell (E K T), 13 Meadow Brown (E A Janes), 14 Great Crested Grebe (C Carver), 16 Lupin (D Bonsall), 16 Water Rail (P R Sterry), 16 Orchid (P R Sterry), 18 Newt (P R Sterry), 21 Flamingo (E K Thompson); *Spectrum Colour Library* 33 Lord Mayor's Show; *M Trelawny* Cover Royal Wedding, 1 Eros, 3 Band, 7 Temple Church, 24 St Paul's, 25 St Martin-in-the-Fields, 25 St Martins, 26 Syon House, 26 Osterley House, 27 St Pancras Station, 28 Albert Memorial, 31 Natural History Museum, 32 Sarah & Andrew, 32 Ceremony of the Keys, 37 Southwark Cathedral, 38 Westminster Abbey, 42 Hayward Gallery, 43 Bear Garden Museum, 43 British Museum, 43 HMS Belfast, 44 London Transport Museum, 44 Madame Tussaud's, 46 Planetarium, 47 Sir John Soames, 52 Buddhist Peace Pagoda, 52 Chiswick House, 53 Hampton Court Palace, 54 Penguin Pool, 54 London Zoo, 56 Burlington Arcade, 57 Purdys, 58 Berwick Street Market, 59 Portobello Road, 60 Old Court Garden, 62 View from Momument, 64 Temple Church Crusader, 65 Trafalgar Square, 66 Fleet Street, 67 Athaeneum Club, 69 Victoria Embankment, 94 War Cabinet, 98 Wig & Pen Club, 99 Covent Garden, 101 St Olave's, 104 Nat West Tower, 106 Jack the Ripper, 108 Keats House, 110 Keats House, 111 Ham House; *Tim Woodcock* Cover Tower of London Guard, Cover Westminster, 5 Hyde Park, 6 Head of Mithras, 7 London Wall, 9 Guildhall, 9 Statue Gog Guildhall, 9 Magog Guildhall, 11 Fire Pump, 21 Black Swan, 24 Greenwich Hospital, 30 Lloyds Building, 33 Horse Guards Parade, 34 Brompton Oratory – Int, 34 Brompton Oratory – Ext, 35 St Clement Danes, 35 St John Smith's Square, 36 St Paul's Dome, 39 Royal Exchange, 44 Horniman Museum, 45 Natural History Museum, 48 Buckingham Palace, 48 Royal Mews, 49 St James's Palace, 49 Kensington Palace, 50 House of Parliament, 51 Ordnance – Tower of London, 55 St James's Park, 56 Harrods, 61 Arsenal v Tottenham, 67 Admiralty Arch, 68 Thames Barrier, 69 Westminster Bridge, 69 Tower Bridge, 109 Cutty Sark.